The Social Psychology of Gender

McGraw-Hill Series in Social Psychology

CONSULTING EDITOR, Philip G. Zimbardo

The Social Psychology of Gender

Shawn Meghan Burn

California Polytechnic State University—San Luis Obispo

McGraw-Hill, Inc.

New York   St. Louis   San Francisco   Auckland   Bogotá   Caracas
Lisbon   London   Madrid   Mexico City   Milan   Montreal   New Delhi
San Juan   Singapore   Sydney   Tokyo   Toronto

This book was set in Palatino by Graphic World, Inc.
The editors were Brian L. McKean and Fred H. Burns;
the production supervisor was Denise L. Puryear.
R. R. Donnelley & Sons Company was printer and binder.

Cover: Scala / Art Resource, New York
Matisse, Henri
Vase of Nasturtiums and "The Dance"
[copyright ARS, NY]
Pushkin Museum of Fine Arts, Moscow, Russia

THE SOCIAL PSYCHOLOGY OF GENDER

This book is printed on acid-free paper.

1   2   3   4   5   6   7   8   9   0   DOC DOC   9   0   9   8   7   6   5

ISBN 0-07-009182-X

Library of Congress Cataloging-in-Publication Data

Burn, Shawn Meghan.
   The social psychology of gender / Shawn Meghan Burn.
      p.   cm.—(McGraw Hill series in social psychology)
   Includes bibliographical references and indexes.
   ISBN 0-07-009182-X
      1. Sex role.   2. Sex differences (Psychology)   3. Social psychology.
I. Title.   II. Series.
   HQ1075.B87   1996
   305.3—dc20   95-15698

About the Author

— ❖ —

Shawn Meghan Burn is associate professor of psychology at California Polytechnic State University—San Luis Obispo, where she teaches social psychology, environmental psychology, research methods, and group dynamics. She received her Ph.D. in social psychology in 1988 from the Claremont Graduate School. She is primarily an applied social psychologist, concerned with applying social-psychological principles to social problems, to particular environmental problems, and to intergroup conflicts. Her current work focuses on factors maintaining traditional gender norms, and the dynamics of social identity in struggles for equality and backlashes to such struggles.

Dedicated to My Son, The Amazing Kane.

Contents

———— ❖ ————

vii

Foreword

———— ❖ ————

W e have become sensitive to the dangers of stereotyping, of creating mental images of others based not on who they are and what they do, but rather on who we think they are supposed to be and what we think they ought to be doing. Many students have gone beyond simple tolerance of individual differences, embracing the rich diversity of people's backgrounds. Yet, is it really possible for these students to rise above the cultural programming that instills our perceptions of race, class, and gender?

For one answer, consider the results of this classroom demonstration I conducted recently with intelligent, "politically correct" psychology students. These students were asked to imagine being the parent of an infant being held in their arms. Half of them chose a name for their baby from among a list containing three female names, while the others selected one from a matched list of three male names. (Neither group was aware of the other group's options.) As they cuddled and cooed the baby, a bearded stranger approached with an attractive Jack-In-The-Box. Their babies looked intently as he wound it up and played its soothing music to them. Suddenly, Jack popped dramatically out of the box. The question posed to each surrogate parent was, "How did your baby react to this unexpected event?"

From a list of fixed alternatives, most selected "startled" regardless of the gender of their baby. But then a curious thing happened when these "student-parents" selected their baby's next reaction. Significantly more of their girls reacted with *"fear"* than did the boys, while more of their boys were *"curious"* than were the girls!

What are the psychological and behavioral implications of these different emotional reactions? Fear leads to distress, to phobias, to denial, to clinging to safe objects, to avoidance and escape, to non-confrontation. And curiosity? Excitement, engagement, challenge, stimulation, approach, and confrontation are its manifestations. So, this differentiation in the emotional reactions of their pseudo-babies reveals that these relatively sophisticated modern parents-to-be have internalized the fundamental biases of gender stereotyping. To the same stimulus event, they are imagining that Michelle will react negatively while Michael will cope positively. Since there are no actual reactions to be observed, they are telling us that some of their stored mental representations are categorized under gender dichotomies, ready to influence their own beliefs, perceptions, and perhaps even important life decisions.

Such gender-based stereotypical differences are reinforced daily by best selling books proclaiming that men and women come from different planets, talk different languages, run with wolves, or sleep with tigers. A recent network special on the gender gap, emphasized all the ways in which men and women are essentially different—in hormones, brain structure and function, morphology, and (especially) evolutionary-based survival behavioral patterns. What such programs choose to ignore is the vast body of research-grounded conclusions that men and women are more similar than they are different, that there is more overlap between them on virtually every measured dimension than there are distinctly separate tails of the two distributions. But the public and media interest in perpetuating myths of essential differences between these apparently different creatures justifies erecting and maintaining foundations of political, economic, religious, and social differences in which men dominate, victimize and women are dominated, victimized.

Here is where systematic, objectively grounded research should enter the scene to clarify, correct, and redirect analyses. And that is precisely what Shawn Burn has given us in this invaluable addition to our understanding of the role and meaning of gender in our lives. In a wonderfully accessible, often charming writing style, she separates fact from fiction, what is real from what we have been misled to believe should be true. The author outlines the hard evidence on which conclusions about gender differences should rest, where apparent differences disappear under the light of impartial evaluation. Shawn Burn focuses our attention on the power of social norms and cultural traditions and on the reward structures inherent in different socialization pressures. She explores how we may escape the limitations of traditional gender roles, changing them for our better mental and physical health and for a fuller enjoyment of life.

Finally, allow me to note one more point about sex and gender. Basic psychology has long ignored sex as a basic aspect of human nature, both as a research topic and even as a topic of discussion in introductory psychology texts. Social psychology has also been reticent to acknowledge the presence of gender, one of the most powerful dialectics that empower interactions in our social context. Shawn Burn's book goes a long way toward correcting this absence of responsible social psychological analysis. I hope that you will enjoy its messages as much as I have in adding its title to the others in our distinguished list of outstanding monographs in social psychology.

The *McGraw-Hill Series in Social Psychology* has been designed as a celebration of the fundamental contributions being made by researchers, theorists, and practitioners of social psychology to our understanding of human nature and to the potential for enriching the quality of our lives through wise applications of their knowledge. It has become a showcase for presenting new theories, original syntheses, analyses, and current methodologies by distinguished scholars and promising young writer-researchers. Our authors reveal a common commitment to sharing their vision with a broad audience starting with their colleagues and extending to graduate students, but especially to undergraduates with an interest in social psychology. Some of our titles convey ideas that are of sufficient general interest that their messages need to be carried out into the world of practical application to those who may translate some of them into public action and public policy.

Although each text in our series is created to stand alone as the best representative of its area of scholarship, taken as a whole they represent the core of social psychology. Teachers may elect to use any of them as in-depth supplements to a basic, general textbook, while others may choose to organize their course entirely around a set of these monographs. Each of our authors has been guided by the objective of conveying the essential lessons and principles of her or his area of expertise in an interesting style, one that informs without resort to technical jargon, and that inspires others to utilize these ideas at conceptual or practical levels.

Since I am writing this foreword on February 14, 1995, I am reminded that it is Valentine's day, a time for celebrating our love for others, for traditional other-sex partners, for same-sex partners, for our children regardless of gender, and for all of human kind without regard for learned categories of mind. That may indeed be the true test of "Love Conquering All"--biases and stereotypes and limitations that close our hearts to the love of kin and strangers alike, who need and desire our love. So give it up today and every day.

Phil Zimbardo
Consulting Editor

Preface

——————— ❖ ———————

The topic of gender is enormously relevant to both the individual and society. One's gender profoundly influences one's life, and gender issues regarding pay, promotion, childcare, and the division of household labor are among the most talked about of social issues. Women's and men's roles in American society are changing but people disagree on how much change is desirable. Scientists view gender as an important topic for study but they too disagree on important issues such as whether the genders are significantly different and whether gender differences are largely the result of fundamental biological differences between the sexes or are due to culture. This book explores these issues by examining research evidence. In particular, it focuses on the role of social norms in the creation and perception of gender differences, how traditional gender roles are limiting to both men and women, and how we perceive gender differences to be much larger than the data justify because of our natural information-processing strategies.

The popular press is full of books in which authors offer up their opinions regarding differences between the genders, but few of these are based on anything more than the authors' impressions. This book is intended as a readable guide to the research literature about the social influences on gender. Academics may find it a useful bibliographic source as well as a source of research ideas. The book is also intended for use in undergraduate and graduate social psychology classes and gender studies courses (an instructor's manual with test items and assignments is available from McGraw-Hill). Some of the most important concepts of social psychology in regard to gender are explored, making the book a useful supplement for social psychology courses. For instance, the role of normative and informational pressure in the creation and maintenance of gender roles is discussed, ingroup-outgroup bias is applied to male-female conflict, and gender as a cognitive category that guides information processing is examined. Instructors and students of gender studies classes may find the book useful for its examination of gender-role socialization, women's work in and out of the home, and the limitations of traditional gender roles for both females and males. Although the book refers to many research studies, I have tried to write a readable text conducive to critical thinking and reflection rather than to slumber-like trances.

My work has benefited enormously from the support of my son Kane and from conversations with friends Carol Stanton, Ted Stolze, Alison Konrad, Lois Scriven, Norma Fitton, Bobbette Beeler, David Carr, and my students at California Polytechnic State University, San Luis Obispo. My mother, Jayne Burn, graciously helped with the final indexing. A number of undergraduate students helped me identify and xerox research articles for the book. In particular I would like to thank Kimberly Weich, Justin Probert, Janet Boynton, Katy O'Neil, Akila Mixon, Roger Biltz, and Brian Nosek. I am also thankful to all of the researchers cited in the book—my path was smoothed by their outstanding work. Reviewers Mykol Hamilton, David Myers, Ann Weber, and Philip Zimbardo provided thoughtful feedback and encouragement. Insightful comments were given by several anonymous reviewers as well. I would also like to thank McGraw-Hill textbook rep Andrew Poy who innocently asked me one day if I had ever thought of writing a book.

Introduction

❖

A Social Psychology of Gender ◆ Diversity and the Social Psychology of Gender ◆ Thinking Critically about Gender ◆ Sex versus Gender ◆ Overview of Book

In her comic strip *Sylvia* cartoonist Nicole Hollander invited readers to identify the sexes of the persons making the statements below, on the coldest day of the year, their ears bright red: (1) "I don't need a hat, cold doesn't bother me." (2) "I don't wear a hat, it makes my hair look funny." I doubt you had any trouble with this task because each statement reflects a common gender stereotype. This book explores the social-psychological nature of gender roles and stereotypes. Such roles and stereotypes profoundly affect our lives, influencing our behavior, self-concepts, career choices, and perceptions of others.

A SOCIAL PSYCHOLOGY OF GENDER

Social psychology is the scientific study of how the social context affects the individual's thoughts, feelings, and behaviors. The social psychology of gender is a research-derived tale of gender as a social norm promoted by culture and by our natural information-processing tendencies. It is an example of the power of social norms and roles and the crippling power of conformity. It is an illustration of some of social psychology's most important concepts such as attitudes, social norms and roles, prejudice and discrimination, social perception and self-perception, self-esteem, and social cognition. In addition, the social-psychological study of gender is a case of social change and the role of social psychology in promoting equality. In this way the social psychology of gender is also consistent with the goals of feminism. Feminism is concerned with the political, economic, and social equality of women and men (Hyde, 1991).

Lott (1991) noted that the fit between social psychology and the study of gender is a good one since "to study the conditions under which social behavior is acquired and maintained is to study how culture constructs gender" (p. 506). However, while social psychology has a long history of concern with stereotyping, prejudice, and discrimination, (cf. LaPiere, 1934), the social-psychological study of gender and women as a discriminated-against social group did not occur in social psychology until the women's movement of the late 1960s and 1970s when traditional gender roles were seriously questioned. Social-psychological research on gender was also stimulated by the women entering social psychology graduate programs in the late 1960s and early 1970s, women who were aware of their minority status in the field and who had difficulty getting accepted into graduate programs due to their sex.

There are several ways to approach a social psychology of gender. One is to focus exclusively on those studies of gender conducted by social psychologists. Another way, and the one I chose, is to develop a unified social psychology of gender using concepts from social psychology as well as other "psychologies" such as developmental psychology. I made this choice because I found that to develop a coherent social-psychological view of gender I had to rely partly on ideas and studies that have originated in other areas of psychology. Much of the work on gender done in other areas of psychology is easily recast in terms of important social-psychological concepts.

DIVERSITY AND THE SOCIAL PSYCHOLOGY OF GENDER

Prior to the 1970s, most of the research conducted by social psychologists (as well as that of other psychologists) used only white male undergraduate students as subjects for study. Part of this was undoubtedly due to the fact that there were more white males in college and therefore more available for study. It is also possible that the behavior of white males was seen as more important due to their higher social status. It is also notable that at that time most social psychologists were white males and may have been studying those with whom they were most comfortable: other white males. In addition, the experimental method used by social psychologists emphasized experimental control—which meant that all variables other than the casual variable of interest (the independent variable) were held constant. This way, if groups that varied on the independent variable differed on some social behavior (the dependent variable) the experimenter could be sure the difference was due to the independent variable, since this was the only conclusion that could be drawn if the groups were identical except for the independent variable. Gender and ethnicity were seen as "nuisance variables" and were controlled by using white male subjects in all independent variable groups (McHugh, Koeske, & Frieze, 1986). Today experimental control is still customary but both male and female subjects are usually used and gender is typically analyzed as an additional independent variable.

Unfortunately, due to a reliance on college students for subjects, subject diversity in terms of age, ethnicity, culture, and social class still remain a problem for social psychology and, correspondingly, the social psychology of gender. While a number of cross-cultural psychology texts have appeared in the last several years, to my knowledge none of these includes a chapter on cross-cultural gender psychology. Part of this is certainly due to the newness of the psychological study of gender in countries other than the United States. It is only in the last several years that gender studies conducted in countries other than the United States have appeared in major psychological research journals. There is also surprisingly little research on subcultural differences, even within the United States. I have included a chapter on gender across cultures and integrated available research on the psychology of gender in different American subcultures throughout the text.

THINKING CRITICALLY ABOUT GENDER

Social psychology is more reliable than our commonsense notions of social reality, which are often biased by our expectations and preexisting beliefs. Social psychologists rarely offer their *opinions* as facts. Instead, social-psychological claims are based on research studies designed to objectively test hypotheses about human behavior. These are typically published in scientific journals complete with detailed descriptions of the study's methodology. Because a biased or poorly conducted study is unlikely to be published in a psychological journal, scientific quality is maintained. Most of this book is based on published research studies. Some I describe at length, but for many I simply provide the authors' names and the year their research was published in parentheses at the end of a sentence summarizing study findings. When you see "et al." after one person's name it means "and others," an indication that there are at least two other authors of the work. Complete references, alphabetized by authors' last names, appear at the end of the book. I recommend that you examine some of these closely, especially when something is said that runs counter to what you have always thought about females and males. Most university libraries carry the research journals in which the articles appear or are able to order articles they do not have from other libraries for you.

Research indicates that people often do not fully understand statistics (Nisbett & Ross, 1980). So keep in mind, as you read this book and research studies, that although there are exceptions to most "rules" regarding human behavior, such rules may still be generally true. When psychologists say that research shows that women do the majority of the housework even when they work full time, they are aware that there are exceptions. Remember: Your thinking of a case which does not fit the research conclusion does not mean that *in general* the conclusion is false. It is also important to understand that when psychologists talk about groups being *significantly different* they have used statistics to determine this, they have not just "eyeballed" the groups and concluded this.

When I first began reading about the psychology of gender 10 years ago, I had not given much thought to gender issues. Since then I have read hundreds of gender studies. Based on research, I am now persuaded that gender differences are largely socially created, that traditional gender roles are limiting to both men and women, and that our natural information-processing strategies lead us to perceive gender differences to be larger than they really are. But do not take my word for it or dismiss me too fast if you think I am wrong. Hear me out and before dismissing my argument, think deeply about your own position. Try to develop clear arguments against my position, ideally seeking good research evidence to support your case. Even if you do not agree with me by the book's end, I sincerely hope that the book stimulates you to think critically about gender issues.

SEX VERSUS GENDER

As you read the book you will notice that I often use the word "gender" instead of "sex." In most contexts, psychologists prefer the word "gender" because it includes the idea that many differences between men and women are culturally created while the word "sex" implies that the differences are caused directly by biological sex (Gentile, 1993; Unger & Crawford, 1993). A further bonus is that the word "gender" provides greater clarity in some cases (e.g., if I called this book *The Social Psychology of Sex* you might get the wrong idea about its contents). There are cases however, when it is appropriate to use the word sex. For instance, when referring to one's biological male or femaleness we are essentially talking about one's biological sex. Deaux (1985, 1993) has said that it is appropriate to use sex to describe the demographic categories of female and male (e.g., it would be acceptable to ask people "What is your sex?" on a questionnaire). However, she recommended that "gender" be used when one is making judgments or inferences about the nature of femaleness and maleness. Unger (1988) noted that the definition of sex typically includes traits caused directly by biological sex whereas gender refers to those aspects of female and male for which causality has not been established. The problem, she said, is that causality is often not clear and may arise from both biological and social influences. This issue of terminology has not yet been resolved by social scientists. Therefore it is customary for authors to define their choice from the outset. In this book, I follow Deaux's (1985, 1993) recommendation and use the term "sex" only as a demographic category based on one's biological sex [although Unger (1988) noted that there are in reality more than two sexes when we consider sex to involve chromosome composition, hormones, and genital structure]. The remainder of the time I use the term "gender" to reflect the socially constructed nature of male and femaleness.

OVERVIEW OF BOOK

Chapter 1 develops the idea that many gender differences which we assume are biological may actually result from social norms which specify different behaviors and interests for females and males. The processes by which we learn appropriate gender-role behavior and our motivations for conforming to them are also discussed. Chapter 2 discusses research on gender differences focusing on mathematics and emotion and several difference areas commonly studied by social psychologists. As you will see, these differences are not nearly as large as popular stereotypes would have us believe and they continue to get smaller as the years pass. Also, a close examination of social norms and socialization practices explains a large part of the remaining differences. Chapter 3 examines the limitations of the traditional female sex role for women while Chapter 4 examines the limitations of the traditional male role for men. I have found that reflecting upon these limitations and the often arbitrary nature of gender roles motivates people to examine the influence of these roles in their own lives and play a part in changing them for the better. Chapter 5 applies social cognition to the topic of gender. It explores some of the cognitive forces driving gender stereotyping and how these interfere with change. Chapter 6 discusses gender across cultures. The vast majority of research studies by psychologists on the topic of gender have used Euroamerican subjects from the United States, and cross-cultural research can offer important insights into the role of culture in the creation of gender differences, Finally, Chapter 7 discusses changing gender roles, examining areas where change has occurred, barriers to change, and how to bring about still-needed changes.

1

$\mathcal{G}$ender $\mathcal{D}$ifferences and $\mathcal{S}$ocialization

Why Women Aren't Really Born to Shop and Men Aren't Biologically Destined to Believe in the Laundry Fairy

———— ❖ ————

I like stand-up comedy and I have noticed that many comedians base their routines on how different males and females are (watch some stand-up comedy and you will see what I mean). For instance, comedian Elayne Boosler

1

once said, "I know how they can motivate women in combat. Just tell them that the guys on the other side said that their uniforms make them look fat." Humorist Dave Barry (1991) said, "Today's man knows that he is supposed to be a sensitive and caring relationship partner, and he's making radical life-style changes such as remembering to remove the used tissue wads from his pockets before depositing his pants on the floor to be picked up by the laundry fairy." If we change the genders of the actors in these jokes, the jokes no longer make sense: The jokes work because they reflect common cultural beliefs about differences between men and women.

Most people assume that gender differences in behavior and social roles arise from biological differences between the genders. To the average person, gender differences are a fact of nature, not nurture. Social psychologists admit that there may be some biological differences between females and males but believe that these far from explain gender differences, and that such biological sex differences exert relatively minor effects on behavior. The purpose of this chapter is to help you consider the possibility that many gender differences are due to culture and socialization, rather than to inborn differences between males and females.

Let us begin by considering my son Kane. Kane has short hair in the front but a long "tail" which stretches halfway down his back. He is adamant about his hairstyle and says, "I wouldn't look like me without my tail." However, Kane's tail has created social problems for him. Throughout kindergarten and first and second grades (at this writing he is in second grade) Kane has come home upset saying that "So-and-So says I look like a girl." Kane will also play with the more "tomboyish" girls and is criticized by many of the boys for being "too nice to the girls." It was clear to him from the way these things were said that his hairstyle and behavior toward girls were unacceptable to many of the other children. Such social disapproval is often enough to cause children to change their behavior to fit social expectations for their gender.

When this happened to Kane for the first time in kindergarten, Kane asked me why boys and girls have to dress differently and play different games. If Kane asked you this question you probably would respond, "Well, that's just the way it is and if you don't want people to make fun of you or think you're weird, you should probably go along with it." In other words, you would communicate to Kane that there are indeed different norms for females and males, and that to receive social rewards one had best conform to these.

SOCIAL NORMS AND GENDER DIFFERENCES

Social norms are essentially social rules which specify appropriate social behavior. According to social psychologists, the explanation for many gender differences lies not so much in the chromosomes or hormones as in the social norms which communicate that different behaviors, attitudes, and interests are appropriate depending upon your gender. Sets of norms that communicate what is generally appropriate for each sex are called *sex roles* or *gender roles*. Some of these social norms are subtly communicated through the mediums of television and literature. Others are communicated explicitly such as when we deviate from expected gender-role behavior and experience social disapproval.

The idea that much of our behavior is shaped by social norms and the social context has a long history in social psychology. Indeed, I think that this is the greatest lesson of social psychology. Eagly (1987) has suggested that gender stereotypes actually constitute social norms. By this she meant that we have beliefs about the appropriateness of particular qualities and behaviors for males and females, that for the most part people agree on these, and that we are typically aware of what is considered to be appropriate behavior for females and males. Social psychologists would expect us to be motivated to conform to these gender expectations for two reasons, sometimes called "normative" and "informational pressure," terms first coined by Deutsch and Gerard in 1955.

The Role of Normative Pressure

Normative pressure results from the fact that we often conform to societal or group expectations (social norms) to avoid social rejection. This obviously plays a role in our adherence to gender roles. Several studies have found that gender-inconsistent behavior is particularly likely to interfere with the popularity of boys (Berndt & Heller, 1986; Huston, 1983; Martin, 1990) and that parents react negatively to cross-sex play behaviors (Fagot, 1978; Langlois & Downs, 1980). These different sets of norms for male and female behavior are operative beyond childhood and even as adults we tend to conform to these different expectations in order to avoid social rejection. Unfortunately, there is little research on the role of normative pressure in the conformity of adults to gender roles. One study (O'Leary & Donoghue, 1978) found that college students find cross-sex behavior acceptable, while two others found that gender-inappropriate behavior led to reduced popularity (Berndt & Heller, 1986; Tilby & Kalin, 1980).

Whenever I think of normative pressure for conformity to gender norms I think of a guy I knew named Cliff. While in college I was a waitress and I shared a shift with Cliff (we called ourselves "waitrons"). Cliff was fascinated with gender roles and decided to violate a few gender norms. He began by wearing pink nail polish and lipstick and eventually waited tables wearing a skirt. We kept track of his tips based on his outfit. When he violated gender norms regarding dress, Cliff was clearly punished by lower tips. Management eventually intervened and requested that Cliff wear pants and less makeup.

Do you think that there is social punishment for deviating from your gender role? Have you ever found it difficult to violate your gender role? Many women tell me that they fear being considered too aggressive (and called a "bitch"), and men fear that if they are too responsive to their female partner's needs they may be perceived as unmanly by their friends. You can probably think of other derogatory names that are only used for one of the genders and reflect different norms for females and males.

Punishment for nonconformity to gender roles can be severe. The Ayatollah Khomeini, leader of Iran from 1979 until the mid-1980s, abolished all laws granting women rights and killed as many as 20,000 women who did not follow strict codes regarding women's dress and conduct (French, 1992). Under ultraorthodox Judaism (*not* followed by the majority of Jews), women who refuse to provide sex to their husbands or neglect household duties may be divorced without their consent and deprived of any property or their children. Hasidic men physically attacked a group of women led by a female rabbi carrying the Torah who wanted to worship at the Wailing Wall in Jerusalem because the Hasidim believe that women should not be allowed to wear worship shawls or even touch the Torah. Over 20 million women in the world have been genitally mutilated in order to preserve their virginity and prevent orgasm. In spite of the severe pain and long-term physical problems that accompany the practice, it persists because men will not marry an unmutilated girl and a girl must marry to survive (French, 1992). Conformity to this mutilation is necessary in order for the women to gain the approval of their societies. Some religions in the United States, such as the Church of the Latter Day Saints and Catholicism, socially pressure women to conform to traditional gender roles and on occasion excommunicate (i.e., expel) women who violate their gender role as defined by the church. In some Protestant religions, women who question women's subservience to men are visited by disapproving pastors who point out those Biblical passages supportive of women's submission to men.

Homosexuality as a Violation of Gender Norms

Another case which illustrates the importance of gender norms to our society and the consequences of not conforming to them is the reaction that many people have to homosexuality. For instance, organizers of a 1994 Boston St. Patrick's Day parade chose to cancel the parade rather than to follow a court ruling allowing gays to participate. We are socialized from a very early age that we are to marry someone of the other sex, have children with them, and assume particular role relationships in regard to the other gender. People who choose not to have children or do not marry (heterosexual or homosexual), or who have romantic and/or sexual relationships with people of their own gender, are often seen as violating their gender roles and experience serious social pressure to conform.

To many people homosexuality is the ultimate violation of gender norms. Kite and Deaux (1987) and Taylor (1983) found that heterosexuals' stereotypes of homosexuals reflect the "inversion theory of sexuality," the assumption that homosexuals are similar to opposite-sex heterosexuals. According to research, however, such stereotypes of homosexuals are actually quite inaccurate (Peplau & Gordon, 1983; Taylor, 1983; Viss & Burn, 1992). For instance, one common stereotype of homosexual relationships is that one partner enacts the traditional male role and the other the female role. Research however indicates that in most gay and lesbian relationships both partners are employed and equitably divide housework (Blumstein & Schwartz, 1983; Kurdek, 1993; Peplau & Gordon, 1983). People with traditional sex-role attitudes are generally less accepting of homosexuals (Black & Stevenson, 1984; Dew, 1985; Herek, 1984; Holtzen & Agresti, 1990; Krulewitz & Nash, 1980). Presumably those who value traditional gender roles devalue homosexuals because they see them as role deviants while those less invested in the roles do not care quite so much (Taylor, 1983).

Like the violation of many norms, homosexuality has a serious social price. For homosexuals this price may be paid in the form of physical attacks, discrimination in employment, personal rejection, and derogatory names and jokes. For most of U.S. history, homosexual behavior has been punishable by law and unequal treatment of homosexuals is still allowed to some extent under the law. For instance, in *Bowers v. Hardwick* (1986), the Supreme Court ruled that the fundamental right of privacy did not extend to private consensual homosexual conduct. Leonard (1991) discussed in detail a number of legal cases heard in the high courts of the United States which reflect the stigmatization of homosexuality.

It was not until 1974 that the American Psychiatric Association removed homosexuality from its list of mental disorders. Psychologists now believe that when homosexuals experience mental health problems it is often because of the covert existences homosexuals feel forced to lead due to society's disapproval (Cain, 1991). (This is not to imply that homosexuals are less mentally healthy than average because research does not support such an assertion; it is just to suggest that some of the difficulties that they face arise from societal disapproval.) Others have noted that great psychological conflict occurs due to a perceived conflict between the perceived ideals of society and the perception of oneself as gay (Hellwege et al., 1988; Thompson, 1992). Given the social unacceptability of homosexuality, it is not surprising that disclosure of one's homosexuality is a difficult decision and one that typically involves a lot of planning and a lot of stress. Disclosure may lead to harassment, loss of relationships, relationship stress, or job loss (Cain, 1991) and loss of one's children. Concealing one's homosexuality also involves a lot of concerted effort and stress.

Secrecy may lead to feelings of dishonesty and interfere with relationship intimacy since an important part of one's identity is being hidden (Cain, 1991). The potential for social stigmatization is a major determinant of whether the gay person "comes out" to others or remains secretive. Several studies have found that a concern with social rejection is a major factor in remaining "closeted" (Franke & Leary, 1991). Being homosexual in a largely heterosexually oriented society is so difficult that, in response to the claim that homosexuality is a choice, some homosexuals reply that they probably would not be homosexual if it were a choice: It is too difficult in a society that does not approve of them (Fairchild & Hayward, 1989).

Deviation from one's gender role is often viewed as evidence of homosexuality, a label many wish to avoid since they know of its social undesirability. For instance, by the fourth grade, boys in the United States use terms such as "fag" or "queer" to insult low-status boys (Thorne & Luria, 1986). Several studies (Deaux & Lewis, 1984; Storms et al., 1981) have found that subjects perceive those who have traits of the other gender as more likely to be homosexual. A desire to avoid this socially stigmatizing label is partly behind conformity to gender roles. Some have argued that the association of gender rebellion with homosexuality has seriously discouraged gender-role change (Phelan, 1993; Silber, 1990). Heterosexual males may be especially negative toward gay males because they are more invested in traditional roles and because deviation from the male role is more likely to be associated with homosexuality than deviation from the female role (Morin & Garfinkle, 1978; Whitely, 1990). Although in principle I recommend that gay people "come out" in order to reduce nongays' stereotypes of homosexuals (Viss & Burn, 1992), it is certainly rational for gay individuals to be selective about whether to come out and whom to come out to. Our society still reflects significant antihomosexual prejudice and gays are likely to experience negative social consequences for deviating from their gender roles.

The Role of Informational Pressure

Informational pressure refers to the fact that we rely heavily on social information to increase our knowledge about ourselves and the world and to gain information about appropriate attitudes regarding social issues (Smith, 1982). In other words, sometimes we conform not simply because we fear social disapproval if we do not but because we really do not know what to think, feel, believe, or do without the guidance of others. Under such circumstances, we turn to others for clues and follow their leads. This makes a great deal of sense when you think about it. We live in a world full of objects, institutions, and situations created by people and unintelligible without them. It is therefore quite adaptive to rely on social information to increase our knowledge about the world and social issues. Cialdini (1993) has pointed out that we determine what is correct by finding out what other people think is correct and we view a behavior as correct to the extent that we see others performing it (he called this "social proof"). In regard to gender roles, when we look around us and see men and women doing different things and hear others (including the media) emphasize how different men and women are, we assume it is so and conform to these expectations. The idea that genders are and should be different is so pervasive in our culture it is not surprising that we would assume it is right. Later in this chapter we will discuss the numerous ways in which such information is conveyed to us. Aronson (1992) has suggested that normative pressure gets its power from our desire to be liked and informational pressure gets its power from our desire to be right. Informational pressure, in combination with normative pressure for compliance to gender norms, partly explains the strong influence of gender norms on our behavior.

Conformity as Cognitively Economical

We may also look at our tendency to conform to social norms as cognitively economical. By this I mean it saves thinking—in a given social situation all we have to do is mindlessly trot out the socially appropriate behavior. In his book *Influence,* Robert Cialdini (1993) made a compelling and entertaining argument regarding the role of social norms in simplifying our lives and reducing the thinking we have to do. Such a tendency, he noted, normally serves us well. Perhaps at an early age we discover just how much simpler life is when we conform to social norms and so we learn to do it virtually automatically. Such is often the case with gender norms. Most people just comply with them unconsciously, without questioning them.

Conformity to Gender Norms: Compliance, Acceptance, or Identification?

While our dominant response may be to conform almost automatically to social norms, there are clearly cases where we do not want to. Social psychologists recognize that just because people conform, doing so does not necessarily mean they agree with the social convention. Sometimes we change our behavior in compliance with social norms even though we do not really embrace them. This type of conformity has been called *compliance* and is guided by *normative pressure* (the desire to avoid social punishment and to gain social approval). For example, the norm at Dee's grandmother's house is for the women to serve the men dinner, carry their empty plates away, and do all the clean-up. Dee does not believe this is right, yet does it at her grandmother's house because if she does not her family gets upset. She only serves her husband there. Her husband conforms as well. He does not normally wait for women to serve him but conforms to the norm at Grandma's by staying seated rather than helping. This example illustrates an important sign of compliance, which is that when the threat of punishment for nonconformity is absent, a different behavior is seen.

Other times, we truly agree with the norms we conform to. This type of conformity is called *acceptance* or *internalization*. For instance, when I was a child, my mother practically waited on my father hand and foot and told me that, because men were superior to women, this is the way it should be. She was not simply conforming externally, she accepted the norm. Informational influence often gives rise to acceptance of social norms and behaviors that are resistant to change since the person truly believes in them. However, if the social context starts offering a different story (as may be the case with women working outside of the home, for example), the person may change. My mother has changed and no longer believes that women are inferior to men and that women should do all the housework.

A third type of conformity, called *identification*, occurs when we do things that peers or role models do, simply because we want to be like them. An example of this would be a male child who greatly admires his traditionally male dad and consequently adopts many of his dad's views. A student of mine wrote about how when she was a child she strongly identified with the character "Mary" from the television show *Little House on the Prairie* (NBC, 1974–1982):

> The years before I began watching *Little House on the Prairie* I was beyond a doubt a tomboy. This changed once I began watching *Little House*. I began changing everything to be just like Mary. I never saw Mary in shorts or pants, she always wore a clean dress. So I began wearing dresses and was careful not to get them dirty. Mary was well-liked by her teacher and worked hard at school, so I did too. My interest in housework increased also. I watched Mary help her mother around the house and because of Mary's influence, I began to set the table and do the dishes without being asked. I would help my mother sort the laundry and I began to make my bed because I noticed that Mary's bed was always made.

As Aronson (1992) pointed out, beliefs due to identification can change if a new identification supersedes a previous one (e.g., you could come to identify with a peer group more than dad). For instance, the young woman who identified so strongly with the character in *Little House on the Prairie* later came to identify with her mother, a career woman.

You might be wondering at this point whether conformity to gender roles is more likely to be due to compliance, acceptance, or identification. Unfortunately, there is little research on this topic although several studies find that both women and men behave more sex stereotypically in public than in private (Eagly & Crowley, 1986; Eagly et al., 1981; Eisenberg & Lennon, 1983). This is suggestive of compliance rather than acceptance or identification. Research on the male role which finds that endorsement of traditional masculinity is weak (Burn & Laver, 1994; Thompson & Pleck, 1986) also suggests the greater role of compliance in conformity to the role.

The two conformity pressures, normative and informational, are not mutually exclusive. Pleck et al. (1993b) have suggested that those who internalize traditional gender roles (presumably via informational pressure) are more likely to be affected by social disapproval for violating them (normative pressure). Conversely, pervasive social information suggesting that conformity to the role is desirable may lead to conformity even in the absence of internalization. After all, most people want to be socially accepted.

Individuals also vary in their adherence to traditional sex roles. Kagan (1964) and Kohlberg (1966) noted that some individuals are highly sex-typed (e.g., strongly feminine if they are female and strongly masculine if they are male) and that such individuals are motivated to keep their behavior consistent with their gender-role standards. Such individuals suppress any behavior that might be considered inappropriate for their genders. Frable (1989) found sex-typed individuals were more likely to accept gender rules designating culturally appropriate behavior for men and women. Societal subgroups within a society may also result in variations in conformity to traditional gender roles. Some religions, for example, strongly reward conformity to traditional gender roles while others are more flexible. Jones and McNamara (1991) found that individuals who had internalized religious beliefs (in contrast to those for whom religion was primarily a source of comfort and social convenience) had more traditional values regarding women. Individual differences in personality and abilities probably affect adherence as well. For instance, a mathematically gifted female may take advanced math courses and a small, delicately boned male probably will not play football.

Last, some individuals have experiences where deviations from their gender roles resulted in feelings of humiliation either because the punishment was objectively severe or because it was perceived to be so because it occurred at a time of personal insecurity. Individuals with such *critical gender socialization experiences* may be particularly motivated to conform to traditional sex roles due to the salience (memorability) of their negative experiences. (This is just a hypothesis at this point; I have not seen any research testing it.) For instance, one of my students told me that her father was named Michelle and her uncle Nicole. These names resulted in a great deal of ridicule as they were growing up. She says that they were two of the most macho men she has ever known (incidentally, they changed their names to Michael and Nick). It is possible that their strong conformity to the traditional male role could be partly a reaction to the ridicule they experienced as children. Likewise, several of my female students have written about haircuts after which they made strong efforts to conform to the female role. One wrote:

> I was eight years old. My school was having a carnival and I was extremely excited about going, but my mom said I had to get a haircut before I was allowed to go. My Dad, being the resourceful guy that he is, took me to his barber shop. When I got to the carnival and saw my mom she broke down in tears and yelled at my father for letting the barber "scalp" me. For the next four weeks I was mistaken for a boy at least once a day. I made up my mind right then and there that I would never be mistaken for a boy again. I grew my hair long and refused to wear anything else but a dress. My senior class voted me "most likely to have ten kids" and I was thrilled.

DIFFERENTIAL SOCIALIZATION

A social psychology of gender views gender as greatly influenced by cultural norms that specify what males and females should do and by social information that tells people how females and males are different. Normative and informational pressures partly explain the process by which these norms are learned, and our motivation to conform to them. In this section, _gender-role socialization_, the process by which we learn what is socially appropriate for females and males, is discussed. Although many of the ideas presented here originated in developmental rather than social psychology, they are quite relevant to a social psychology of gender.

Developmental psychologists use the term _differential socialization_ to describe the process by which we teach females and males that different things are appropriate depending upon an individual's gender. Socialization, of course, is the process by which we teach individuals appropriate social behaviors, values, etc. According to the _cognitive-developmental theory_ of gender developed by Kohlberg (1966), all this information regarding appropriate gender behavior is represented mentally in _gender schemas_. These schemas consist of all the information the individual has learned about gender. Schemas guide information processing by influencing what we pay attention to and, because it is easier to encode into memory information that fits with what we already believe, schemas influence memory as well. Developmental psychologists have focused on gender schemas in childhood while social psychologists have focused on gender schemas and their role in gender stereotyping in adulthood. These cognitive roots of gender are explored extensively in Chap. 5. In Chap. 6, we will see that differential socialization is a pancultural phenomenon—in all cultures male and female children are socialized differently.

The beginnings of differential socialization can be seen even before a baby is born. Why do you think prospective parents want to know whether their baby will be a girl or a boy? Why do you think other people also want to know? (Did you know that pregnant women are constantly asked if they know whether the child is a girl or boy and whether they want a girl or a boy?) These inquiring minds want to know because they think of children differently depending on gender. Parents want to know because the gender of their child will determine the name they will give it, the clothing, toys, and decorations they will buy, and the activities they anticipate doing with their child. One study of infants (Shakin et al., 1985), conducted at suburban shopping malls, found that 90 percent of the infants were wearing clothing which was sex-typed in style or color. In Mexico, parents pierce the ears of infant girls so that the sex of the child is clear to observers. Elastic ribbons with bows for infant girls are currently popular in American culture. As we will see throughout the book, gender is a very important social variable. It is also one parents do not want observers to make any mistakes about.

Differential Reinforcement and Differential Modeling

There are two main mechanisms by which differential socialization occurs: differential reinforcement and differential modeling (Mischel, 1970). Differential reinforcement means that we reward appropriate gender-role behavior and punish inappropriate gender-role behavior and that different behaviors, interests, etc., are rewarded and punished depending upon one's gender. Rewards often take the form of social approval. Conversely, straying from what our culture defines as appropriate gender-role behavior is likely to be punished by social disapproval. For example, several studies found that boys who deviate from same-sex play norms suffer more peer ridicule and are less popular with peers than those who conform to sex-role stereotypes (Berndt & Heller, 1986; Steriker & Kurdek, 1982). Perry et al. (1989) surveyed fourth through seventh graders and found that boys expected less parental disapproval for aggression than did girls. Lytton and Romney (1991) statistically combined studies on parents' differential socialization conducted in the period from 1966 to 1986 and concluded that parents encourage sex-typed activities.

Children clearly identify themselves as female or male (this is called gender identification) by age 3. At this time, children begin to notice that males and females tend to do different things, look different, and be interested in different things. Adults often unintentionally encourage gender identification by regularly referring to the child's gender ("that's a good/bad boy/girl") and by saying to children "girls/boys do/don't do

(if someone (female) is in control with a high self-esteem, they may be considered as masculine)

this." By age 7, and often as early as age 3 or 4, children achieve *gender constancy,* an understanding that gender is constant and cannot be changed (Bem, 1989; Emmerich et al., 1977; Martin & Halverson, 1983b). Even before they begin elementary school, children demonstrate considerable knowledge of sex-typing of toys, clothing, activities, objects, and occupations (Serbin et al., 1993).

Once gender identification occurs and the child notes that there are differences between males and females, the child typically pays careful attention to same-sex models in order to be the best girl or boy possible (called *self-socialization,* a term coined by Kohlberg, 1966). As part of this process, girls and boys tend to model themselves after different models of behavior, with the boys usually modeling males' behaviors and the girls modeling females' behavior. This is called *differential modeling* and is based on *social learning theory* (Bandura, 1977), a theory that postulates we can learn behaviors by observing other people and whether they are rewarded or punished for what they do. Most boys between the ages of 2 and 3 try to wear their mother's shoes, play with makeup, and wear nail polish. However, once gender identification and constancy occur and they realize that these activities are reserved for girls, they begin to model the behavior of other males.

Differential modeling explains why females usually like to shop and usually do all the planning for holiday celebrations and men do not. We grow up seeing that these are things that women do, and if we are female, we watch more closely than if we are male. The same goes for other household chores like doing the laundry. Likewise, the concept of differential modeling can be used to explain why more males than females watch sports on television.

Smetana and Letourneau (1984) suggested that gender constancy seems to motivate children to seek social interactions where they might acquire information about sex appropriate behavior. Bussey and Bandura (1992) found that the sex-role behavior of younger children is motivated by external social pressure but eventually children construct their own personal standards relating to gender-linked conduct. After this occurs, children guide their own conduct by sanctions they apply to themselves. They call this a *social cognitive theory of gender self-regulation.*

Although there is evidence that children watch and learn from adults of both genders (Maccoby & Jacklin, 1974), research indicates they are more likely to *perform* gender-appropriate behaviors (Martin & Halverson, 1981, 1983a). Perry and Bussey (1979) found that children observe the frequencies with which males and females perform certain behaviors and then use these as a guide to their own behavior. They also found that children are more likely to imitate an adult's behavior if they think the model's behavior is a good guide to appropriate gender role behavior. This is why children of parents who display nonstereotypical gender-role behaviors may adopt behaviors typical of their gender roles anyway; it is clear to them from observing other adults that their parents are not typical, therefore they do not model their parents' behavior.

Many people have told me they know someone who, despite their best intentions to raise a gender-neutral child, ended up with a gender-stereotyped one. They have then concluded that this must be because biological gender differences overrode the attempted parental socialization. However, you must keep in mind that parents are not the only agents of socialization nor are they a child's only role models. You should also keep in mind that gender-role socialization is an on-going lifelong process reflecting changing circumstances and experiences. Throughout the life-span, gender is constructed or learned from what culture systematically pairs with femaleness and maleness (Lott & Maluso, 1993).

The message that females and males are and should be different is communicated in a myriad of ways throughout our culture. And, as we discussed earlier, it is probably in our nature to rely on social information to help us understand and function in our confusing world. This information sometimes comes directly from other individuals but it is also communicated through other cultural messengers. As Williams and Best (1990a, p. 240) wrote: "Beliefs concerning the psychological makeup of women and men are absorbed into myth and religion, into oral history and written literature. Heroes and heroines, real or fanciful, embody the stereotypic characteristics of the sexes and serve as potent modes for sex-appropriate characteristics."

Nonparental Sources of Gender-Role Socialization

Children's Literature
Teachers, other children, other children's parents, books, relatives, toys, and television all communicate to children what society views as gender-appropriate behavior. Most of the research on sexism in children's literature has focused on documenting content rather than its effects on behavior. However, one experimental study found that exposure to sex-stereotyped books contributed to an increase in children's sex-typed play behavior (Ashton, 1983).

Although recent research (such as Purcell & Stewart, 1990) has found improvement in the portrayal of the genders in books published in the 1980s (the good news), libraries are full of books predating this period (the bad news). Such books tend to have more male characters than female, and they portray females almost exclusively in domestic roles while portraying males in a wider variety of roles (McDonald, 1989). These stories may suggest to children that with the exception of childrearing it is a "man's world" and that females are less important than men.

Crabb and Bielawski (1994) analyzed illustrations in Caldecott Medal and honors books from 1937 to 1989 for changes in "gender marking."

These books are prominent in libraries and bookstores and the authors assumed them to be representative of children's actual reading material. An object's gender marking indicates whether it should be used predominantly by females, or predominantly by males. Gender marking is important because, as discussed earlier, children observe the frequencies with which males and females perform behaviors and are more likely to imitate a behavior if it is seen as gender-appropriate. Results from the study were that a significantly larger proportion of female characters were portrayed with household objects (e.g., cooking utensils, brooms, etc.) and that this proportion did not change over the 53-year period. The proportion of male characters using household objects, however, was found to significantly increase over time. Males were significantly more likely to be depicted with production objects (objects used for work outside of the home) than were females, while the proportions of female characters using production objects did not increase significantly over the 53-year period. This study suggests that, with the exception of a greater number of boys depicted using household objects, children's picture books have changed relatively little over the years in their depiction of gender-based labor.

Television
Gerbner and Gross (1976) viewed television as having a unique ability to cultivate basic assumptions about the nature of social reality because it reflects and magnifies the status quo, its images are portrayed with great realism, and people make wide and selective use of it. Bandura (1969) suggested that television competes with parents and teachers as a provider of role models for emulation. Research suggests that the media are part of our gender-role socialization and analyses of television suggest that what is modeled on television are stereotypical and traditional female and male images. One of my students wrote about the impact the television show *The Brady Bunch* had on her gender-role socialization. This show first ran on ABC from 1969 to 1974 and is still seen in syndication:

> As a child my favorite past-time was watching *Brady Bunch* re-runs. At that time my goal in life was to be the perfect wife like Carol Brady, to have six or seven kids, and to let my husband take care of me. That was still my goal when I came to college. In fact it wasn't until last year that I seriously started considering a career and changed my major from home economics to psychology.

Signorielli (1989) analyzed week-long samples of prime-time network dramatic programs broadcast between 1969 and 1985 and found that approximately 71 percent of the people on prime-time television and 69 percent of the main characters were male. Trend analyses revealed relatively little change over the 16-year period. On television women were, on average, younger than the men; more attractive and nurturing; portrayed in the context of romantic interests, home, and family; and more likely to be victimized. Only three out of 10 married female characters worked outside of the home (in the real world, over half of married women work) and when women did work they were usually cast in traditional female occupations. In contrast, men were not only portrayed significantly more frequently, but they were portrayed in high-status jobs such as doctors and lawyers or masculine jobs such as police officers. Atkin et al. (1991) described a comprehensive study of 555 television characters, and in regard to female characters wrote that "the vast majority conformed to male fantasies of scantily clad half-wits who need to be rescued" (p. 679).

VandeBerg and Streckfuss (1992) analyzed 116 prime-time television program episodes covering 2 weeks of programming from each of the three major U.S. networks. Not only did they find male characters to outnumber female characters by 2 to 1 (65 percent to 35 percent), but they found that working women were significantly less likely to be portrayed as decision-makers, assertive corporate politicians, and socially and economically productive working persons. In addition, they noted that women in upper-level management positions on television typically inherited these positions from their spouses or relatives. Although male characters on television are more frequently portrayed and are often shown as more powerful than women characters, their portrayal also leaves something to be desired. VandeBerg and Streckfuss pointed out that men are often presented as tough, self-centered, and aggressively competitive. Furthermore, men are more likely than women to be depicted as negative characters and women are more likely to be portrayed as interpersonally sensitive.

Davis (1991) analyzed the entire spring 1987 network programming. He found that there were significantly more male than female characters (65 percent were male versus 35 percent female). He also found that adult females were significantly younger than adult males (by about 10 years), and that women were four times more likely to be blonde than men and four times more likely to be provocatively dressed than male characters. According to Tavris (1992), an analysis of television by Brett Silverstein in the late 1980s found that 69 percent of women on television are very thin compared to 17.5 percent of men. Davis (1991) suggested that the portrayal that emerges is that of the young, attractive, sexy female who in many shows is more ornamental than functional. Davis concluded that such portrayals suggest to us that women are valuable in as much as they are young and fulfill traditional cultural definitions of beauty and femininity. Ask the women you know what they think about this.

Sports media are also notable in their portrayal of the sexes. In a review of research on images of men in sports media, Sabo and Jansen (1992) concluded that men are portrayed in sports as dominant, masculine, and valued while women are shown as subordinate, feminine, and devalued. For instance, they reported that sports media often inferiorize women as sex objects (the famous *Sports Illustrated* swimsuit issue is the most obvious example) and that 85 percent to 95 percent of media coverage is given to male sports. The women's sports that receive the most coverage are those that are most feminine, such as figure skating. The coverage itself is also interesting. In the case of male sports, it is dominated by descriptions of physical power and domination. For female sports, the coverage is often framed in terms of appearance, attractiveness, and grace, while strength is played down (Sabo & Jansen, 1992).

Content analyses of television commercials indicate that they too largely portray males and females in sex-stereotyped ways. Such studies (Bretl & Cantor, 1988; Lovdal, 1989) have found that the voice of authority in commercials is almost always male, that females appear predominantly in commercials selling domestic products, and that men are portrayed in three times the variety of occupations. Bretl and Cantor estimated that the average American views approximately 714 television commercials a week. Strate (1992), in an analysis of beer commercials, concluded that such ads exploit traditional images of masculinity to sell beer and constitute a guide for becoming a man.

What does the research say about changes in the way television presents the genders? Atkin et al. (1991) did find that the number of female leads on programs increased through the 1980s. Furthermore, they pointed out that most of the shows featuring nonstereotypical women originated with female producers. In an analysis of the family as portrayed in prime-time television, Moore (1992) found the percentage of employed mothers shown went from 3 percent in the 1950s to 30 percent in the 1980s. Moore's analysis of family shows from 1950 to 1990 led him to conclude that television has actually exaggerated changes in male roles, with its large number of male single-parent portrayals and portrayals of men who emphasize family roles over work roles.

Are people really influenced by television? By the sheer quantity of it Americans watch you would certainly expect so. Television watching is up to $7\frac{1}{4}$ hours per home per day and by the time they graduate from high school students will have spent more time watching television than in the classroom (Davis, 1991). According to Kimball (1986), children who watch television have more strongly sex-typed attitudes that those who do not. Other studies (e.g., Cobb et al., 1982; McGhee & Frueh, 1980; Steeves, 1987) have found a positive relationship between exposure to sex-stereotyped media content and sex-stereotyped perceptions, attitudes, and behaviors. Of course these findings are correlational and it is possible that the direction of the relationship is the opposite (researchers call this the "directionality problem"). In other words, individuals with sex-stereotyped attitudes may be more likely to watch sex-stereotyped programming. Or it could be that children whose parents let them watch sex-stereotyped programming are more sex-stereotyped than parents who do not allow such viewing and that it is not the viewing but rather the parental attitudes that are responsible for the relationship between childrens' viewing and their stereotypes (researchers call this the "third-variable problem").

Several experimental studies (which control for "third" variables and "directionality" problems) have found that televised models can influence children's perceptions of the genders. Ruble et al. (1981) found children played less with a neutral toy after seeing a television commercial where a child of the other sex was playing with it and were more likely to consider such a toy to be appropriate for an opposite-sex sibling. A similar study by Cobb et al. (1982) is discussed later in this chapter. Experimental studies by Geis et al. (1984) and Jennings et al. (1980) found that the viewing of sex-stereotyped commercials influenced the career aspirations, conformity, and self-confidence of female subjects. For example, Jennings et al. (1980) randomly assigned women to one of two groups. One independent variable group viewed a set of four replicas of television commercials on the air at that time that portrayed women in traditional roles in relation to men (domestic or sex-object roles). For example, one commercial was a replica of a "Hungry Man" frozen dinner commercial where a diminutive wife proudly serves her gigantic husband his meal. The other independent variable group viewed the same four commercials except that each of the roles was played by a person of the other sex.

Jennings et al. (1980) hypothesized that the women who viewed the traditional commercials would show less independence of judgment and lower self-confidence (the dependent variables) than the women who viewed the reversed-roles commercials. The researchers measured independence of judgment by having half of the subjects participate in another study (bogus) to find out "which cartoons people thought were funny." Subjects announced their "funniness" ratings of 16 cartoons. Before they did this, though, the experimenter casually pointed to a large blackboard showing the ratings of alleged previous subjects and told each subject that her responses would be added to that list. The women who viewed the traditional commercials conformed significantly more to the false ratings.

To measure the effects of the commercials on self-confidence, the other half of the subjects participated in a study on "opinions about the media" (also bogus). These subjects gave a 4-minute extemporaneous speech on their choice of either "harmful or misleading television commercials" or "television programs that showed violence." An experimenter, unaware of the treatment conditions of the subjects (did not know which commercials the subjects had seen), rated these subjects on seven nonverbal behaviors found by research to indicate speaker confidence (eye contact, fidgeting, etc.). Women who viewed the traditional commercials were significantly less confident than women who viewed the reversed-role commercials.

Face-ism

A number of studies show that the sexes are frequently portrayed engaging in different types of activities and social roles, but there are also more subtle cultural messages that may contribute to our differing perceptions of women and men. Archer et al. (1983) suggested that media depictions of women and men also differ in facial prominence, and called this *face-ism*. In particular, they suggested that media photos emphasize men's faces but women's bodies by showing photos of men from the neck up but full body photos of women. They found this to be true of print media in the twelve countries they studied. Nigro et al. (1988) also found that men received greater facial prominence than women in *Time, Newsweek, Good Housekeeping,* and *Ms* magazines in the 1970s and 1980s. At first glance this may not seem worthy of concern. However, as Archer et al. remarked, the face and head are the "centers of mental life—intellect, personality, identity, and character" (p. 726), and it is therefore noteworthy that media portrayals associate these more with males than females. Furthermore, in an experiment where face-ism was manipulated by these researchers, it was found that greater facial prominence led to more favorable attributions regarding intelligence, ambition, and physical appearance.

Language

Our language may also contribute to stereotyped perceptions of males and females. Henley (1989) pointed out that there are many ways in which our language treats males and females differently and, in so doing, trivializes, ignores, and demeans females. Why, for instance, do we have a special title for married women (Mrs.) but not for married men? What does this communicate? That a woman's marital status is relevant to how we perceive and respond to her while a man's is not? Why is it worse to be called a "sissy" than a "tomboy?" Henley (1989) also cited research showing that there are six to ten times as many words describing females in negative ways as males in negative ways (think for example of all the ways we have to label a sexually promiscuous female). Such words provide information about what our culture sees as gender-appropriate behavior.

Psychologists are especially concerned with the use of the "masculine generic." Although subtle, the use of the pronoun "he" and words like "man" or "mankind" to refer to the human species or the generic person, or the use of terms such as "the right man for the job," "the brotherhood of man," "the man in the street," may influence our perceptions of the genders. In my son's 1991 *Encyclopaedia Britannica* for young children, the masculine generic is rampant. So what's the big deal? The big deal is that research indicates that the generic masculine is generally not perceived as including both sexes by children (Hyde, 1984a; Switzer, 1990) or by adults (Gastil, 1990; MacKay, 1980; Moulton et al., 1978; Todd-Mancillas, 1981; Wise & Rafferty, 1982). Such studies find that the use of the generic "he" usually leads listeners to think of male images. Such uses of words, as Henly (1989) pointed out, ignore females by designating human beings as male.

I understand that you may think it is ridiculous to use "s/he" instead of "he" or to change words such as "fireman" to "firefighter" or "chairman" to "chairperson" but think about how these words communicate gender appropriateness and perhaps you will change your mind. We often grow up thinking that females cannot or should not do particular things because our language suggests that this is the case. For instance, Briere and Lanktree (1983) found that job descriptions written in the generic masculine decreased females' interest in those jobs and led readers to assume that females did not have the ability to perform the job. Psychologists are so convinced of the negative effects of the generic masculine that professional psychological journals no longer permit it.

Toys
Children's toys also appear to play an important role in differential socialization. In contrast to girls' toys and games which typically aid in the practice of domestic and mothering activities and the development of expressive skills and cooperativeness, research indicates that boys' toys and games are more likely to encourage inventiveness and manipulation of the environment, help develop skills that promote abilities relevant to the development of spatial abilities and mathematics, and promote independence, competition, and leadership skills (Block, 1979; Connor et al., 1978; Emmot, 1985; Miller, 1987; Peretti & Sydney, 1985; Pitcher & Schultz, 1983).

Go to a toy store and examine the toys. It will be clear to you that most of them are clearly intended for either boys or girls, but usually not for both. Girls' toys are easy to identify. They are usually in pink or pastel colored boxes, have a picture of a female and not a male on the box, and are either grooming-related (e.g., play cosmetics), caregiving-related (e.g., baby dolls), or housekeeping-related (e.g., vacuum cleaners, little stoves, dishes, etc.). Boys' toys are in boldly colored boxes, have boys playing with the toys on the boxes, and are often building-related (Legos, Tinker Toys, blocks) or action-oriented (action figures, guns, etc.). Miller (1987) found that children's toys continue to be differentiated with respect to gender—forty-one of the fifty toys rated in her study were considered by subjects to be differentially appropriate for girls or boys. The toys stereotyped by subjects as female were domestically oriented toys like tea sets and dolls and stuffed toys whereas boys' toys included vehicles, balls, guns, and construction toys.

The gender-appropriateness of a toy is often communicated by its name or packaging. Think about the popular hand-held computer toy known as "Game-Boy." When my son was five he asked why it was called this. "Girls can play with it, right?" he asked. "Sure," I replied. "Well, then it ought to be called 'Game-Child' so that girls know it's okay for them to play with it," he said. The problem is not just that playing with gender-appropriate toys communicates traditional sex roles, but that playing with gender-appropriate toys can also affect the skills girls and boys learn (Eccles, 1990). For example, Sprafkin et al. (1983) found that male-preferred toys such as blocks and puzzles improved children's visual-spatial skills. Etaugh and Liss (1992) found that children who received male gifts did not want female occupations and children that received female toys for gifts did not want male occupations. McClurg and Chaille (1987) found that female and male children in fifth, seventh, and ninth grades showed spatial skills gains after playing spatial-type computer games. Furthermore, Linn (1985) found that boys are more likely than girls to use computers in play.

Adults buy more sex-typed than non-sex-typed toys for young children (Pomerleau et al., 1990; Thompson et al., 1988). For example, Bradbard (1985) found that 9- to 16-month-old boys received cars and trucks and spatial-temporal toys for Christmas and girls received domestic items. I am aware that you could suggest that this is because boys and girls prefer different toys and therefore request different toys. Indeed, research (such as that by Etaugh & Liss, 1992) has found that girls want and ask for female toys while boys want and ask for male toys. For instance, my son Kane professes a strong dislike for Barbie dolls while his friend Samantha loves Barbie. Kane has never asked me for a Barbie while Samantha often asks for a Barbie and Barbie-related paraphernalia when a gift-giving occasion arises. In other words, it appears to be true that boys and girls often prefer different toys. But is this due to a "natural" preference or a socially created one?

A number of studies (Bell & Carver, 1980; Culp et al., 1983; Seavey et al., 1975; Sidorowicz & Lunney, 1980) have indicated that adults begin shaping toy preferences in infancy. For instance, in the Sidorowicz and Lunney (1980) study, subjects individually interacted with a 10-month-old child ("Baby X"). Subjects were randomly assigned to one of three groups. One group was told the baby was a girl, one group was told that the baby was a boy, and one group was not given information on the child's gender. Three toys were present during the interaction period: a rubber football, a doll, and a teething ring. If we give boys and girls different toys due to differences in their behavior we would expect the subjects would choose toys based on the infant's actual gender rather than the label they were provided with. This is not what happened, though. The infant's actual sex made little difference although the gender label did. When the infant was thought to be male, 50 percent of the male subjects and 80 percent of the female subjects chose the football (20 percent of both groups chose the teething ring for the presumably male infant). When the infant was identified as female, 73 percent of the female subjects and 89 percent of the male subjects chose the doll. None of the males chose the football for the female-labeled child and only 28 percent of the female subjects did.

Did you ever experience a negative reaction from your parents when you played in a way thought to be more appropriate for the other gender? One time when I was a child, my friend's brother played dress-up with us. From his parents' reactions you would have thought a felony had been committed. Indeed, research indicates that parents typically react more positively to their children who play with sex-appropriate toys, especially boys (Fagot, 1978; Fagot & Leinbach, 1989; Langlois & Downs, 1980; Martin, 1990). Even in preschool, children who do not play with sex-appropriate toys are likely to be ignored by other children or criticized by them (Carter & McCloskey, 1984; Fagot, 1978). Etaugh and Liss (1992) found that generally both boys and girls received the gender-traditional toys they asked for but did not receive the gender-nontraditional toys they asked for. Research by Japanese psychologists has also found that parents choose toys based on their child's gender, and that children's toy choices can be influenced by manipulating the gender label of the toy (see Shirakawa et al., 1992, for a description of these studies).

Even if parents and relatives do not deliberately offer their male and female children different toys, self-socialization may result in different toy preferences. Take an afternoon or Saturday morning to watch children's television programming and you will discover that almost all toys are marketed as either boy toys or girl toys (the average child watches 4 hours of television a day). Remember that once the child clearly identifies him- or herself as male or female, and notes that males and females tend to do and like different things, the child will tend to model from same-gender models. My son noticed early on that boys do not play with dolls although we intentionally did not communicate this to him. He has even said to me while watching television, "I would like to have that toy but there are only girls playing with it in the commercial—so, it must be only for girls." He immediately realized that no one could stop him from buying it, but he said that he wouldn't "feel right" about buying a toy that was supposed to be only for girls.

A well-conducted experiment conducted by Cobb et al. (1982) provided evidence supportive of the notion that televised models can influence toy preferences in young children. The subjects were children 4 to 6 years old randomly assigned to view one of three videotapes using *Sesame Street* Muppets. In all three films, a male and female Muppet discussed the sex appropriateness of a set of toys previously shown to be chosen for play equally by boys and girls. In one version, the Muppets provided reasons why the toys were "boy toys," in the second version reasons why they were "girls toys," and in the third version why they could belong to either girls or boys. After viewing one of the 20-minute films, each child was left to play in a room with the set of toys described in the film and a set of toys demonstrated by other research to be both gender-neutral and preferred by children less than the film toys. Both boys and girls spent more time playing with the test toys when they were identified as sex-appropriate than with the comparison toys. Conversely, when the test toys were identified as sex-inappropriate, children spent more time playing with the less desirable comparison toys. In short, the researchers found that toy preferences based on gender could be created by televised models who indicated that a toy was more appropriate for one gender or the other. Because the researchers used only toys that had been demonstrated to be gender-neutral, and used the same toys for all three conditions, gender-based preferences following the videotape viewing had to be due to the televised models.

Toy manufacturers are showing some increased awareness of this issue. Mattel's "Talking Barbie" says that "computers are fun" but she also said that "math class is tough" until the American Association of University Women persuaded Mattel that this sent the wrong message to girls. There are some toys considered appropriate for both boys and girls which depict both girls and boys on the box. I recently saw a commercial with a boy and a girl enthusiastically playing with a toy washer and dryer. There are even special blocks for girls—but they are pink and lavender and the container shows little girls building living rooms and kitchens.

Scarr and McCartney (1983) suggested that male and female children may have different dispositions which lead them to have different toy preferences, and, that differential socialization practices are a reaction to these "natural" differences. They call this thesis the *evocative genotype → environment effect*. Results from several studies can be interpreted in ways which seem to support this hypothesis. For example, Snow et al. (1983) did find that fathers were less likely to offer dolls to their 1-year-old sons than they were to their 1-year-old daughters, but even when they did offer dolls to their boys, the boys played with them less than the girls. In another study, 18-month-old children showed greater involvement in play with sex-typed toys although parents did not appear to promote sex-typed play overtly (Caldera et al., 1989). Unfortunately, we cannot rule out the possibility that some differential socialization had already taken place and influenced the children's toy preferences. A number of studies have found that differential socialization begins in infancy (Bell & Carver, 1980; Culp et al., 1983; Shakin et al., 1985; Sidorowicz & Lunney, 1980). Another plausible hypothesis is that biology creates individual differences in preferences, and that if those are consistent with the child's sex role then they are encouraged but if not they are discouraged (especially among boys). For example, research suggests that boys with temperaments that predispose them to play in a more cross-sex way are likely to be punished or discouraged (Berndt & Heller, 1986; Fagot, 1978; Fagot & Leinbach, 1989; Langois & Downs, 1980; Martin, 1990; Steriker & Kurdek, 1982).

The high incidence of tomboyism also casts some doubt on the premise that girls and boys have naturally different play preferences. "Tomboys" are female children who engage in traditionally male activities and play with traditionally male toys, although some still play with other females and engage in some traditionally female play as well. In one study, 63 percent of junior high girls reported that they were tomboys and, in a sample of adult women, 51 percent reported having been tomboys (Hyde et al., 1977). In a later study of fourth, sixth, eighth, and tenth graders, over 50 percent of the girls identified themselves as tomboys (Plumb & Cowan, 1984). Likewise 50 percent of 193 university and community college women surveyed by Burn et al. (1994) said that they were tomboys during childhood. Also interesting is that several studies (Burn et al., 1994; Plumb & Cowan, 1984) found tomboylike behavior to decline significantly at puberty. Hyde (1991) suggested that this occurs because gender-role pressures are intensified during adolescence. When Burn et al. (1994) asked adult women who identified themselves as tomboys during childhood, "Why did you stop being a tomboy?" the majority of responses fell into four categories: social pressure from junior or high school peers, social pressure from parents or other adults, wanting to attract boys, and physical development. Perhaps menstruation and physical development make the tomboy's "femaleness" more noticeable and this leads the tomboy and others to increasingly apply female gender norms to her behavior.

*A*NDROGYNY

Benefits

In this chapter we have discussed the process by which we become gendered. In some cases, differential socialization may result in the development of different psychological traits in females and males. For instance, sex-differentiated toys may encourage a caring orientation toward others in girls and competitiveness and assertiveness in boys. However, in reality, social norms and socialization do not create perfectly masculine males and perfectly feminine females. Psychologist Sandra Bem (1974) pointed out that femininity and masculinity do not exist as polar opposites, and an individual may possess both masculine and feminine qualities. Furthermore, Bem believes that it is desirable to be *androgynous*, that is, to combine the best of both sex roles.

Prior to the 1970s, psychologists saw the display of "masculine" traits by women and "feminine" traits by males to be a source of concern. This is a common belief among nonpsychologists as well and one that makes people hesitant to accept cross-sex interests and behaviors in children. However, recent research does not support the view that deviation from sex-role standards leads to psychological maladjustment (O'Heron & Orlofsky, 1987, 1990). Indeed, Bem (1974) suggested that mental health should be genderless and that androgyny is positively related to psychological well-being. Androgyny has been linked to situational flexibility (i.e., being assertive or other-centered, depending upon the situation) (Bem, 1975; Vonk & Ashmore, 1993); high self-esteem (Mullis & McKinley, 1989; Orlofsky, 1977; Spence et al., 1975); achievement motivation (Spence & Helmrich, 1978); effectiveness as a parent (Baumrind, 1982); and subjective feelings of well-being (Lubinski et al., 1981). In addition, Zammichieli et al. (1988) found that couples in which both partners were androgynous reported higher levels of marital satisfaction than couples where both were sex-typed or one was sex-typed and the other was not. Ickes (1993) discussed a number of studies finding that relationships in which at least one person is androgynous are more satisfying, although recent research suggests that marital satisfaction is particularly linked to the femininity of one's partner—male or female. This is explained by the fact that nurturance, caring, being affectionate, etc., are associated with a feminine identification and these things increase the quality of relationships (Ickes, 1993).

✳ Bem's Sex Role Inventory

Bem's Sex Role Inventory (BSRI; Bem, 1974) is the most widely used measure of sex-role stereotyping in adults (Hargreaves, 1987). Adults indicate, using a 7–point scale, how true each of sixty adjectives are of them. Twenty of the adjectives make up the masculinity subscale (e.g., masculine, analytical, ambitious, aggressive, dominant), twenty make up the femininity subscale (e.g., feminine, warm, loves children, sensitive to the needs of others), and twenty are neutral (e.g., reliable, solemn, tactful, jealous, conceited). These adjectives were chosen on the basis of what was gender-appropriate at the time the scale was developed so as to locate gender in the context of culture rather than in the personality of the individual (Bem, 1993). Subjects who score high on both the femininity and masculinity scales are labeled androgynous; those who score high on the feminine but not the masculine scale are labeled feminine; and those who score high on the masculine but not on the feminine scale are identified as masculine. An "undifferentiated" label is applied to those who are low on both the feminine and the masculine scales. A sex-typed person is one whose self-definition and behavior match what their society defines as gender-appropriate.

Some studies have examined the BSRI scores of non-Euroamerican groups. Interestingly, this research often does not confirm common stereotypes. DeLeon (1993) found both male and female African-Americans and Puerto Ricans to be more androgynous than Euroamericans. Other studies have found African-American women to score higher in androgyny than Euroamerican women (Binion, 1990; Dugger, 1988). This is explained by the historically low pay and high unemployment rates of black men which have led to the consistent presence of black women in the labor force in comparison to white women. The historical experiences of black women are at odds with culturally dominant conceptions of gender and, as a consequence, their conceptions of womanhood have come to include self-reliance, strength, resourcefulness, and autonomy (Dugger, 1988). In a 1983 study of college students, Pugh and Vazquez-Nuttall found that black women scored highest on masculinity, followed by Hispanic women, and then white women (reported in Vazquez-Nuttall et al., 1987). Similar findings were obtained by DeLeon (1993).

Kranau et al. (1982) found that the BSRI scores of Mexican-American women were more feminine for women highly acculturated into American society although they exhibited fewer feminine behaviors. A recent study, however, did not find Puerto Rican women living on the island to be more feminine in orientation than Puerto Rican women living in the United States (DeLeon, 1993). DeLeon (1993) compared African-American, Puerto Rican, and Euroamerican men on the BSRI. The highest percentage of males classified as feminine and the lowest percentage of men classified as masculine were in the Puerto Rican group. Puerto Rican males had significantly higher femininity scores than did males in the African-American and Euroamerican groups. DeLeon (1993) suggested that this was because Puerto Rican culture emphasizes familism, concern for others, and nurturing, traits that lead to a classification of feminine on the BSRI. These studies point to the role of culture in the creation of gender-typedness as well as the need for more research in this area. In Chap. 6 we will discuss further the relationship between culture and gender.

Debate over Bem's Inventory and the Concept of Androgyny

The BSRI has generated a great deal of debate, much of it on complex methodological issues (Baldwin et al., 1986; Bem, 1979; Hargreaves et al., 1981; Kottke, 1988; Locksley & Colten, 1979; Lubinski et al., 1981; Marsh & Byrne, 1991; Pedhazur & Tetenbaum, 1979; Spence & Helmrich, 1981; Taylor & Hall, 1982). Other measures of androgyny include Spence, Helmrich, and Stapp's (1974) Personal Attributes Questionnaire (PAQ); Baldwin et al.'s (1986) Sex-Rep instrument; the ANDRO Scale (Berzins et al., 1978); and the Sex-Role Behavior Scale (Orlofsky et al., 1982).

Even the concept of androgyny has come under attack (Ashmore, 1990; Sedney, 1989). Bem (1981, 1993) herself has lamented that the androgyny concept still presupposes some desirable qualities are "masculine" and some "feminine" and in so doing encourages the very gender polarization it was intended to reduce. Many gender psychologists recommend that we abandon the terms "femininity" and "masculinity" because they perpetuate gender differences and stereotypes (Betz, 1993). Spence and Helmrich (1981) recommended that instead of using those terms, *instrumentality* be used to refer to the capabilities of self-assertion and competence (key aspects of traditional masculinity) and *expressiveness* be used to represent qualities traditionally associated with femininity such as nurturance, interpersonal concern, and emotional expressiveness and sensitivity (Betz, 1993).

In her 1993 book, Bem acknowledged that the concept of androgyny is far from current reality, and that it suggests change should occur at a personal level when in fact the elimination of gender inequality will require changes in social institutions. Another thorny issue stems from the possible loss of a positive social identity should we reduce the female-male dichotomy. As we will see in Chap. 5, there are self-esteem benefits associated with strongly identifying with our sex and emphasizing the ways in which it differs from the other. Still, a world of individuals who are both expressive and instrumental sounds desirable to me. I must agree with Bem (1993) that, in spite of its problems, androgyny provides a vision of utopia and mental health where individuals do not have to banish from the self those attributes and behaviors which their society deems gender-inappropriate. The concept is also important because it suggests that it is as desirable to have qualities traditionally viewed as feminine as qualities traditionally viewed as masculine. This is important given that masculine qualities have generally been seen and presented as more normative and desirable (cf. Bem, 1993; Miller et al., 1991; Tavris, 1992).

CONCLUDING REMARKS

This chapter focused on the role culture plays in the creation of gender, the various ways cultural norms regarding gender are relayed, and our motivations for conforming to our culture's gender-role expectations. Yet I understand that at this point you may still be reluctant to accept a nonbiological explanation for gender differences. You may, for example, agree with sociobiologists like E. O. Wilson (1978). Sociobiologists suggest that differences in male and female behavior were naturally selected for, that is, that such differences contributed to the survival of the species and therefore became more frequent in the gene pool. And indeed, it is plausible that certain sexual divisions of labor did make survival sense at one time. As Williams and Best (1986) noted, women's mobility was restricted because it was always necessary for the women to nurse infant children. Therefore, because women were "stuck at the cave" it made sense for them to assume other child-related and household responsibilities. Conversely, hunting and fighting required mobility as well as strength, and consequently these became the duties of men. Also, it was best for the group if men rather than women performed such dangerous tasks because a group that loses too many of its childbearers risks extinction.

Psychologists Buss and Barnes (1986) and Kenrick et al. (1990) also assumed that traits such as male dominance and female nurturance may have originated in natural selection and evolution. According to their *biosocial* or *evolutionary perspective,* males were chosen for traits related to dominance and social status while females were chosen for traits indicative of reproductive potential and the potential for nurturance toward offspring. Again, the presumption is that such traits increased reproductive success, and then became more frequent in the gene pool. A number of studies on mate selection have found that females are more attracted to males who appear socially dominant while males are more attracted to females who are physically attractive and youthful and that these differences occur in most cultures (Buss, 1989; Buss & Barnes, 1986; Kenrick et al., 1990). The authors of these studies assumed that such differences are consistent with an evolutionary model where males contributed in terms of food and protection to offspring and females contributed via gestation and nurturing.

Unfortunately, science is not yet at the point where we can directly demonstrate that such gender differences in human mate preference (or other behaviors and psychological qualities) are genetically encoded or hormonally determined. Indeed, the research conducted by and referred to by sociobiologists to support their view of naturally selected-for gender differences is fraught with error and provides questionable support for sociobiological explanations of gender (see Fausto-Sterling, 1985, for a critique of that research). Furthermore, alternative explanations suggest plausible social sources of such gender differences. For example, Kenrick et al. (1990) found that females rated "earning capacity" as more important for a mate than men did. This could be due to the fact that both women and men know that women's earning potentials are lower and so they both look to men to be the dominant wage earners. It could be due to social norms that communicate to men and women that a man's value is determined in part by his earning power. For instance, many a little girl has been told to grow up and marry a rich man and many a young woman has had her parents grill her boyfriend on his future career and earnings. Could these norms have evolved because until the midtwentieth century advent of infant formula and birth control, childbearing made women economically dependent upon men?

Let us say, though, that at one time it contributed to the survival of the human species for males and females to behave differently. Does this mean that these differences have been genetically encoded? No, not necessarily. Indeed, it is quite possible that the mechanism by which these differences were transmitted was social. Many people see that sex differences are instinctual in nonhuman animals and infer that such is the case with all humans as well. Keep in mind that our large brains leave less to instinct and more to learning than do smaller animal brains. This is why humans successfully live all over the world and display incredible variations in behavior. The rapid (historically speaking) changes in women's roles in the last century seem to testify to the part that culture plays in creating or eliminating gender differences. Such changes seem more revolutionary than evolutionary. For example, biology does not explain why male and female scores on mathematical and spatial tasks are becoming smaller and smaller as the years pass. As Rosenthal and Rubin (1982, p. 711) said, such changes are occurring "faster than the gene can travel."

Myers (1990) pointed out an additional relevant critique regarding sociobiology and gender roles. Remember that the sociobiologist assumes that gender-role differences exist because they contribute to the survival of the species. However, Myers (1990) noted that you could easily argue that other gender-role arrangements could have contributed positively to survival as well. For instance, he said, strength and aggressiveness in women should have been naturally selected for since a strong, aggressive woman would have been better able to protect her young.

We should also note that, even if it once made sense for women to be the primary caregivers of children (after all, they have mammaries and infant formula is a relatively recent development) or for men to be aggressive, it does not mean that these behavioral differences are still adaptive (contribute to the survival of the species). Myers (1990) pointed out that evolutionary wisdom is past wisdom—it tells us what behaviors were adaptive in times past, not whether such tendencies are still adaptive and desirable today. Bem (1993) argued that sociobiologists pay far too little attention to the ability of humans to transform their environments through cultural intervention and consequently to transform themselves. She provided a number of examples where culture and technology have liberated humans from what seemed to be intrinsic biological limitations.

Kenrick (1987) pointed out that modern society is information-oriented and physical strength and aggressiveness are not very relevant to success in such a world. Also, because most women now work outside the home in order to eat, to maintain a decent standard of living, or to fulfill themselves, it no longer is adaptive for women to be the primary caregivers of children; greater involvement of fathers in raising children is now adaptive as well. As Hoffman and Hurst (1990) noted, it is ironic that, although in many societies the original reasons for the division of labor have ceased to be obvious or compelling, the traditional arrangement has persisted.

While Freud once said that "anatomy is destiny," we now know that women do not have to be the primary caregivers of infants or have children at all and men do not have to be aggressive. Yes, the fact that women have uteruses and mammary glands makes it more likely that they, not men, will have and care for babies. And the fact that men tend to be larger and stronger may make it more likely that in comparison to women they

SINGLE SLICES By Peter Kohlsaat

He's Soooo Cool. Last week he had a couple of sensitivity genes spliced into his DNA.

SINGLE SLICES- year 2020

Because of evidence suggesting that gender differences are socially created, most social psychologists doubt that sex differences in emotional sensitivity are genetic.

will be physically aggressive. However, as Degler (1990) pointed out, even if there is a biological or evolutionary base for human behavior, this does not mean that what humans do has to be dictated by it. Sociobiologists such as E. O. Wilson (1978) and Donald Symons (1985) have suggested that natural selection favored men who were aggressive and polygamous and whose commitment to their children ended at fertilization. But men can be monogamous, nonaggressive, and concerned about their offspring. As Degler (1990) said, our values are determined by us, not by evolution or natural selection.

Of course we do not want to deny the influence of our evolutionary past. Indeed, the great influence social context and culture has on our behavior may itself be rooted in evolution. For instance, it is possible that our tendency to form social units and be influenced by social information was naturally selected for, since humans who lived in groups and who paid attention to the behavior of others were more likely to survive. We also do not want to deny that biology affects human behavior. Indeed, there is compelling evidence that up to 50 percent of an individual's personality is determined through genetic inheritance and that many psychological disorders are rooted in physiology. However, biology may be more powerful in explaining differences between individuals than it is at explaining differences between human groups, be they ethnic or sex differences. In short, biology is important but there is a lot more to human behavior than biology and we will not get very far in understanding gender, or reducing gender inequality, without first examining the sociocultural contexts in which humans operate.

✳ SUMMARY

- Gender stereotypes often operate as social norms. We are compelled to conform to gender norms due to normative and informational pressure. Normative pressure to comply to gender norms occurs when we conform to gender roles in order to receive social approval and avoid social disapproval. Informational pressure to conform to gender norms occurs when we assume that gender norms are appropriate because social information suggests that this is the case. We live in a culture in which men and women typically do different things and gender differences are treated as facts of nature; therefore we accept and conform to gender norms.

- Conformity to gender norms may be in behavior but not in belief (compliance) or in behavior and in belief (internalization), or may be due to wanting to be like a peer or role model (identification). Also, individuals vary in their conformity to gender roles. Some individuals are highly sex-typed and conform strongly to traditional gender roles. Those who have had critical gender socialization experiences where deviation from their sex roles resulted in severe negative social consequences may be especially likely to be sex-typed.

- Through a process known as differential socialization, we are taught that different interests, behaviors, and psychological qualities are appropriate depending upon our gender. Differential socialization occurs through differential reinforcement and differential modeling. Differential reinforcement occurs when females and males are rewarded and punished for different behaviors, interests, etc. Differential modeling occurs once children clearly identify themselves as male or female and begin to pay more attention to the behavior of same-sex models and imitate it.

- Parents are not the only agents of differential socialization. Information about appropriate gender-role behavior is found in children's literature, television, and the English language. Research indicates that these sources contribute to stereotyped perceptions of males and females.

- Children's toys may play a role in the development of sex-typed skills and qualities. Research indicates that boys' toys are more likely to promote skills relevant to spatial skills and mathematics whereas girls' toys encourage the development of domestic and social skills. Children ask for and receive more sex-typed toys and research suggests that these preferences are socially created beginning in infancy.

- Although there is considerable debate surrounding the measurement of androgyny, there is reason to believe that it is desirable to possess a balance of female and male traits.
- Sociobiologists and evolutionary psychologists believe that differences in male and female behavior were naturally selected for since they contributed to the survival of the species. However, even if differences once contributed to the survival of the species, this does not necessarily mean the differences are genetically encoded, that they are relevant to a modern world, or that we must let biological gender differences dictate our values.

2

Research on Gender Differences

The Not-So-Opposite Sexes

❖

*W*e think of males and females as being quite different. Williams and Best (1986) reported that in comparison to women, men are seen as ambitious, rational, independent, and unemotional while women are believed to be affectionate, sensitive, emotional, and sociable. These beliefs about females and males are common in our popular culture. For instance, one comic said that when it comes to emotional sensitivity women have satellite dishes and men have coat hangers with foil on them. Dave Barry (1991) said that women want to be loved, listened to, desired, respected, needed, and trusted and men want tickets to the World Series. Jacklin (1989) suggested that speculation about differences between males and females is a national preoccupation. Erlich (1973) once said that stereotypes about ethnic groups are part of the social heritage of a society. The same could be said of gender stereotypes. They are, it appears, part of the dominant social consciousness.

Even in science, small differences in brain anatomy between the sexes are presented as more significant than the data warrant and are likely to receive great media attention (see Unger & Crawford, 1992, and Tavris, 1992, for a discussion of this point). In psychology, only four differences between the sexes (spatial ability, mathematics performance, verbal ability, and aggression) were identified by Maccoby and Jacklin's famous review (1974) of the topic, yet it is these that are consistently reported in psychology texts, usually with little or no mention that the sexes are more similar than different (Unger, 1988) and little or no mention that recent research finds these differences to be small and very situation-specific (a point explained in this chapter).

The study of gender differences in psychology dates back to the late 1800s, but until the 1970s it was largely focused on demonstrating differences and how these justified the differential treatment of females and males (Denmark & Fernandez, 1993). There are over 20,000 published articles on sex differences from the last 20 years alone (Myers, 1990), some of them reporting that the sexes are different. Please keep in mind though that when differences are found, they are relatively small, usually about 10 percent or less—there is typically about 90 percent overlap between the distributions of males and females (Basow, 1986; Hyde, 1991; Maccoby & Jacklin, 1974; Pleck, 1978; Spence et al., 1974). As Hyde (1991) pointed out, when we say that females and males are significantly different on some

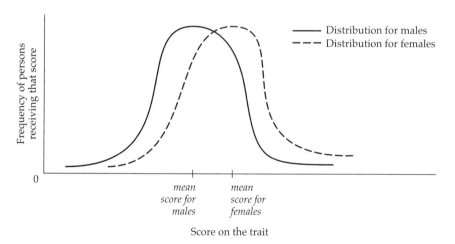

FIGURE 2.1
Examples of distributions of scores for males and females that might lead to statistically significant gender differences for a trait (From J. S. Hyde, *Half the Human Experience*, Heath Publishers, 1995, p. 75. Reprinted by permission.)

trait, this does not necessarily mean that the difference is large. For instance, Fig. 2.1 shows two curves, one representing the distribution of scores for males, the other for females. Statistics would probably find the difference between these two distributions to be "significant." However, look at how much the two distributions overlap. Even the means are not dramatically different.

Another problem with the literature on gender differences is that journals tend to be more interested in differences than similarities, so research finding differences is more likely to get published than research finding similarities (Basow, 1986; Unger, 1988). Finally, as discussed in Chap. 1, when differences are found, we often assume that they are due to fundamental biological differences between the sexes. However, closer examination suggests that these differences arise because of the differing requirements of the female and male gender roles and the different experiences we have based upon our genders.

Because of the large number of gender difference studies, I will focus primarily on two areas in which we normally perceive men and women to differ: mathematics and emotional expressivity and empathy. These are used to illustrate the social-psychological nature of gender. In addition, difference areas customarily studied by social psychologists such as aggression, conformity, and altruism are also discussed. Gender differences in power, status, leadership, and relationship intimacy are discussed in Chaps. 3 and 4. For detailed reviews of other areas studied for gender differences, see Halpern (1992), Basow (1986a), or Hyde (1991). A volume edited by O'Leary, Unger, and Wallston (1985) also focuses on gender-related topics in social psychology and discusses research on gender differences in performance attributions, achievement motivation, and conceptions of justice, as well as influenceability, aggression, and altruism. You may also use your library to locate reviews of research on particular difference areas.

META-ANALYSIS

Before we proceed, you should be familiar with a research technique called *meta-analysis*. Following Hall's (1978) meta-analysis of gender differences in nonverbal decoding, the technique quickly became a powerful tool in the study of gender differences. Meta-analysis is a statistical technique where information from many studies is combined in order to arrive at an overall estimate of the size of the differences between groups; in other words, it is an analysis of other analyses (see Glass et al., 1981; Hyde & Linn, 1986; and Rosenthal, 1991, for extensive explanations and statistical discussions).

Meta-analysis tells us whether there is a difference between groups on some variable and gives us an estimate of how large the difference is. Prior to the development of meta-analysis, researchers examining the research literature on particular difference areas used a "voting" method to ascertain whether a given gender difference was reliably found by the research. The voting method involves collecting a large number of studies on the topic of interest, and counting the number that found a gender difference and the number that did not. For instance, Maccoby and Jacklin's (1974) famous book on sex differences was essentially an exhaustive review of the existing literature on the subject (a narrative review) and a tabulation of studies finding or not finding gender differences.

One problem with the voting method is that individual research studies may lack *statistical power,* the ability to detect a difference between groups. The statistics which determine whether groups differ significantly from one another on some variable take into account how large the difference is between the groups, and how much variability there is within each group on the variable. In other words, how different are males and females on the variable, and how much do females differ from other females and males from other males? In order to declare the groups significantly different, the difference between the groups must exceed the differences within the groups. For example, if women differ as much from each other on the variable as men and women differ from each other, then the groups would not be found to differ significantly from one another.

It is more difficult to obtain a significant effect when differences or effects are small, especially if you do not have many people in your study. In other words, small effects and sample sizes reduce statistical power. This may result in the failure of a statistical test to detect a difference that is actually there (this is called a "type II" or "beta error" in statistics lingo). Thus, you could falsely conclude there is no difference between the groups when there is. Because meta-analyses combine data from a number of studies, statistical power is boosted. This means that sometimes a meta-analysis will find a difference between groups that was not revealed by the voting method (Lipsey & Wilson, 1993). Also, meta-analysis gives us an idea about the size of the difference, called the *effect size,* usually represented by the letter symbol d.

A high-quality meta-analysis involves the collection of all available research studies on the topic, including unpublished ones. An effect size (d) is computed for each study by subtracting the mean of one group from the mean of the other (in this case the mean for females is subtracted from that for males) and this difference is divided by the pooled within-group standard deviation (Eagly & Carli, 1981; Hyde, 1992; Hyde & Linn, 1986; Lipsey & Wilson, 1993). Cohen (1969) suggested that a d of .20 indicates a small effect size, .50 a medium effect size, and .80 a large effect size. A large effect size means that males and females differ more from each other than they do from other members of their own sex (Eagly, 1987). The d's from each study are then averaged to get an idea about the overall size of the effect across studies (add up the d's, divide by the number of d's). For example, Table 2.1 shows effect sizes for gender differences on an eighth-grade mathematics test for

TABLE 2.1 NATIONAL SEX DIFFERENCES ON EIGHTH-GRADE
MATHEMATICS TEST

Country	Mean for boys	Mean for girls	$X_M - X_F$ difference	Effect size
Superior Performance of Boys				
France	17.02	14.18	2.84*	.37
Israel	18.79	17.74	1.05*	.11
Luxembourg	13.34	11.74	1.60*	.25
Netherlands	22.00	20.23	1.77*	.17
New Zealand	14.60	13.51	1.09*	.10
Ontario, Canada	17.72	16.94	.78*	.08
Swaziland	9.29	7.89	1.40*	.21
Equal Performance				
British Columbia	19.55	19.27	.28	.03
England-Wales	15.38	14.92	.46	.04
Hong Kong	16.59	16.09	.50	.05
Japan	23.84	23.80	.04	.004
Nigeria	9.50	9.05	.45	.07
Scotland	16.83	16.68	.15	.01
Sweden	10.70	11.18	− .48	− .06
United States	14.98	15.12	− .14	− .01
Superior Performance of Girls				
Belgium-French	19.44	20.54	− 1.10*	− .12
Finland	13.24	14.87	− 1.63*	− .17
Hungary	22.36	23.62	− 1.26*	− .13
Thailand	12.09	14.16	− 2.07*	− .22

*Indicates female and male scores were significantly different according to an F test,
$p < .01$. Note effect sizes, which are all in the small range.
SOURCE: From Baker and Perkins-Jones, "Creating Gender Equality: Cross-National Gender
Statification and Mathematical Performance," *Sociology of Education*, 66, #2, Table 2-1. Amer-
ican Sociological Association, 1993. Reprinted by permission of the American Sociological
Association and the authors.

nineteen countries. You could average the effect sizes for those countries
where boys' performances were superior to girls' (you would get a *d* of
.18), and you could average the effect sizes for countries where girls' performances were superior to boys' (you would get a *d* of .16). In other
words, even when females and males differ significantly in math performance, it is a small difference.

A comparison of *d*'s from studies from different time periods, or using
different measurements, methods, age groups, or contexts, may also be
undertaken in order to see how differences change over time and across
situations. Such analyses typically show that whether gender differences
are found in a given area depends greatly on the gender norms salient in
a particular time and place. In this chapter meta-analyses on math, aggression, altruism, and influenceability are discussed. Meta-analyses on
gender differences in leadership and gender biases in performance evalu-

ations are presented in Chap. 3. Hyde and Frost (1993) have presented an excellent summary of meta-analyses of gender differences.

GENDER DIFFERENCES IN MATHEMATICS SKILLS

Research Findings

Research on gender differences in mathematics skills has been conducted for over 30 years. In general, studies find no differences between females and males prior to junior high (Callahan & Clements, 1984; Dossey et al., 1988; Siegel, 1968), or find differences that favor females (Brandon et al., 1985, in Friedman, 1989; Hawn et al., 1981, in Friedman, 1989). Studies conducted with junior high students sometimes find that females outperform males (Tsai & Wahlberg, 1979), males outperform females (Hilton & Berglund, 1974), or there are no differences (Connor & Serbin, 1985). More consistent are studies with high school students finding that males outperform girls (Friedman, 1989). In general, girls get better grades than boys in all subjects, including math, until high school, when males begin to outperform females in math (Stockard & Wood, 1984; Wentzel, 1988).

This divergence between males and females in math performance which occurs at puberty could be the result of hormonal changes at that time which influence these skills or the result of social differences between males and females. The "hormonal" thesis seems unlikely when you examine recent data indicating that these differences have become smaller and smaller over the years (e.g., Becker & Hedges, 1984; Friedman, 1989; Hyde et al., 1990a), a tendency seen all over the world in countries that have made progress toward gender equality (Baker & Perkins-Jones, 1993). Meta-analysis is an especially important tool in the study of gender differences in mathematical tasks over time. This is because a large number of studies from one period of time can be statistically compared with a large number of studies from another period of time.

Friedman (1989) conducted an impressive meta-analysis of 98 studies that took place between 1974 and mid-1987 on sex differences relating to mathematical tasks. The study is impressive because of its thoroughness and attention to factors found by past researchers to increase the validity of meta-analyses. The studies included dissertations, journal articles, and large national studies using elementary students to senior high school students. Friedman's (1989) results indicate that average sex differences on mathematical tasks are now very small. Also, when effect sizes from meta-analyses from different time periods are compared, it is clear that sex differences relating to mathematical performance in favor of males have decreased over time. For example, the median effect size (d) reported by Hyde (1981) was .43 (recall that .20 is considered to be a small effect size, .50 a medium effect size) but fell to .22 in Friedman's (1989) meta-analysis, and was .05 in Hyde et al.'s (1990a) meta-analysis of 100 studies. Feingold (1988) in a meta-analysis using the norms for several commonly used standardized tests (e.g., PSAT, SAT, DAT) also found gender differences in mathematical performance to decline over the years.

Although the size of the mathematics gender difference has gotten smaller, Feingold (1988) and other researchers (Becker & Hedges, 1984; Benbow & Stanley, 1980, 1982) found that mathematically talented adolescents are disproportionately male. Also, when Hyde et al. (1990a) combined studies from elementary through high school the gender differences were basically zero. However, when high school and college studies were analyzed separately, it was found that differences in problem solving (applications in the form of word problems or story problems) showed up in high school ($d = .29$) and college ($d = .32$), with males performing better. (Note that it is not a large difference, but a small to moderate one.) There were still no differences in computational ability or understanding of mathematical concepts. As Eccles and her associates have pointed out, though, such studies did not measure effort or prior exposure to mathematics and thus it cannot be concluded that these were real differences in aptitude and not due to gender differences in experience (Eccles & Jacobs, 1986; Eccles et al., 1990).

Kenrick (1988) suggested that sex differences in math performance are not due to differences in cognitive ability. He maintained that these differences are due to sex differences in aggressiveness and its offshoot, competitiveness. Furthermore, he postulated that this "hyperactive dominance drive" is due to the greater levels of testosterone possessed by males. To support his position he pointed to the finding that females do much better than males under the more relaxed schedule of the formal math class, but worse under the time pressure of the SAT-M. While there is reason to believe that males are more competitive than females, it is not clear that this difference is hormonal since the male gender role clearly encourages competition to a greater extent than the female role. Furthermore, contrary to the media stories on this topic you may have read, research on the relationship between sex hormones and cognitive abilities (e.g., Golub, 1976; Hampson & Kimura, 1988; Heister et al., 1989) has provided only the weakest of support for the hormone-cognitive abilities hypothesis (see Halpern, 1992, pp. 120–133, for a discussion of this research). As the discussion which follows here suggests, there is also good reason to believe that social factors play a role in the sex differences in math which emerge at puberty.

Why Male-Female Performance Diverges in High School

Why might male and female performance on mathematical problem-solving tasks suddenly diverge in high school? There are several compelling explanations.

1. *Females may lack confidence in math abilities and not expect to do well.* Some research (Eccles, 1989; Fennema & Sherman, 1977, 1978) has suggested that females take fewer math courses not only because to do so is to risk feeling socially deviant, but because they lack confidence in their mathematical abilities and do not expect to do well. Eccles (1989) discussed her research showing how females' confidence in their math abilities begins to decline in seventh grade and continues to decline throughout high school. Fennema and Sherman (1977, 1978) provided evidence supportive of the relationship between confidence in learning math and performance. Research also shows that men have higher expectations for success in problem solving than women (Meehan & Overton, 1986). Eccles et al. (1990) found that gender differences in self-perceptions of abilities leads females and males to select different educational training programs and to aspire to different occupations.

Hyde et al. (1990b) in a meta-analysis on gender and mathematics attitudes found only a small gender difference in mathematics self-confidence although they did find greater gender differences in confidence in the high school years. They concluded that other factors, such as those discussed below, may be more powerful explanations for the gender differences in mathematics which arise at puberty.

2. *Math achievement may represent gender-inappropriate behavior for girls.* This explanation suggests that many females believe that doing well in math is gender-inappropriate, and consequently they make little effort to achieve in this domain. It is interesting that girls and boys do not differ in their liking for math until adolescence (Etaugh & Liss, 1992). Hyde et al. (1990b) found that high school males see mathematics as a more masculine domain than females do (the effect size was a large .90 across all age groups and was at its highest in the 15- to 18-year-old age group). They suggested that these attitudes may lead males to indicate to their female peers that mathematics achievement is unfeminine. According to Wentzel (1988, p. 693), research evidence suggests that "characteristically male achievement domains (e.g., mathematics) may come to represent salient, negatively defined performance contexts for female students as they grow older." In other words, being liked and attractive to boys is very important to adolescent females and being good at math is perceived by adolescent females to reduce their attractiveness to others. Indeed, girls express less interest than boys in taking advanced math classes, are less likely than boys to enroll in advanced high-school math classes, and are less likely to aspire to careers in mathematically related fields such as engineering (Eccles, 1984a, 1984b). Halpern (1992) wrote of a student-guided tour she took of the University of California at Los Angeles where her guide explained that females studying mathematically related fields are called "science dogs." The experience of one of my students (a home economics major) also illustrates this point:

> Throughout our education from kindergarten to high school, my sisters and I had different expectations than my brothers. It is definite that my sisters were

not confident with their intelligence, and were more interested in popularity and social interaction than trying their best in their classes. Unfortunately, in junior high and high school, a lot of girls feel that they need to choose one or the other. On the other hand, I had always done well on the tests they give every year to show how you compare to students nationwide. Therefore I was placed in a gifted and talented education program. This is a title I spent my adolescent years trying to live down. I used to be good at math, but my social needs took over in the eighth and ninth grades, and my math performance plummeted.

Also supportive of the idea that some females perceive mathematical achievement to be socially unacceptable is a study by Selkow (1985) demonstrating that gender differences in problem solving were reduced by controlling for sex-role identification. In other words, females with a strong traditional sex-role identification performed more poorly than those who lacked such a strong identification, probably because they perceived proficiency at mathematics as inappropriate for females. Of course it is possible that girls who have poor math abilities come to more strongly identify with the traditional female role since their chances of success are greater in that role than in a less traditional female role.

It is also interesting that, in spite of the evidence that girls really are good at math, they are less likely than equally qualified males to pursue careers in science and engineering (Kimball, 1989). Baker and Perkins-Jones (1993) suggested that student performance in a subject is linked to anticipated future opportunities. Eccles (1989) found that, by eighth grade, females start seeing math as less and less relevant to their future goals and become less and less likely to take advanced math classes. As Baker and Perkins-Jones (1993) wrote:

> If male students are afforded the possibility of greater future educational occupational opportunities as a function of their performance in mathematics, then they may try harder, teachers may encourage them more, and parents and friends may help them see that mathematics is a domain of performance that should be taken seriously. On the other hand, female students, who are faced with less opportunity, may see mathematics as less important for their future and are told so in a number of ways by teachers, parents, and friends. (p. 92)

Baker and Perkins-Jones (1993) reasoned that, if their hypothesis was correct, cultures that provide greater mathematically relevant opportunities to women should show smaller mathematical sex differences than those that are strongly gender-stratified and for which mathematically related careers are clearly identified as male. This is precisely what their study of 77,602 eighth-grade students in nineteen countries showed (mathematical performance was measured by a standardized math test). Table 2.1 shows the mean for boys and girls on the forty-item test as well as the effect size for each country. As you can see, they found considerable cross-cultural variation in sex differences in mathematical performance:

In seven countries boys did better than girls (France, Israel, Luxembourg, Netherlands, New Zealand, Ontario, Canada, Swaziland); in eight there was no sex difference (British Columbia, England-Wales, Hong Kong, Japan, Nigeria, Scotland, Sweden, United States); and in four girls outperformed boys (Belgium, Finland, Hungary, Thailand). The authors pointed out that this, along with data showing that sex differences in math in many of the countries decreased as opportunities for women increased, contradicts biological models of cognitive differences which see social factors as secondary to biological ones.

3. *Parents and teachers are less likely to encourage girls in math.* The low confidence many females have in their mathematical abilities may originate in parental and teacher expectations and support. Hyde et al. (1990b) found that parental and teacher stereotyping of math as a male domain peaks in high school. In a series of studies, Dweck and her colleagues (Dweck & Bush, 1976; Dweck et al., 1978; Dweck et al., 1980) demonstrated that teachers used positive feedback in ways which suggested more to boys, than to girls, that their successes were due to ability. Boys' failures were more likely to be attributed to temporary factors such as lack of effort. The researchers also demonstrated that such attributions diminished the academic self-confidence of girls despite the fact that girls' academic performance tends to be better than boys. This then led to decreased persistence or impaired performance following failure or threatened failure experiences (Dweck et al., 1978). This problem may be even greater for African-American girls, who receive even fewer opportunities to respond in the classroom than white girls and for whom teachers have lower expectations (Bell, 1989).

Parsons et al. (1982) found that parental encouragement and confidence in their child's abilities strongly influenced the child's confidence in his/her own abilities and influenced the child's course selection. In their meta-analysis, Hyde et al. (1990b) found that males were more likely to make ability attributions for their mathematics success than were females. Furthermore, gender-differentiated perceptions of parents exist although their female and male children do equally well on both their school grades and on standardized tests (Eccles et al., 1990; Eccles-Parsons et al., 1982). The Baker and Perkins-Jones (1993) study of nineteen countries discussed earlier also found that gender differences in parental support for mathematical performance were associated with gender differences in math performance. Sex differences in parental support were also related to sex differences in access to mathematics curricula. The good news, however, is that in the Hyde et al. (1990b) meta-analysis a trend toward fewer gender differences in parental and teacher support was found.

In addition, the research conducted by Eccles et al. (1990) has suggested that, when their female children do well at math, parents tend to attribute the success to effort, rather than to ability, while the opposite holds true for their male children. These parental expectations and attributions then influence the children's self-perceptions and possibly lead female children to avoid more "masculine" activities such as mathematics and science. However, it should be noted that Raymond and Benbow (1986) found that parents equally encouraged boys and girls who showed extremely high mathematical ability.

Even when females take as many math classes as males, they may be less likely to receive the encouragement from teachers and guidance counselors to pursue math and science-related fields. Recently, a female aeronautical engineering student told me that her engineering professor proclaimed on the first day of class, "I don't expect the females to do well in this class." Another female engineering student told me that when her female friends have difficulties in that major they are advised to consider another major, while her male peers are advised to "stick it out." The experiences of these women are consistent with research by Matyas (1987) finding that college, math, science, and engineering professors pay more attention to male students and are more likely to encourage male students to get involved in research and go on to graduate school.

Most teachers do not intentionally treat male and female students differently, but research suggests that teachers do subtly encourage boys more, especially in math (Brophy, 1985; Eccles & Blumenfeld, 1985). Parsons et al. (1982) compared classrooms in which boys' math expectancies were higher than girls' to classrooms where there were no sex-related differences in expectancies. They found that, in classrooms where the expectancies did not differ, girls interacted more with the teachers than did boys and received more praise. The reverse was true in classrooms where boys had higher expectancies. In a study of geometry classes, Becker (1981) found that boys were spoken to more, were called on more (even though females had their hands up just as much), and received more feedback, individual instruction, praise, and encouragement than girls. That research also found that girls received 30 percent of the encouraging comments and 84 percent of the discouraging ones. Teachers were also more persistent with boys; all of the contacts lasting more than 5 minutes were with boys.

A report from the American Association of University Women (1992) reviewing over two decades of research indicates that teachers give less attention to girls than boys and that the educational system tracks girls toward traditional, sex-segregated jobs and away from areas of study that lead to careers in science and technology. Teachers often reward passivity and punish assertiveness in girls (Sadker & Sadker, 1982) and in this way make it hard for girls to compete with boys for greater teacher attention (Bell, 1989).

4. *Females' experiences out of the classroom may provide them with fewer mathematical and problem-solving experiences.* Girls' experiences out of the classroom may provide them with fewer mathematical problem-solving experiences than males and this may partially explain male-female differences in mathematical problem solving. While this possibility has not

There is some evidence that teachers treat boys and girls differently, and that this may contribute to skill and career differences.

been extensively studied, several studies do show that boys have more science and mathematically related experience than girls do (Kahle et al., 1985; Linn & Petersen, 1986). In Chap. 1 we discussed how children's toys may encourage the development of different skills in girls and boys.

*E*MOTIONAL EMPATHY AND EXPRESSIVITY

Common stereotypes suggest large gender differences in empathy and emotion. Dave Barry (1991) once said that women should essentially give up expecting sensitivity from males: "If you were to probe deep inside the guy psyche, beneath that macho exterior and endless droning about things like the 1978 World Series, you would find, deep down inside, a passionate heartfelt interest in: the 1978 World Series. Yes, the truth is, guys don't have any sensitive innermost thoughts and feelings. It's time you women knew!"

Dave Barry echoed what most people think: In regard to differences between males and females, we often consider women to be better at expressing emotion and more sensitive to the feelings of others (empathy) than men. Indeed, the belief that females are more emotional than males is one of the most consistent findings in research on gender stereotypes (Birnbaum et al., 1980; Fabes & Martin, 1991). Ickes and Barnes (1978) have explained that masculinity is typically associated with achievement, autonomy, and striving for control—the type of control that encourages the capacity to alter the expression of awareness of one's feelings. In contrast, they described femininity as being associated with interpersonal communication, communality, and the awareness and active expression of one's own feelings.

Emotional differences between men and women can be examined on several different levels. One has to do with the ability to be aware of others' emotional states (empathy) and to express this awareness (empathic expression). The second has to do with one's own experience of emotion (emotional experience) and with the tendency to express one's own emotions (emotional expression). Both have important implications for mental health and interpersonal relations, a point developed at length in Chap. 4 on the limitations of the traditional male role.

Empathy

Are women more empathic than men? If they are it is probably due to social norms. Would you expect males or females to be more empathic, or better at identifying the emotional states of others? If you are like most people, you probably feel fairly confident that females are more empathic than males. Researchers are less confident than you probably are. The data regarding gender differences in empathy are inconsistent and seem to vary depending upon the particular method used to measure empathy. Eisenberg and Lennon (1983) in an extensive review of research studies on this topic found that, the less obvious it was that empathy was being measured, the smaller the sex differences found. For example, large sex differences have been found in studies using scales where individuals report on how empathic they tend to be, small differences in studies using self-report measures where subjects report on their feelings following the presentation of emotion-provoking situations, and no differences in studies using physiological measures or measures of facial expression. In other words, findings like these suggest that males may be less willing to portray themselves as empathic because it is not consistent with the male gender role. Conversely, an important part of the female gender role is to be caring and nurturing. Therefore, males may be just as capable of identifying and internally sympathizing with the emotional states of others as females, but they may be less likely to show behavioral evidence of this. This may be especially true for males who strongly identify with the traditional male sex role and perceive empathic responding to be gender-role-inappropriate. In Chap. 4 we will discuss the male gender role in more depth and how part of the male role is to avoid behaviors associated with femininity.

I suppose it would not be surprising if men expressed less empathy than women. After all, males have more socialization experiences which encourage the suppression of empathic responses. We have already discussed traditionally male and female toys. Female toys such as dolls encourage empathic expression while boys' toys typically do not. It is also the case that males often find themselves in situations where they are expected to be powerful, competitive, independent, and dominant, behaviors which are not very compatible with empathic responding. This pressure to be independent and competitive often begins in childhood. Block (1973) followed the development of a group of females and males over a 40-year period. She found that parents treated their sons and daughters differently throughout that period. In particular, daughters were encouraged to express their feelings and to relate well to other people. Sons were encouraged and rewarded for being independent, and for controlling their emotions. Perhaps males have less practice with empathic responding and are simply less likely than females to know how to respond to others' emotional distress.

Tavris (1992) suggested that gender roles are responsible for differential empathy in men and women. So-called "women's jobs" such as child-care provider call for empathic responding. She pointed out that research studies on single men who were caring for their children due to widower-hood or wife's desertion (and did not choose to be their children's primary caregivers prior to such events) have found that such men exhibit typically female traits such as nurturance and sympathy. In other words, it is not because they are so nurturant that they are children's caregivers, it is because they are children's caregivers that they are so nurturant. It is the social role which calls for empathic behavior, and women typically occupy such social roles.

Social Roles Theory

Tavris's reasoning is quite similar to Eagly's (1987) *social roles theory.* According to social roles theory, many gender differences are the products of the different social roles occupied by females and males—social roles that sustain or inhibit different behaviors. In other words, the sex-differentiated experiences that arise out of gender roles cause women and men to have somewhat different skills and attitudes which then give rise to different behaviors (Eagly & Wood, 1991). Social roles theory also suggests that social roles often lead to social stereotypes (in addition to stereotypes leading to social roles). In other words, we see men and women doing different things and infer that they are correspondingly different. Deaux and Lewis (1984) found that subjects judged females who had adopted masculine roles as more masculine in personality than females in feminine roles and males in feminine roles to be more feminine in personality than males in masculine roles. Similarly, Eagly and Steffen (1984) had subjects give their impressions of fictitious women and fictitious men employed either outside of the home or who were full-time homemakers. Regardless of gender, those who worked outside the home were viewed in more masculine terms and the ones who stayed at home full-time were viewed in more feminine terms.

Williams and Best (1986) suggested that stereotypes about the genders evolved as a mechanism to support sex-role differentiation. Females, they suggested, ended up with the homemaking role because nursing infant children limited their mobility and homemaking tasks were compatible with this restriction. Having found it useful for women and men to assume different roles, societies try to reassure themselves that these roles are appropriate by developing beliefs about the qualities of males and females to serve as further justification that these roles are for the best. Once established, these beliefs serve as norms for the behavior of adults and provide models for the socialization of children.

Tavris (1992) also described how people, regardless of gender, are sensitive to nonverbal signals when they are low in power. Such sensitivity makes sense because, to survive, "subordinates" need to be able to read and respond appropriately to the behavior of powerful others. In other words, women's sensitivity to what others are feeling is an adaptive response to their typically low power. For instance, until recently it was customary for most of the power in a marriage to be held by males. Women who were not submissive and subservient were reprimanded by their husbands and families. In such cases women had to watch carefully and wait until their husbands were in the "right" mood before they could broach certain subjects and have a reasonable chance of success. Snodgrass (1985) conducted a study with male-female dyads where sometimes the man was the leader and sometimes the woman led, and found that subordinates, regardless of gender, were more sensitive to nonverbal cues than leaders, regardless of gender. We will discuss in Chap. 3 the alarming evidence that women are still lower in power than men.

Although the evidence for gender differences in empathy is far from strong, Hall's (1984) analysis of 125 studies on gender differences in sensitivity to nonverbal cues did find that women tend to be better at reading the emotions of others than men. If women are better "decoders" then they might be expected to experience more empathy than men (Eisenberg et al., 1989). Still, we must remember that most studies have found no gender differences in empathy and those that have typically found weak effects. Think for a moment about all the men you know and all the women you know. We all know some extremely empathic men and some unsympathetic, selfish women. Are the differences between the men and women you know really large enough to justify perceiving men as significantly less empathic than women? Do we really want to accept gender differences in empathic expression as fundamental biological differences? Should not everyone, regardless of gender, be encouraged to respond appropriately to other people's emotional distress and self-disclosures?

Emotionality

Are women more emotional than men? It depends. Empathy has to do with sensitivity to others' emotions. But what about the individual's own experience and expressions of emotion? Do you believe that women are more emotional than men? Do you believe that women are more likely to express their emotions than men? Unfortunately there is not a lot of research on this topic but what there is suggests that men and women are equally emotional, but express emotion differently because of different norms regarding emotional expression for men and women.

Eisenberg et al. (1989) found modest sex differences in facial and self-report indexes of emotion, with females being somewhat more responsive. However, one of the most interesting things about their findings was that this gender difference increased with age. For example, with preschool children there were few gender differences but by second grade sex differences had begun to emerge. The authors also reported that "the masking and inhibition of negative facial expressions increase with age in childhood, especially for males" (p. 115). Other studies, some conducted with adolescents (Stapley & Haviland, 1989), some with college students (Snell, 1989), and some with adults (Saurer & Eisler, 1990), have found that females are more emotionally expressive than men. These findings, especially the ones showing an increasing trend in this direction as children age, suggest that through socialization we learn to express or repress our emotions in socially appropriate ways. Our society may have different expectations and norms regarding emotional expression by males and females. These different expectations are communicated to us throughout our lifespans. For example, emotional toughness is an important part of being a "man" (a point to be discussed further in Chap. 4) and, in some social settings, deviation from this results in being labeled as less than a man (many of us have witnessed the less-than-macho male being called a "wimp" or "wuss" or "sissy"). Likewise, many females grew up being told to act like a "lady," which among other things included restraining or avoiding expressions of anger that could endanger interpersonal relations (Kaplan et al., 1983; Lemkau & Landau, 1986).

I am sensitive to the norms regarding the emotional expressivity of males because I realize that my nontraditionally male child is a target for social rejection and, like most parents, I do not want my child to suffer. When Kane was 5, he worked very hard on valentines for his kindergarten classmates. Not only did he write "To so-and-so, from Kane," but he wrote "I love you" on every one. As he did this, I found myself in a quandary. Should I tell Kane not to do this, knowing that boys are not supposed to express their feelings of love for their peers? I decided that the social repercussions at age 5 of this behavior were likely to be few but I knew that within a few years such a behavior would be punished severely by his peers. Kane also hugged and kissed his friends, both male and female, hello and goodbye. In kindergarten, Kane's affection was tolerated quite well by his peers. However, it did not take a psychic to predict that these behaviors would wear socially thin in just a few short years, especially with the boys. Indeed, by the third week of first grade it was clear to Kane that these behaviors had severe social consequences and he stopped performing them. By second grade he crossed out the word "love" on his store-bought valentines for his classmates and wrote in "like." If Kane were female, perhaps the statute of limitations would have been longer. Indeed, research (Brody, 1985; Eisenberg et al., 1989) has found that sex differences in emotionality are generally more obvious in adolescents and adults than in children. It takes time to create them.

It is also interesting to think about crying as an emotional expression and how gender differences in crying may be based in part on differences in gender roles. When I was a child, an adolescent, and a young adult I cried very easily when frustrated, hurt, or angry. Now I never cry in these situations. Why the change? I want to be perceived as competent and in control and I know that crying interferes with this perception. What is interesting about this is that being competent and in control is an important part of the male role and as I, a female, have moved into the workplace and competed with men, I have come to adopt these norms. Unfortunately, I have gotten so good at controlling this response that I now have a hard time crying even when I feel like I want to. I imagine that many men also feel this way.

Johnson and Schulman (1988) found that adults estimated that females display communal feelings (e.g., concern for others' feelings, needs, or desires) more than males. Males were estimated to express more self-oriented feelings (e.g., needs, desires, interests of the self) than females. Other research has found that females are more comfortable expressing fear and sadness than males (Blier & Blier-Wilson, 1989; Brody, 1984) although people do not perceive males and females as differing in the experience of fear and sadness (Fabes & Martin, 1991). Males are also perceived to express, but not to experience, more anger than females (Fabes & Martin, 1991) and Averill (1982) found that, in everyday life, women's experience of anger was just as frequent and intense, and occurred in response to the same things, as men's. Kopper and Epperson (1991) did not find that women suppress their anger more than men although those who scored masculine on the Bem Sex Role Inventory were more likely to get angry and to express anger outwardly. Fabes and Martin (1991) explained that males are more likely than females to behave aggressively, and this may lead individuals to believe that men express more anger.

SOME OTHER COMMONLY STUDIED GENDER DIFFERENCES

Aggression

Gender differences in aggressive behavior are among the most reliable of gender differences, but like the other differences we have discussed, they are not nearly as large nor as clearly connected to biological differences between the sexes as we might expect. In their famous review of the gender differences literature, Maccoby and Jacklin (1974) concluded that aggression was the only social behavior for which there was evidence of a clear-cut sex difference. Three meta-analyses of the psychological literature conducted in the 1980s (Eagly & Steffen, 1986; Hyde, 1984b; Hyde, 1986) also concluded that there is a gender difference in aggressive behavior. However, Eagly and Steffen (1986) concluded that it was a relatively small difference for adult subjects ($d = .29$). Hyde's (1984b) analysis included a large number of studies with child subjects and found a moderate effect size (d) of .50. This means that only about 2 to 5 percent of the variation in aggressive behavior is explainable by gender (i.e., 95 to 98 percent of the variation comes from other sources). Part of the reason we perceive gender differences in aggression to be large is because murderers and rapists are overwhelmingly male. However, as pointed out by Burbank (1994), these behaviors are performed by a small minority of males. With respect to these behaviors, the behavior of most men resembles that of most women. Another reason we see the difference as large is because of a cultural belief that males' higher levels of the hormone testosterone lead them to be more aggressive. In fact, research has not consistently demonstrated the testosterone-aggression link in humans (Bjorkqvist, 1994).

Bjorkqvist and Niemela (1992) concluded that whether males are more aggressive than females depends upon the gender of those involved, the type of aggression, and the situation. For instance, Lagerspetz et al. (1988) in a study of 11- and 12-year-old Finnish students, found that females were more likely to use indirect forms of aggression such as rumor-spreading and making a new friend in "revenge" while males were more likely to express their anger directly in the form of yelling, striking, or pushing. Bjorkqvist et al. (1994) suggested that physical aggression makes less sense for the physically weaker female, who consequently resorts to verbal or indirect means of aggression. Indirect aggressive strategies have been reported by a number of cross-cultural researchers to occur more often among females than among males although there is quite a bit of cultural variation (Bjorkqvist, 1994).

Hyde's (1984b) meta-analysis found that gender differences in aggression tended to be larger among preschoolers and smaller among college students. Research indicates that by early adulthood men, like women, begin to express their aggression verbally or indirectly not only through gossip but through critical remarks, interruptions, insinuations without direct accusation, and "do-not-speak-to-me" behavior (Bjorkqvist et al., 1992, 1994). Bjorkqvist et al. (1994) noted that middle-class social norms in European and North American cultures discourage physical aggression in adult males.

Whether gender differences in aggression are found may depend upon the type of aggression and on the setting. Bjorkqvist and Niemela

(1992) noted that the majority of studies examining sex differences in aggression have defined aggression as physical, a type which may be more likely in males. Indeed, the strongest predictor of sex differences in aggression in the Eagly and Steffen (1984) meta-analysis was whether the situation provided an opportunity for physical rather than psychological aggression (men were more likely to aggress when it was a situation calling for physical aggression). Eagly and Steffen (1984) also pointed out that the majority of social-psychological studies on aggression have focused on aggression toward strangers in short-term encounters. Cross-cultural studies of aggression which examined both physical and indirect forms of aggression in interpersonal relationships have found that there is good reason to doubt the assumption that males are more aggressive than females (see the special 1994 issue of the journal *Sex Roles*, Vol. 30, Nos. 3 and 4, on cross-cultural studies of aggression in women and girls).

Eagly and Steffen (1986) used social roles theory to discuss gender differences in aggression. They wrote that such differences may be explained in part by gender roles that encourage some forms of aggression for males while discouraging aggressiveness in females (e.g., aggressiveness is incompatible with several major components of the female role such as being caring and avoiding physical danger). Research by Campbell and Muncer (1987) and Campbell et al., (1992) suggests that men may feel publicly pressured to aggress when their self-esteem or public integrity has been challenged and when they perceive that observers are likely to view their passivity negatively. In contrast, women feel embarrassed if they aggress in public. Perry et al. (1989) found that, by age 10, boys expect less parental disapproval for aggression than girls do. Eagly and Steffen (1986) also noted that males are more likely to occupy and anticipate occupying roles calling for aggressiveness (e.g., military and athletic roles), thereby gaining more skills and experience in being aggressive. In contrast, aggressive behavior is inappropriate for most roles occupied by women (e.g., mother, secretary, teachers, nurses) and would be more likely to create guilt and anxiety in females because of its incompatibility with the female role's emphasis on caring and concern for others.

Conformity and Influenceability

Social stereotypes about the genders might lead us to believe that, in comparison to men, women are more conforming, easier to persuade, and more easily led because they are more dependent and submissive (Eagly & Wood, 1985). Early conformity studies did not explicitly address the issue of gender differences. Sherif's (1937) study on informational pressure used only male subjects. Asch (1956) apparently collected data from both sexes for his study on normative pressure but did not report the findings from the female subjects. Although both male and female subjects were often used in later research and although gender differences in influence-ability were not always found, the view that women are more easily influenced than men was expressed with great confidence in social psychological texts and the *Handbook of Social Psychology* well through the 1970s. This was in spite of the fact that 82 percent of the studies comparing females and males on persuasion and 74 percent testing for gender differences in conformity had failed to find a difference (Eagly, 1978; Eagly & Wood, 1985).

Using the newly developed technique of meta-analysis, Eagly and Carli (1981) analyzed 148 social influence studies from 1949 to 1977. In their meta-analysis a small but statistically significant effect for gender on influenceability was found (d was estimated to be in between .16 and .26; remember .20 indicates a small effect and .50 a medium effect size). The effect was largest for studies on group pressure where the subject was pressured by other group members to change beliefs or behavior (d in between .23 and .32). This may have occurred because females are more "communal" and committed to preserving social harmony and good feelings among group members (Eagly, 1978; Eagly & Wood, 1985) or because men conform less due to social norms suggesting that men should be independent and not easily influenced (Eagly et al., 1981). Eagly et al. (1981) found that men conformed less when they thought group members had access to their opinions than they did when others presumably did not know what their opinions were. Women's conformity was not affected by this.

Eagly's (1978) article noted that of the twenty-two studies on persuasion conducted and published before 1970, 32 percent found greater influenceability among female subjects whereas only 8 percent of the forty studies published after 1970 found such a difference. She remarked that the social psychological impact of biological sex is apparently contingent upon the cultural context. Eagly also reasoned that, because we are more likely to conform when we are unsure of our opinions or abilities, sex differences would be more likely for those studies using topics which were more familiar or interesting to one gender versus the other. For instance, a number of the earlier studies for gender differences involved military or political topics (Eagly, 1978). Sistrunk and McDavid (1971) and Goldberg (1974, 1975) found that males conformed more than females when feminine items were used and vice versa. Maupin and Fisher (1989) also found that gender differences in influenceability are influenced by the gender-related content of the influencing task and whether female or male superiority on the task is evident. However, a study by Eagly and Carli (1981), where male and female subjects rated eighty-three topics used in persuasion studies from 1949 to 1977 on interest and self-knowledge, did not find that researchers overrepresented topics for which males had greater interest and knowledge although more masculine topics were associated with greater female influenceability.

One of the more curious findings on gender and influenceability is that the sex of the researcher seems to make a difference in whether gender differences are found. Eagly and Carli (1981) found that 79 percent of the studies finding that females are more influenceable were conducted by men, and male researchers tended to find larger differences than female researchers. Eagly and Carli (1981) suggested that perhaps researchers are more likely to design, implement, and report their studies in ways that flatter their own gender.

Although research by Eagly (1978) and Eagly and Carli (1981) found the gender difference in influenceability to be very small, the stereotype that women are more conforming and more easily influenced than men persists (Eagly & Wood, 1982). Eagly and Wood (1982) and Eagly (1983) suggested that this perception persists because of women's lower social status in both the home and workplace. Persons who are lower in power and status generally must yield more to the influence of higher-status others. They wrote that because individuals have seen more instances of males than females occupying higher status roles they have also seen more instances of females being submissive and conforming than males. Thus, the stereotype. They conducted several experiments supportive of this hypothesis. In other words, females are not fundamentally more submissive and yielding than men although their lower status means that it often behooves them to behave in this way. Unger and Crawford (1992) also noted that gender differences in submissive behaviors are often the result of status differences between females and males. Eagly and Wood (1982) concluded that, as the distribution of males and females into social roles becomes less gender-typed, such gender stereotypes should diminish as well.

Altruism

Common stereotypes of females as nurturant and compassionate suggest that they would be more helpful than men but a meta-analysis of social-psychological studies of helping conducted by Eagly and Crowley (1986) found that males are more helpful than females. According to those authors, this result can be explained by the fact that the typical social-psychological study of helping involves the short-term helping of strangers, a type of helping more likely to be done by males. Eagly and Crowley (1986) wrote that neither males nor females are more helpful, although there are sex differences in helping depending upon the type of helping, a hypothesis supported by their meta-analysis.

These differences in when males and females help can be understood from an examination of the different social roles occupied by females and males. Recall that according to Eagly's social roles theory, it is not so much that differences between men and women lead them to occupy different social roles as that different social roles result in men and women being different. In regard to helping, the idea is that norms governing helping are different for the male and female roles. For instance, the female gender role suggests that women should care for the personal and emotional needs of others and help them accomplish their goals ("caregiving help"). The male role encourages more "heroic" types of helping involving non-routine and risky acts of rescuing others as well as "chivalrous" types of helping such as carrying heavy things or holding open doors. Eagly and Crowley (1986) noted that females' helping occurs primarily in close relationships for two reasons: the potential danger involved in helping strangers, and the fact that females are more likely to occupy social roles which require them to provide caregiving help. For example, women are more likely to occupy domestic roles, and roles such as secretary and nurse, which require assisting others to reach their goals. In contrast, men are more likely to occupy roles which require heroic help-giving (e.g., firefighter, police officer, soldier). Eagly and Crowley (1986) further pointed out that the occupation of these different roles (and the anticipation of occupying these different roles) fosters the development of different helping skills.

Piliavin et al. (1981) explained gender differences in helping in terms of cost-benefit considerations. According to their cost-reward model of helping, we will help when we assess the benefits of helping to outweigh the costs of helping. Males and females are likely to make different cost-benefit assessments depending upon the physical strength required for and danger involved in helping. For instance, a series of helping studies was conducted on subways where appropriate intervention included lifting a collapsed male. Not surprisingly, such studies found strong sex effects favoring men as helpers in these cases (Piliavin & Unger, 1985). Some types of helping, as pointed out by Eagly and Crowley (1986), may be more or less socially appropriate depending upon gender, and as Piliavin and Unger (1985) noted, sex-appropriate helping may be perceived as less costly.

CONCLUDING REMARKS

The theme of this chapter was that gender differences are not nearly as large as popular stereotypes would have us believe. Also, there is evidence that different norms exist for females and males, norms which encourage the development of different skills and abilities. Furthermore, the fact that gender differences are getting smaller as the years pass suggests that there is more to gender differences than biology.

Some research findings are difficult to explain by differential socialization. Halpern (1992), for instance, viewed studies finding that left-handedness is associated with good spatial skills in women while the reverse is true for men as evidence that cerebral lateralization is a contributing factor in cognitive sex differences. Males, she pointed out, also have a higher incidence of stuttering and severe reading disabilities—differences that are hard to explain by differential socialization. Geary (1989) quite reasonably has suggested that nature and nurture interact to produce sex differences. He wrote that culture may attenuate or exaggerate early biologically related gender differences and, as culture changes, we can therefore expect the size of sex differences to change as well. There is still the question of the relative influence of biology and socialization on sex differences. I suspect that socialization and culture play the larger roles in the creation of gender differences for four reasons. One is that sex differences, when found, are relatively small. The second is that there is strong research evidence suggestive of differential cultural expectations for men and women. A third reason is that the size of sex differences is getting smaller as we change these cultural expectations. And the fourth is that meta-analyses of gender difference areas consistently reveal that whether a difference is found in an area depends markedly on how the behavior is conceptualized and measured as well as a myriad of other factors such as the research setting and social context.

As we conclude this chapter on gender differences, we must remember that even where differences are found they are quite small and certainly do not justify our perception of men and women as "opposite sexes" nor do they justify treating the sexes as differently as we often do. As Linn (1986, p. 217) said in the concluding chapter of a book on meta-analyses of gender differences: "Gender differences in intellectual and psychosocial tasks are relatively small compared to the massive differences in participation of males and females in powerful, remunerative, satisfying, and secure careers." Similarly, in a 1990 meta-analysis Hyde et al. (1990b) found relatively small gender differences in performance, confidence, and attitudes toward mathematics. They concluded that, to explain the substantial underrepresentation of women in mathematics-related occupations, we must look beyond abilities and intrapsychic factors to influences such as sex discrimination in education and employment. In Chaps. 3 and 4 we will discuss the limitations of traditional gender roles for both men and women. Keep in mind as you read these chapters that these limitations are not easily justified by differences in biology.

Tavris (1992) once said that our tendency to magnify differences between the genders obscures the reality of their similarities. However, as Eagly (1987) pointed out, in spite of the similarities between men and women (on important things like intelligence, memory, analytic ability, etc.) that have been documented by research psychologists, the average person still perceives males and females to be quite different. She suggested that this perception is to some extent correct: When we look around, we see men and women occupying different social roles, roles which often require stereotypically masculine or feminine qualities. For instance, we see mostly female nurses, mothers, and secretaries and mostly male engineers, computer technicians, and businessmen. It is no wonder, then, that we see males and females as so different—they often do very different things in our society. However, as Tavris (1992) noted, we need to avoid confusing differences in what women and men *do* in their lives with differences in their basic psychological capacities. I would add that we also need to avoid confusing differences between what men and women are socially rewarded for with differences in their basic psychological capacities. Both men and women are motivated to conform to societal expectations for their genders in order to avoid social disapproval. Indeed, several studies (Klein & Willerman, 1979; LaFrance & Carmen, 1980; Putnam & McCallister, 1980; Serbin et al., 1993) have shown that whether males and females exhibit sex-stereotypic behavior depends greatly upon the situation and what is perceived to be "appropriate" in that situation.

This tendency to assume that female-male gender-role differences are due to fundamental differences between them rather than to socialization or the social roles they occupy is reminiscent of the *fundamental attribution error*. This is the name given by social psychologists to the tendency to underestimate the role of the situation in creating behavior (Ross, 1977). The F.A.E., as it is sometimes called, suggests that we are more likely to assume that individuals' personal traits and attitudes are responsible for their behavior than we are to attribute their behavior to external/situational causes. Geis (1993) noted that it is the fundamental attribution error which makes high-status characteristics appear to be the internal personality traits of men and subordinate characteristics the internal dispositions of women. She gives the example of how when seeing Marcia wait for Marc's directions we assume that Marcia is dependent and Marc is dominant, ignoring the fact that Marcia is Marc's secretary and is simply behaving in accordance with her role.

One reason given for the F.A.E. is that we may not be aware of the situational forces which gave rise to the behavior. As David Myers put it (1990, p. 79), "causality is found where our attention is drawn." In the case of gender differences, society focuses our attention on biological sex as an attribution in and of itself. Thus we assume that behavioral differences between females and males result from internal personality differences originating from biological sex differences. We often fail to realize that the different social roles occupied by males and females call for different behaviors and encourage the development of different qualities. I believe that this tendency is so widespread as to constitute a *fundamental gender attribution error* (F.G.A.E.!). One of the goals of this book is to draw attention to some of the situational forces behind gender roles and behaviors in order to reduce this error.

SALLY FORTH By Greg Howard and Craig Macintosh

Reprinted with special permission of King Features Syndicate.

Sally makes the fundamental gender attribution error.

I would like to conclude this chapter on gender differences by trying to reconcile social psychology's desire to promote diversity with the perspective that we should minimize gender differences. *Difference feminists,* feminists who celebrate the very differences suggested by gender stereotypes, are concerned that androgyny and other perspectives which minimize male-female differences will result in a melting pot where women will be melted into models of males. They also argue that the female qualities suggested by gender stereotypes have been unjustly maligned. Likewise, the *mythopoetic men's movement* (so-called because fairy tales and myths are used to illustrate men's "fundamental masculine nature") suggests that natural male qualities have been unjustly villified, and that men have become too "wimpy" and "feminized" (Kimmel & Kaufman, 1994). In some ways, these ideas are consistent with current criticisms of the cultural "melting pot." The "melting pot" idea where people from many different cultures come together and eventually meld together (assimilate) is out of vogue. The problem is that assimilation into the dominant culture often results in the loss of unique cultural traditions and identities. The melting pot metaphor has been replaced by the "salad bowl" metaphor which reflects how different cultures may come together while retaining their own flavor. The "salad bowl" model encourages and values cultural diversity.

Does valuing diversity mean that we should value gender differences? My personal position is that we should value qualities associated with both genders but not as gender differences. As Chaps. 3, 4, and 5 will demonstrate, the artificial separation of qualities into female and male unnecessarily limits both genders and contributes to gender conflict. While we should certainly value some of the qualities that have been labeled in the past as female, or as male, we should not insist that an individual has to be a particular gender in order to possess them. The issue gets more complicated, however, when we consider the self-esteem and identity benefits of emphasizing the differences between the genders. We will explore this issue in Chap. 5.

Summary

- When gender differences are found they are relatively small. Females and males are more similar than different in regard to most behaviors and skills.
- Meta-analysis, a statistical technique where information from many studies is combined in order to estimate the size of differences between groups, is an important tool in the study of gender differences.
- Gender differences in mathematics skills are waning and the differences that do remain appear in high school. It is at this time that females seem especially sensitive to social pressures to fit their gender role. There is also evidence that parents and teachers may communicate to females that the pursuit of mathematics is inappropriate for females, evidence that females have low confidence in their mathematics ability, and evidence that girls receive fewer experiences outside of the classroom which prepare them for careers in science and mathematics.
- Common stereotypes suggest large sex differences in empathy and emotion but such stereotypes are not strongly supported by research. Self-report measures of empathy find larger sex differences than do physiological measures. This suggests that males may be unwilling to portray themselves as empathic because doing so is inconsistent with the male gender role. Research suggests that whether and how a person expresses emotion is influenced by gender norms.
- Gender differences in aggressive behavior are commonly found but depend upon the gender of those involved, the type of aggression, situational factors, and gender norms. Studies on gender differences in influenceability have indicated that whether differences are found depends upon the situation and whether the research was carried out by a female or male experimenter. Gender differences in altruism also depend upon the type of helping involved and whether it is gender-role-appropriate.
- Social roles theory suggests that many of the differences between men and women are created by the different demands of male and female roles. For example, female social roles (such as childcare provider) are more likely to require empathic responding while male roles often require that men be powerful, competitive, and dominant—qualities that are at odds with empathic responding.

Likewise, gender roles encourage some forms of aggression in males while discouraging aggressiveness in females.

- It is not surprising that we view men and women as fundamentally different since they often occupy different social roles and our culture emphasizes how different men and women are. However, assuming that gender differences in behavior are due to biological sex differences when they may be due to differences in roles and norms may constitute a "fundamental gender attribution error."

3

L imitations of the
T raditional *F* emale *R* ole

❖

The Homemaker ◆ Women in the Paid Labor Force ◆ *Household Labor and the
Employed Woman* ◆ *The Male-Female Earnings Differential* ◆ The Low Power and
Status of Women ◆ *Women's Power in Organizations: The Glass Ceiling* ◆
Explanations for the Glass Ceiling ◆ Concluding Remarks ◆ Summary

S ocial psychologists are interested in gender because it is a fascinating example of how social norms are learned and influence our behavior. But their interest goes deeper than this. Most social psychologists feel that traditional
gender roles often limit individuals and lead to social inequality.

People often say to me: "Men's and women's roles are separate but they're
equal so why change them?" They think of traditional female and male roles as
complementary and as arising from biological differences between males and females. In previous chapters we critically examined the assumption that role differences are "natural." In this chapter we will examine the assumption that
women's roles are separate but equal. We will see that the research evidence suggests that women's roles are dramatically unequal when it comes to work, pay,
status, and power in our society. There are other limitations to the female role
which are not explored here. These include such things as the fact that women are
disproportionately victims of sexual assault and poverty, and that cultural standards suggesting that women are valued to the extent that they are young, thin,

59

and physically attractive produce low self-esteem and contribute to eating disorders.

*T*HE HOMEMAKER

Many of us were raised to believe that a woman's place is in the home, but only about 40 percent of women stay at home full time (this figure includes female senior citizens). The percentage of families with a working husband, stay-at-home wife, and two or more children comprise only about 7 percent of the nation's families (Duxbury & Higgins, 1991). While it may sound good not to have to go to work outside the home each day, it is a mistake to think that the woman staying home full time does little work. In fact the average housewife spends between 48 and 70 hours on housework a week (Hyde, 1992). Furthermore, paid work fulfills many needs for individuals—not only economic needs, but social needs and recognition, respect, status, and stimulation needs. These needs may be harder to meet for the individual who stays at home full time.

In 1963 Betty Friedan's book *The Feminine Mystique* was published. Friedan used the term "feminine mystique" to refer to the cultural belief that true feminine fulfillment was to be found in the life of the American suburban housewife. The difficulty, Friedan noted, was that many such women found themselves dissatisfied and ashamed of their dissatisfaction since they knew they were supposed to feel lucky. In her interviews with homemakers, Friedan found that this dissatisfaction occurred even in women whose greatest ambition had been to be a wife and mother. The main problem according to her interviews was that women mainly function as support personnel for others and have no identity of their own. Yes, their role is important since they make it possible for their children and husbands to achieve, but vicarious living—living through others—is not the same as living yourself. Yet the feminine mystique tells us that this is the ultimate in feminine existence. The other problem with the homemaker role, according to Friedan and her interviewees, is that it keeps women from sharing in human destiny and becoming fully human: "Love and children and home are good, but they are not the whole world, even if most of the words written for women pretend they are" (Friedan, 1963, p. 67).

Friedan's book was written 30 years ago but to some extent I think the feminine mystique and its accompanying problems live on. Crosby (1991), for example, talked about the continued idealization of motherhood and how there is almost a conspiracy of silence about how difficult motherhood is: "Many young women and men look forward to parenthood as an idyllic time filled with smiles and coos and hugs. Most likely you did too . . . [but] did you anticipate the sleepless nights, the hours of pacing . . . did you foresee the mountains of laundry, the rashes, the temper tantrums, and the boredom?" (pp. 49–50). The "housewife syndrome" is a term coined by Tavris and Offir (1977) to refer to the frustration experienced by many women whose sole identity is that of a housewife. Think about it. Not only is the work never done (as soon as you get the house clean, someone messes it up again), but it is often boring and not appreciated as the work it is. And although children can be the most wonderful creatures imaginable, having children is not like having days filled with Kodak moments. The reality is that they must be fed, clothed, and washed (imagine the labor this amounts to), they fight with each other and with you, and once they reach a certain age they really do not want to have a lot to do with you.

Ferree (1980) noted that homemakers often feel socially isolated. She suggested that geographic mobility, suburban living, the large number of working women, and the unpredictable schedules of small children and infants all contribute to this isolation. The growth in numbers of women in the workplace may also contribute to the perception that staying home full time is leisurely or lazy (Ferree, 1980) and this decline in the prestige of homemaking has probably led to a greater dissatisfaction with housework (Gove & Tudor, 1973). Perhaps this is why some researchers (cf. Shaver & Freedman, 1976) have found that homemakers have a lower sense of self-worth than employed women. Some studies (cf. Ross et al., 1983) have even found stay-at-home wives to be more depressed than employed wives. Gove (1972) suggested that homemakers have a higher incidence of depression because they have only one source of gratification and because housework is tedious, repetitive, and low in status.

Still, not all studies have found homemakers to be more depressed and less satisfied with their lives than employed women. Shehan (1984) reported that, while housewives found housework to be boring and isolating, they did not suffer from decreased psychological well-being because their housewife role allowed them enough time to pursue hobbies and belong to clubs and organizations. Ferree (1987) pointed out that

BABY BLUES By Rick Kirkman and Jerry Scott

Reprinted with special permission of King Features Syndicate.

Children are wonderful, but many women find full-time homemaking to be less than satisfying intellectually and socially.

there are some rewards associated with housework such as meeting the needs of loved ones and the satisfaction that comes from doing a good job. The conflicting results seen in the research on this topic probably have resulted from the different samples used in the different studies. Neither "homemakers" nor "employed women" are uniform, homogenous groups. Their family incomes, their religious backgrounds, their reasons for staying at home or working, their jobs, the amount of social support they have for their choice, their achievement motivations, whether they like or dislike housework, and the ages and number of their children all differ. All these things affect satisfaction with a domestic or employed social role. Krause (1983) found that full-time homemakers who endorsed nontraditional expectations for the female role but who felt their husbands held traditional views regarding the female role were significantly more dissatisfied with their role and more depressed than homemakers who endorsed the traditional female role. Perry-Jenkins et al. (1992) also found that women's satisfaction with their home and work roles depended upon the meaning they gave to these roles. For instance, employed women who viewed their incomes as equally important to the family as their husbands' incomes were more satisfied than employed women who viewed their incomes as secondary or who were ambivalent about working outside the home.

While the research is somewhat equivocal about the effects of the stay-at-home role on women, it is less equivocal on the point that contributing financially to the household increases a woman's power within it. According to *family power theory,* the person with the greatest economic resources in the family is usually the one with the greatest power as well (Stroh et al., 1992). In the case of the homemaker, her economic dependence on her male partner gives her less power in the home since it is "his" money and he is the one doing the "real" work (because women's labor in the home is unpaid people often assume it is not as valuable as paid labor). Several studies have found that employed wives have a greater say at home than housewives (Beckman & Houser, 1979; Crosby, 1982; Mason & Bumpass, 1975). Ericksen et al. (1979) found that husbands who have jobs high in occupational prestige are especially likely to dominate domestic decisions. As Steil and Turetsky (1987, p. 75) put it, "gender differences in marital influence parallel gender differences in occupational resources outside marriage." These studies do not demonstrate definitively that the greater household power comes directly from having more money or a high status job. However, it certainly makes sense that when we are economically dependent upon someone and they have a higher social status they would have greater power over us than we over them.

In short, the life of the homemaker is not the idyllic one portrayed on television and those who occupy this role deserve greater power and status than they currently enjoy. We must also ask ourselves why this role continues to be reserved almost exclusively for women and consider the part that socialization plays in the development of any skills that may make them seem better suited for it than men. It is also interesting to note that, in addition to gender stereotypes and differential socialization which suggest that women would be better at staying at home and men belong in the workplace, women's lower pay for work outside the home is often the decisive factor in determining who stays home with the children. A number of couples have told me that they decided the mother should stay home because the loss of her salary would be less of a blow to the household income than the loss that the father's would be. This gender pay differential is one of the topics explored in the next section.

WOMEN IN THE PAID LABOR FORCE

According to the 1993 *Statistical Abstracts of the United States* (U.S. Department of Commerce, 1993), slightly under 60 percent of women in the United States are employed in comparison to about 75 percent of men. About 67 percent of women who are married with children under age 18, 78 percent of divorced women with children, 58 percent of mothers with preschool aged children, and 55 percent of women with children under age 3 work outside the home. Unfortunately, as discussed below, women who work for wages are usually expected to satisfy the traditional female role at home while in the workplace they are still not treated as equal to men.

Household Labor and the Employed Woman

One significant limitation of current women's roles is that employed women continue to be responsible for the bulk of childcare and household labor. After working a shift outside the home, most women come home and work a second shift. Because of this *second shift*, women experience a *leisure gap* in comparison to men (Hochschild, 1989). In comparison to the women they live with, black men do 40 percent of the household labor, white men 34 percent, and Hispanic men 36 percent (Shelton & John, 1993). Although research has found that husbands have significantly increased their household work time in the last 10 years (Zick & McCullough, 1991), when both partners are employed women still do, on average, 69 percent of the household work (Berardo et al., 1987). For women, increases in labor market hours translate into only small reductions in family work and the amount of time they must devote to child-care tasks (getting children ready for school, doctor's appointments, etc.) remains unchanged (Presland & Antill, 1987).

Using data from a national survey of 3000 married and cohabiting couples, Blair and Lichter (1991) found that females contribute twice the amount of total household labor than males (33 hours a week versus 14 hours). Blair and Lichter (1991) and Gunter and Gunter (1990) also found that tasks in the home are gender-segregated and pointed out that "women's" tasks tend to be those daily tasks which must be done within a certain time frame (such as meal preparation and dishes) while "men's" tasks provide more discretion as to when they are to be done (yard work and household repairs). However, Shelton and John (1993) found that household labor was less gender-stratified in black homes than in white or Hispanic ones. Research has also found that women assume more responsibility than men for managing the household finances (Gunter & Gunter, 1990). We will see in this chapter that traditional divisions of household labor also create problems for women in the workplace. In the final chapter of the book, we come back to this issue, examining why this household labor differential persists, and the problems it creates for female-male relationships.

The Male-Female Earnings Differential

A cartoon shows a little boy and girl looking into their diapers. Its caption reads, "Oh, so that explains the difference in our pay!" Euroamerican women working year-round full-time jobs earn about 68 percent of what Euroamerican men make. African-American women make even less, 61 percent of what white men make and 90 percent of what white women make. Hispanic women make 53 percent of what white men make and 78 percent of what white women make. Black and Hispanic men still make more than black and Hispanic women (84 percent and 82 percent, respectively) but this difference is not as large as the discrepancies between white men and all groups of women. Although women's pay has improved since 1979 when women's earnings were only 60 percent that of men's, women, especially nonwhite women, are still overrepresented in low-paying jobs. Furthermore, they earn less than men even when working the same jobs. (All statistics are from the U.S. Department of Labor, 1993.) In the next section we explore explanations for the gender pay gap.

Explaining the Gender Pay Differential

The two most common explanations for the gender pay differential are that women are paid less because they choose to work in jobs that pay less, and that women are less valuable to the organization due to lack of experience and qualifications. Another explanation suggests that women get paid less because they expect and accept lower pay. Let us take a critical look at each of these explanations.

1. *Women customarily choose to work in female-dominated jobs that pay less than men's jobs.* The *compensating differentials* explanation suggests that

women choose lower-paying jobs in exchange for pleasant work conditions which offer good social relations, the opportunity to serve others, flexible hours, or easy work (Filer, 1985, 1989).

The workforce is *sex-segregated,* that is, most jobs are occupied by predominantly one gender or the other. For instance, 98 percent of secretaries are female (U.S. Department of Labor, 1993). It is also true that most "women's work" pays less than jobs traditionally held by men even when the job requires quite a bit of skill. Konrad (1988), using data from a nationally representative sample, found that individuals in female-dominated industries and occupations earned less than individuals in male-dominated ones. For example, at the university where I teach, the starting salary for a painter (a job held by males) is greater than the starting salary for a registered nurse (by $170.00 a month) or an executive secretary (by $386.00 a month). Only one of the nineteen nonadministrative, nonmanagerial, nonfaculty jobs typically held by females has a top salary exceeding $3000.00 a month (registered nurse at $3138.00) while seventeen of the nineteen male-dominated ones exceed this level. Jacobs and Steinberg (1990) also found that the proportion of women in a job title depresses the wages associated with that job—the more women, the lower the salary accorded to that job.

It is true then that women are not typically found in jobs customarily held by men, and that the salaries in "female" jobs are lower. Does this mean that women choose these jobs over higher-paying men's jobs because they are more pleasant or conducive to mothering? Not according to research. Female jobs do not offer more flexible hours, lower levels of exertion, and other characteristics that would facilitate parenting (Glass & Camarigg, 1992). In fact, Glass and Camarigg (1992) found that the opposite was true: Greater concentrations of females in professional and blue-collar jobs were related to less flexibility, greater supervision, and less control over the timing and pacing of tasks. An analysis of 1600 jobs by Jacobs and Steinberg (1990) suggested that female-dominated jobs involve somewhat different, but not necessarily fewer, undesirable working conditions than male-dominated jobs. Women's jobs are more likely to involve working with difficult clients, cleaning others' dirt, mindless repetition, and low autonomy (lack of control over one's work). Furthermore, they found that undesirable working conditions typically have a *negative* effect on wages for both men's and women's jobs because unpleasant jobs tend to be held by those who are low in power and cannot command the higher wages needed to offset the unpleasant conditions.

Another problem with the compensating differentials approach is the assumption that women *choose* to work in lower-paying gender-segregated jobs. A U.S. Department of Labor report from 1990 (*Facts on Working Women*) concluded that a variety of barriers limit women's access to "male" occupations. These include requirements for nonessential training or credentials that women lack, and factors in the work climate such as harassment. For instance, until 1993, the Los Angeles Police Academy had a height requirement of 5 feet 8 inches for police officer candidates, which resulted in the exclusion of the majority of female applicants. Since that time a number of women under that height have passed the grueling physical examination.

Access discrimination (e.g., hiring or not hiring someone because of their membership in some social group, including gender) may also be responsible for gender-segregated hiring (Martinko & Gardner, 1983). Research indicates that women are less likely than equally qualified men to be hired for nontraditionally female jobs (Olson & Frieze, 1987). Glick et al. (1988) found that negative access discrimination is likely to occur when either females or males apply for jobs traditionally held by the other gender. They suggested that employers hire based on beliefs regarding the traits desirable for an occupation as well as beliefs about whether males or females are more likely to have those traits. A survey of career planning and placement professionals supported this hypothesis (Glick, 1991). Glick et al.'s (1988) study findings suggest that if an employer receives clear information that an applicant has the traits called for by a job, this can override the tendency toward sex discrimination. The problem is that women often do not have the type of past experience which would be enough to convince employers they do not fit the stereotype; past discrimination prevents them from having the weapons to fight future discrimination (Glick et al., 1988).

Most women, though, do not even consider traditionally male jobs. Women may be more comfortable with "female jobs" since they are more familiar and socialization has provided women with the appropriate skills (Ragins & Sundstrom, 1989). Research has also found that women expect to receive negative interpersonal consequences if they pursue masculine occupations (Condry & Dyer, 1976) and that both men and women perceive that a masculine occupation will negatively impact upon a woman's desirability as a romantic partner (Pfost & Fiore, 1990).

Women may also avoid "male" jobs because they anticipate a negative social climate within the workplace should they assume those roles. Yoder and Aniakudo (1994) described the "chilly work climate" often experienced by females in the male-dominated workplace, which includes their being ignored, their competence being disregarded, their mistakes being magnified, the use of double standards in how rules are applied to them, their encountering unwanted sexual comments and direct unwelcoming comments, and their having difficulties in obtaining adequate equipment. Unfortunately, there is evidence that male coworkers' reactions to women in "male" jobs are indeed negative (Padavic & Reskin, 1990). For instance, Yoder and Aniakudo (1994) found that 77 percent of a sample of African-American female firefighters had been sexually harassed by coworkers, 64 percent felt their competence was disregarded, and 82 percent felt their mistakes were magnified. Gutek and Morasch

(1982) contended that, when women are numerically rare in a job, their gender is highly salient (noticeable) and this causes them to be seen as women first, and employees second. They found that women in male-dominated work experienced more sexual harassment (unwanted sexual attention) than did either women in more traditional female jobs or women in gender-integrated jobs. Similar findings were obtained by Gutek and Cohen (1987) and Mansfield et al. (1991). We do not yet know whether the anticipation of such negativity causes women to avoid even considering a traditionally male job. However, Gutek and Morasch (1982) reported that 20 percent of the women in their sample who had worked in nontraditional female jobs quit due to sexual harassment and another 9 percent said they lost their jobs because they had complained or refused to go along with such harassment.

2. *Women get paid less because they are less valuable to the organization than men.* We have been talking about how sex-segregated the workplace is and how jobs customarily held by women typically pay less than jobs customarily held by men. However, even when working the *same* jobs as men, women get paid less. U.S. Department of Labor statistics from 1991 indicate that women computer programmers make 83 percent of what their male counterparts make, female financial managers 67 percent of what male financial managers make, females in sales make 58 percent of what males make, female elementary teachers make 89 percent of what male elementary teachers make, etc. Women's starting salaries tend to be lower than men's and this has long-term consequences because salary increases are usually awarded as percentages of base pay (Gerhart & Rynes, 1991).

One common explanation for the discrepancy between male and female salaries, even when the job is the same, comes from the *human capital approach.* This approach suggests that job rewards depend upon the individual's past investment in education and job training (Blau & Ferber, 1987). The suggestion is that women earn less because they are less skilled, less educated, or less experienced than men and therefore less valuable. Although differences in job qualifications and time on the job explain part of the male-female earnings differential, statistical analyses controlling for education, tenure in the occupation, and age have found that 75 percent of the gap remains unexplained (Rytina, 1983). Similarly, Stroh et al. (1992) in a study of male and female managers in *Fortune* 500 organizations found that, after controlling for number of years in the workforce and number of years in the company, female managers' salaries had increased 54 percent while male managers' salaries had increased 65 percent.

Do women deserve less money because they do not work as hard? Bielby and Bielby's (1988) research, reported in an article titled "She works hard for the money," found that women put more effort into paid work than men. In a laboratory experiment using college students, Major et al. (1984a) found that, for the same amount of money, female subjects did more work, worked longer hours, completed more correct work, and were more efficient than male subjects.

Is there bias in the evaluation of men's and women's work? Are females paid less because the quality of their work is perceived to be poorer than males'? Evidence on gender bias in evaluation is mixed. A meta-analysis of 104 studies on the evaluation of men and women's work found that the most common result was no difference in how the work of males and females was judged (Swim et al., 1989). However, the majority of the research studies used in the Swim et al. (1989) meta-analysis were laboratory experiments with college student subjects. Other research has found that under certain conditions sex bias does occur in the performance appraisal process. Robbins and DeNisi (1993) discussed a number of factors such as whether the ratee is performing an out-of-role occupation and whether the rater is sensitive to issues of gender bias. Research conducted in real-world work settings also suggests that bias does occur at times, especially in jobs where evaluation criteria are subjective, where information is minimal, when women are being evaluated in what are traditionally male jobs, and when people are being considered for high-level positions (Dobbins et al., 1988; Haberfeld, 1992; Martinko & Gardner, 1983; Nieva & Gutek, 1980; Ruble et al., 1984).

3. *Women get paid less because they expect lower pay.* It has been proposed that women have lower pay expectations than men. If women expect less pay than men expect, then they are likely to be offered less pay than similarly qualified men (Jackson et al., 1992). In one study, subjects playing employers offered salaries based on the pay expectations communicated by applicants, such that those with lower expectations ended up with lower pay than equally qualified persons with higher expectations (Major et al., 1984b). Furthermore, when female subjects did not know how much others were paid, they asked for less money than did males who did not know how much others were paid. Major and Forcey (1985) found that college-aged women thought they deserved less pay for their work than men. Significant differences in the career pay expectations of male and female students in business-related fields have also been found (Major & Konar, 1984; Martin, 1989; McFarlin et al., 1989). Jackson et al. (1992) found that regardless of occupational field, senior college women had lower expectations than their male counterparts for career-peak pay despite the fact that the women had higher grade point averages.

It is not yet clear how common sex differences in pay expectations are in the "real" world since most of the research on this topic has been conducted with college students. There are also a number of possible explanations for their occurrence. One study suggested that women may expect less to compensate for their dual commitment to the family and that males have higher job performance expectations than women and therefore expect greater pay (Jackson et al., 1992). Others have proposed that women believe they have less to contribute and are therefore worth less. There is some laboratory support for this hypothesis (McCarty, 1986) but field research does not support it (Snyder et al., 1992). It may be that women estimate their salaries based on the salaries of other women who are underpaid (i.e., women use different social comparison standards). For example, Bylsma and Major (1992) found that gender differences in personal entitlement vanished when both women and men knew that others were highly paid. Perhaps men are more "wage aware" because of a society that values men based on how much money they earn, encourages them to earn as much as possible, and discusses acceptable pay and methods of wage negotiation with them. Women may be less likely to be exposed to discussions about pay and consequently may have lower expectations because of a lack of familiarity with what particular jobs pay. Jackson et al. (1992) and Jackson and Grabski (1988) found that female subjects had lower pay expectations than men not just for themselves, but for others as well.

It is important to keep in mind that women's lower salary expectations are only a minor contributor to women's lower salaries. Most women can only get traditionally female jobs—jobs that pay less than traditionally male jobs and for which pay is not negotiable. Furthermore, some research indicates that women are offered lower starting salaries than men even when their pay expectations are equal to men's and they negotiate as much as men (Gerhart & Rynes, 1991). Employers may have stereotypes that women will accept less money than men, and this may lead them to offer less to women. For instance, my student Mary Kay was a router/dispatcher for a trucking company and worked very hard and was promoted. While training her male successor she discovered that his annual salary was $3000 more than her salary at her *promoted* job. When she confronted her boss, he said he was sure her male successor would not work for the low salary that she was willing to work for.

Equity Theory and Women's Reactions to Pay Differentials
Mary Kay quit her job when her boss refused to increase her salary. Her reaction may be symbolic of some important changes in women in the last 20 years. My personal experience suggests that women are less accepting of pay inequities and other gender differentials than they once were. Although I could not find any studies directly addressing this issue, I did find some Gallup polls that seem to support my perception. For instance, 32 percent of Americans surveyed in a Gallup poll conducted in 1975 said that men have better lives than women in the United States; in 1989 this percentage went up to 49 percent, and in 1993 to 60 percent (Newport, 1993). Forty-eight percent of Americans polled in 1975 said that women have equal job opportunities to men; this decreased to 42 percent in 1989 and 39 percent in 1993 (Newport, 1993). Only 30 percent of women in 1993 felt that women in the United States have equal job opportunities to men,

and 70 percent felt that men had better lives than women (a breakdown by gender for the other years was not available).

To decide whether what we are getting is fair we often compare ourselves to others. This is the essence of *equity theory* (Adams, 1965). Originally a theory about personal relationships, equity theory says that people are motivated to have their inputs and outcomes be equivalent to the inputs and outcomes of others. Applied to work, the idea is that we put things in (such as time, energy, qualifications, etc.) and we get things out (such as pay, promotions, etc.). To decide whether what we are getting out based on what we are putting in is fair or equitable, we look at how our situation stacks up with what "comparison others" are putting in and getting out. Who you compare yourself to can therefore very much affect whether or not you perceive equity. *Relative deprivation theory* (Crosby, 1982) is based on a similar idea. It suggests that feelings of deprivation are not based simply on some objective standard but rather depend on how "deprived" we are relative to some reference group or comparison other.

Research indicates that women have not typically used men as comparison objects (Chessler & Goodman, 1976; Zanna et al., 1987). Instead, they have used other women, and as long as other women in the workplace were getting approximately equivalent outcomes given their inputs, equity was perceived. Using data collected in 1974, Zanna et al. (1987) found that, although most of the women in their sample compared themselves to women, those women who used a male reference group experienced greater feelings of deprivation and resentment regarding their work. Research summarized by Crocker and Major (1989) suggests that women are more likely to compare themselves to other women because sex segregation makes other women more available for comparison and because we tend to select comparison persons who are similar to ourselves. Major and Forcey (1985) found that, when performing sex-appropriate jobs, subjects preferred to compare themselves with same-sex others but when performing sex-inappropriate jobs they did not. Major et al. (1984a) used a sex-neutral task and found that subjects generally ignored the sex of comparison others when determining what was fair pay for themselves. It appears then that women will compare their outcomes to the outcomes of men in similar job positions.

According to equity theory, when you experience underpayment inequity (i.e., that you are getting less for your inputs than the comparison other), you are motivated to restore equity. In the case of the woman who comes up short when she compares her input/outcome ratio with the input/outcome ratio of a male in the workplace, equity can be restored in a number of ways. Underpayment inequity can be dealt with by the woman quitting her job or decreasing her inputs (e.g., not doing as much) but these are often not realistic options. Equity can be achieved by the woman changing her comparison other to one that yields a more equitable comparison (e.g., she can compare herself only to women). Another option is for her to rationalize the inequity (e.g., "I must not be as good at my job as he is . . .," "He must have more experience," etc.). Most women, however, probably prefer to achieve equity by increasing their outcomes ($). This is usually done by asking for a raise and, in rare instances, suing the employer for equal pay.

For women working the same jobs as men, paying them less is illegal according to both the Equal Pay Act of 1963 and Title VII of the 1964 Civil Rights Act. Why then do so few women pursue the legal avenue to equity? There are several reasons. One is that, even when discrimination is obvious, the legal system is often not very responsive. The Equal Employment Opportunity Commission (EEOC), the federal agency charged with handling such cases, is notoriously backlogged and underfunded. Another reason why legal action is infrequently taken is the way these laws are worded and practiced. Currently you must prove that the discrimination was intentional and not simply due to the market value of a particular job. Because our labor force is largely sex-segregated, it is hard to prove that women's jobs in an organization pay less because of sex discrimination.

According to the concept of *pay equity,* or *comparable worth* as it used to be known, people performing jobs in the same organization judged to be of equal worth or difficulty should be compensated equally. Some people argue that comparing two different jobs (for example, the male painter job and the female clerical job) is like comparing apples and oranges and cannot be done fairly. However, the development of rating systems permitting the comparison of different jobs on the basis of the knowledge and skills they require, the mental demands they make, and work conditions they involve renders this argument obsolete. Why then are pay equity programs so rare? Two reasons really—they result in increased labor costs, and there is little legal pressure for their adoption. Thus, pay equity programs are likely to remain scarce without significant legal changes or group struggle (strikes, unionization, etc.).

*T*HE LOW POWER AND STATUS OF WOMEN

Not only do women make less money than men for their work, but evidence abounds that women are also lower in status than men. For instance, the majority of society's most prestigious and professional jobs are held by males: 80 percent of scientists, 84 percent of doctors, 61 percent of college and university professors (females make up only 10 percent of tenured professors—the highest status), 78 percent of lawyers and judges, 87 percent of architects, and 94 percent of engineers are male [figures are from the federal government's 1991 *Statistical Abstracts of the United States* (U.S. Department of Commerce, 1991)].

There is also a great deal of evidence pointing to women's lower power in comparison to men. As we will see, women are less likely to occupy roles where they have control over resources and determine what goals are pursued and how. This occurs in part because male gender stereotypes are more compatible with what we see as the qualities needed for the attainment and wielding of power. Therefore, males are seen as better suited for power roles.

Women's low power in comparison to men's is apparent when one looks at the relative absence of women in politics, a point to which we will return in Chap. 6. In spite of the declaration of the November 1992 election as the "Year of the Woman" in politics and, relatively speaking, recent dramatic improvements in women's overall political visibility, women are still poorly represented in government. For instance, although women comprise 51 percent of the U.S. population, the voting in 1992 resulted in only six women being elected to the 100-person U.S. Senate and forty-seven women to the 435-person House of Representatives (the Senate gained two women and the House twenty-four). Women now make up 10 percent of the voting members of Congress—the largest percentage ever (U.S. Department of Labor, 1993). Three of President Clinton's fourteen Cabinet appointees are female. For the first time in U.S. history, two female justices sit on the nine-member Supreme Court—Sandra Day O'Connor, the first female justice, appointed in 1981, and Ruth Bader Ginsberg, appointed in 1993. Only once has a woman been a major party candidate on a U.S. presidential ticket. That was Democrat Geraldine Ferraro in 1984, Walter Mondale's vice-presidential candidate.

Women's Power in Organizations: The Glass Ceiling

Men have significantly more power than women in organizations as well. About 39 percent of U.S. managers are women (up 26 percent from 1978!), but the higher you go in the organization, the fewer women you find— only 1 to 2 percent of top executive jobs are held by women (U.S. Department of Labor, 1989). A survey by *Fortune Magazine* of 799 of the largest firms in the United States found that only 19 of the 4012 highest-paid officers and directors were women, less than half of 1 percent (Fierman, 1990). Jacobs (1992), using nationally representative sample data from 1970 and 1988, found that while the number of women in management had dramatically increased from 18 to 40 percent, women managers still trailed their male counterparts in both earnings and authority.

Women who do make it out of the lowest levels of organizational management often encounter a *glass ceiling*. This term is a metaphor for the fact that in many organizations there is an invisible ceiling on how high women and non-Euroamericans may go. President Bush's Secretary of Labor, Lynn Martin, defined the glass ceiling as "those artificial barriers based on attitudinal or organizational bias which prevent qualified individuals from advancing upward in their organization into management positions. . . .Qualified women and minorities are too often on the outside looking into the executive suite" (U.S. Department of Labor, 1991b, p. 1).

Black, Latina, Asian-American, and Native-American women represent approximately 4 percent of women in management, leading some theorists to call the ceiling minority women face a concrete one. Unfortunately, the majority of research on women in management has ignored the problems faced by minorities. Although you may believe that minority women are doubly advantaged in an organization (the "two-fer" theory, as in "two for the price of one"), research does not support this perception (Nkomo & Cox, 1989). Instead it appears that minority women often face the dual burden of racism and sexism in organizations, sometimes called a "double whammy" (Bell et al., 1993).

Explanations for the Glass Ceiling

Psychologists once assumed that there were few women in higher-status positions because women had personality traits or behavior patterns that made them ill-suited for managerial positions. For example, Horner (1969) suggested that women were fearful of success because they perceived an incompatibility between achievement and femininity. But by the mid-1970s and early 1980s, it was apparent to social psychologists and sociologists that there was a lot more to the male-female organizational power differential than person-centered explanations which emphasized the qualities of women as the main culprits in their lower status. Kanter's 1977 book *Men and Women of the Corporation* was one of the first to provide situation-centered explanations for the power differential such as discriminatory personnel practices, stereotypes, and organizational politics.

Based on extensive research, situation-centered factors are now believed to be the major sources of women's lack of representation at higher organizational levels. As Stroh et al. (1992, p. 251) said: "Studies of managerial women have ruled out lesser skills, abilities, and motivations as explanations for women's slower career progression." Catalyst (1990) found that 79 percent of *Fortune* 500 chief executive officers admitted that there are identifiable barriers to women getting to the top of organizations.

Now we take a closer look at some of the most common explanations for women's stagnation at lower organizational levels.

1. *Women bring less human capital to the organization.* One popular person-centered explanation for the glass ceiling is the *human capital approach* discussed earlier as an explanation of the gender pay differential. According to this approach, pay and occupational attainment are tied to "human

capital," the resources individuals bring to the organization such as experience and education. It is assumed that women earn less and are not promoted at the same rate as men due to gender differences in human capital.

Human capital theory does explain differences in pay and promotions but it does not do a good job of explaining the gender organizational power differential. Gender is actually a better predictor of a person's rank in the organization than length of time in the organization (Ragins & Sundstrom, 1989). In a federal social service agency (a field with a high proportion of women), sex accounted for a significant portion of the variance in organizational position after the effects of age, education, and length of time in the organization were accounted for (Snyder et al., 1992). Konrad and Cannings (1993) found that the human capital approach predicted men's promotions at two large corporations, but not women's advancement. In a comparison of male and female managers in *Fortune* 500 companies, Stroh et al. (1992) found significant sex differences in career progression although there were no significant differences in education or relocation. They noted that, while "doing the right stuff" (e.g., being willing to relocate, having experience, etc.) is a more powerful predictor of career progression than gender, it is disturbing that women's following the traditional male career model was still not enough to eliminate men's career advantages over them.

2. *Women do not lead as well as men.* The explanation for why women are typically found in more dead-end managerial staff positions and not in "line" positions leading to the executive suite often goes something like this: Although they may possess managerial skills, women do not customarily possess leadership qualities. Available evidence, however, suggests that women are no less effective leaders/managers than men (Bass, 1981; Eagly & Johnson, 1990; Hollander, 1983; Powell, 1990); that female managers often have higher levels of work motivation than male managers (Donell & Hall, 1980); and that female managers are comfortable and capable in conflict management roles (Duane, 1989). Indeed, a U.S. Department of Labor report on the glass ceiling (1991b) cited research finding that a majority of women in both line and staff positions had leader-style management skills and a greater proportion of women in staff positions displayed a greater leadership orientation than men in line positions. This study suggested that women are actually well-suited for leadership positions.

In a meta-analysis of 162 studies comparing the leadership styles of men and women, Eagly and Johnson (1990) found that women leaders were slightly more interpersonally oriented than male leaders and more likely to use a democratic style. This should operate in women's favor since research finds that subordinates prefer a democratic style from both men and women (Kushell & Newton, 1986). Eagly and Johnson (1990) suggested that women's social skills probably facilitate a managerial style that is democratic and participative. They also wrote that female leaders may use a participative and collaborative mode in order to win acceptance from skeptical subordinates. In general however, Eagly and Johnson (1990) found the differences between male and female leaders to be quite small. They noted that this is not surprising since organizations usually provide very clear guidelines about expected conduct in these roles, and individuals who wish to be successful adhere to these expectations, regardless of gender.

3. *Stereotypes of women may cause us to perceive women as inappropriate for leadership and managerial positions.* Morrison and Von Glinow (1990) cited several studies (Freedman & Phillips, 1988; Heilman & Martell, 1986; Ilgen & Youtz, 1986) indicating that gender stereotypes suggesting that women are inappropriate for leadership positions are so strong that contrary data are often ignored in managerial selection and other managerial decisions affecting women. If it is believed that a woman's place is in the home and/or that women are ineffective as leaders and decision makers, then women will be denied leadership positions (Stevens, 1984). Darley (1976) suggested that, because of our tendency to make inferences about individuals' personalities from their social roles, we may forget that the nurturing, emotional, people-oriented wife-mother can be an assertive, rational high-achiever in her work role. Since our dominant images of women are in traditionally female roles that often call for different behaviors than those called for by a manager role, we may have a hard time envisioning women as leadership material.

Common stereotypes of women suggest that women cannot lead. A number of studies have found that successful managers are believed to have personality traits more consistent with male than female stereotypes (Brenner et al., 1989; Heilman et al., 1989; King et al., 1991; Massengill & DiMarco, 1979; Powell & Butterfield, 1984; Schein, 1973, 1975; Schein et al., 1989). Schein and Mueller (1992) found males in the United States, Great Britain, and Germany to believe this. They found that women in Germany sex-typed managerial positions almost as much as males in Germany, females in Great Britain also sex-typed them, but not as much as German women, whereas women in America saw both genders as equally likely to possess the traits needed for effective management. For instance, many people hold stereotypes of women as emotional and indecisive— qualities that are clearly undesirable for a leader. Frank (1988) found that business students perceived female managers to be humanitarian, sympathetic, and dependent, qualities that in previous studies (Best & Spector, 1984; Garlen, 1982) were associated with attributions for management failure. Conversely, competitive behavior is seen as male behavior.

Glick (1991) found that jobs are generally seen as "masculine" or "feminine" and that job applicants are seen as more or less suitable for different jobs depending upon the applicant's sex. If you asked a number of people to imagine a leader, most of them would imagine a (white) man. This protypical leader image may interfere with the hiring of women.

Several research studies have suggested that gender-based stereotypes associate power with men and not women (Ragins & Sundstrom, 1989). This, in combination with the fact that there are relatively few women in positions of power, may make it hard for some people to imagine a woman in such a position. Dion and Schuller (1990) have also pointed out that research suggests we rely more on stereotypes when the target person's membership is salient. Because women tend to be a numerical minority in the corporation, their gender is quite noticeable to perceivers. Therefore, they are likely to be judged and evaluated on the basis of gender stereotypes. In support of this, Eagly et al. (1992), in a meta-analysis of experimental studies on gender and the evaluation of leaders, found that the tendency for male leaders to be more favorably evaluated than female leaders was most pronounced for roles occupied mainly by men.

Gender stereotypes may also lead those in power to view a woman's success in a traditionally male job to be due to effort rather than ability (Deaux & Emswhiller, 1974; Geis, 1993). A woman's success at male-typed tasks may violate observers' expectations and consequently reduce ability attributions (Greenhaus & Parasuraman, 1993; Heilman, 1983; Nieva & Gutek, 1980). Greenhaus and Parasuraman (1993), in a study of 748 managers and their supervisors, found that the performance of successful female managers was less likely to be attributed to ability and that ability attributions were positively correlated with career advancement prospects.

Being perceived as leadership material is not as simple as exhibiting stereotypically male-oriented characteristics. On the one hand, if women are too feminine they will not be perceived as management material; on the other hand, if they are too masculine they will be devalued as well (Maupin, 1993). Geis (1993) called this the "damned if she does, damned if she doesn't" dilemma. Women must do what is not expected of them, while doing enough of what is expected of them to gain acceptance (Morrison et al., 1987). One famous example of this led to a legal suit of sexual discrimination [*Price Waterhouse* v. *Hopkins* (1990)] and social psychologist Susan Fiske was called as an expert witness (S. P. Fiske et al., 1991).

Ann Hopkins was a top performer at one of the nation's largest accounting firms (Price Waterhouse) and applied for partnership in 1982. She had brought in business worth $25 million and had logged more billable hours than anyone else proposed for partner that year, but was denied partnership. She alleged sex discrimination but Price Waterhouse contended that she had interpersonal skills problems. Her evaluators said she was "macho," and "overcompensated for being a women"; and one colleague recommended that she improve her chances by being more feminine. Social psychologist Fiske testified that, according to research, stereotyping is most likely to occur when the target is an isolated, one or few-of-a-kind individual in the environment, is in a job that is nontraditional for her or his group, and evaluative criteria are ambiguous. All of these applied in the Hopkins case. Of the 662 partners at Price Waterhouse, only seven were women. She was the only woman of 88 candidates for partnership that year, and she was criticized for her interpersonal skills (a subjective judgment). It was also apparent from the evaluator comments that her gender was relevant in the evaluation process (Fiske et al., 1991). The judge concluded that gender-based stereotyping played a role in Price Waterhouse's decision not to make Ann Hopkins a partner.

Cann and Siegfried (1990) referred to a number of studies that found an overlap between stereotypes of the "good manager" and a "typical male." They pointed out, however, that most leadership models as well as leadership studies suggest that good leaders are directive and task-oriented (stereotypically male qualities) *and* people-oriented and interpersonally skilled (stereotypically female qualities). Their research found that the behaviors relevant to successful leadership included those that are viewed as feminine. They concluded that the stereotype of a masculine leader represents a very narrow view which ignores an important dimension of effective leadership. Schein et al. (1989) suggested that the business curricula in higher education should teach a broader view of the traits necessary for successful management.

4. *Organizational norms may dictate the hiring and promotion of males over females into management positions.* If organizational norms do not explicitly advocate hiring women into high-level positions, then those doing the hiring are likely to follow standard operating procedures and hire men. A 1991 Department of Labor report on the glass ceiling noted that, in general, managers high up on the corporate ladder do not communicate corporate values regarding equal employment opportunity. In some cases organizational norms may clearly communicate that women are not appropriate for high-level positions. Individuals within the organization may then comply with these norms regardless of their personal feelings regarding the appropriateness of women in leadership positions. Larwood and her colleagues (1988) provided evidence that people in organizations who are not themselves prejudiced or sexist may still discriminate against women or minorities if they perceive that doing otherwise might interfere with their own power or success in the organization. Larwood et al. (1988) call this the *rational bias theory of managerial discrimination* (e.g., it is rational to be biased if you may be punished if you are not). Similarly, a qualified woman may not be promoted if upper management feels that employees' or clients' stereotypes might interfere with her effectiveness (e.g., if management feels employees or clients will not be comfortable taking orders from a woman or will not find her a credible authority). Wiley and Eskilson (1983) found that, in comparison to female managers, male managers were perceived to be better liked by coworkers and were expected to get more cooperation from subordinates.

5. *Within the organization, women may not receive the experiences needed*

to advance in the organization. Most organizations have entry-level jobs that lead up the organizational ladder. According to economist Bergmann (1989), these jobs are typically ear-marked for men. Kanter (1976) argued that women are usually placed in jobs with less power and limited mobility, and in this way they are "structurally disadvantaged" in the organization. Baron et al. (1986) analyzed job ladders (jobs that provide promotion opportunities as opposed to so-called "dead-end" jobs) in 100 organizations. Jobs in these organizations were pervasively segregated by sex (only 73 of the 1071 jobs studied had both female and male incumbents), while 71 percent of the promotion ladders in the sample were occupied exclusively by men, 6 percent exclusively by women, and 22 percent by both men and women. Ragins and Sundstrom (1989) noted that women in prestigious male-typed organizations are usually segregated into female-typed specialties that offer fewer resources for power or are hired into departments with little power.

Women often do not get the assignments that would make them good candidates for higher-level positions. In this way management may create a *self-fulfilling prophecy.* Self-fulfilling prophecies occur when people's stereotyped attitudes lead them to behave toward those they stereotype in a way that makes the stereotype come true. For example, supervisors may have the expectation that women are not appropriate for leadership positions, so they do not give them the experiences needed to develop or demonstrate leadership qualities; then they say, "We just don't have any women with the experience for the promoted position." Other organizational practices work in a similar way. The 1991 Department of Labor report on the glass ceiling described a study of nine randomly selected *Fortune* 500 companies which found that, in all nine, "developmental practices and credential building experiences, including advanced education, as well as career enhancing assignments were often not as available to minorities and women" (p. 5). The result? A pool of candidates for higher-level positions in the organization that does not include women or individuals from other traditionally underrepresented groups. The report also noted that the recruitment practices used by the majority of the companies surveyed kept the female candidate pool small. The three most common sources for management candidates did not typically refer women, African-Americans, Hispanics, or Asians. (The three sources were word-of-mouth referrals from other—presumably male—executives, employee referrals, and executive search firms.)

Women's progress may also be limited by their relative lack of access to the political network and lack of mentoring. Mentoring occurs when a more senior organizational member helps guide the career of a more junior member by sharing what the senior member knows about how to succeed in the organization. Because of their gender and concerns about intimacy and sexual attraction, women are often excluded from the informal social relationships shared by their male counterparts where power transactions and mentoring occur (Bhatnagar, 1988; Nelson et al., 1990; Noe, 1988; Powell & Mainiero, 1992). For instance, power transactions often take place over drinks, or on the golf course, or at racquetball/handball/squash or tennis courts. Women can, of course, mentor other women, but as noted earlier, there is a shortage of women in power positions in most organizations. One study found that men and women were equally willing to mentor, but that women perceived a greater risk to their own careers should their proteges fail, and were more likely to believe that they lacked the time to be mentors (Ragins & Cotton, 1993). The authors explained that women's visibility in the organization makes it more likely that a protege's performance will be viewed as a reflection of the mentor, and that the greater barriers to advancement faced by women may mean they need to spend their time advancing their own careers rather than helping others.

6. *Women's responsibilities to home and family may prevent upward mobility in the organization.* Women's responsibilities in the home may prevent the devotion of the extra time and energy needed to climb the organizational ladder. It may not be possible for a woman to assume a leadership position if she is unable to work late or on weekends, or if she has to miss work because of childcare problems. She may even select a job with fewer opportunities for promotion but one that allows her to meet her familial obligations with less conflict (the *self-selection hypothesis*).

A number of research studies leave us with little doubt that, in comparison to their working male partners, working women do the majority of housework and childcare (Blair & Lichter, 1991; Hochschild, 1989; Model, 1982; Yogev, 1981, among others). For some women, these demands mean that they are unable to put in the extra hours or travel time necessary for rapid advancement in the organization. Valdez and Gutek (1987) in a survey of 827 working women found that, in comparison to women who were not in management, women with managerial positions were more likely not to be married. They also found that, as levels of commitment and preparation required for a job go up, there is an increase in the proportion of childless women and a decrease in the proportion of women with three or more children holding such positions. Stroh et al. (1992), in a study of male and female managers in twenty *Fortune* 500 companies, found that male managers were significantly more likely to be married than female managers (86 percent versus 45 percent) and to have children at home (62 percent versus 20 percent). Research also indicates that women are significantly more likely to interrupt their careers for family-related reasons than men and that such interruptions affect later job advancement and career decisions, especially for women (Powell & Mainiero, 1992).

Working women who are single parents may be especially likely to experience conflict between their work and family roles. In 1994 approximately 40 percent of children in the United States lived in a single-parent household and 90 percent of these households were headed by women. Most fathers with visitation rights do not see their children at all by the time the divorce is 3 years old (Podilchak, 1990). In one nationally representative study, almost half of the children of divorced parents aged 11 to 16 had not seen their fathers in a year (Furstenberg, 1988). Because single-parent working women must typically assume complete responsibility for their children, they may have difficulty doing things that are often required for promotion such as staying late, traveling, and working on weekends.

Because high work involvement is incongruent with the traditional female gender role, women who work often experience anxiety and guilt (Burke & McKeen, 1988). This, in combination with the burden of holding a highly demanding management job while simultaneously being responsible for the bulk of the childcare and housework, may lead women to choose career tracks (sometimes called "mommy tracks") that minimize these conflicts. As Powell and Mainiero (1992) noted, marriage or family is seen by few men as a constraint on the emphasis they place on their careers, while multiple and conflicting role demands related to parenthood frequently affect women's career choices.

For women identification with the family is strongly linked to responsibilities and time commitments within the household; for men it is not. Instead, many men feel they satisfy their family demands by being "breadwinners" (Bielby & Bielby, 1989; Duxbury & Higgins, 1991). Furthermore, because the traditional male sex role emphasizes giving careers top priority (Pleck, 1977), men may experience less guilt than women when their work takes them away from their involvement in the home or detracts from their partner's career progressions. Bielby and Bielby (1992) found that men were less likely to let their spouses' jobs affect their career advancement than women were, although this was less true for couples with nontraditional gender-role beliefs.

7. *The* perception *that women's primary commitment is to home and family may interfere with promotion.* Many women sustain high levels of commitment to work and family roles, yet find themselves disadvantaged in the workplace because of assumptions employers make about women's commitment to work roles (Bielby & Bielby, 1989). The U.S. Department of Labor report (1991) on the glass ceiling stated that many male managers assume women with children are not interested in being considered for promotions or assignments requiring longer hours. Ironically, while employers view marriage and family as a hindrance for a woman's career, they are regarded as assets to a man's career (Valdez & Gutek, 1987).

Even when women with children exert the same work effort and performance levels as they did before giving birth, their job commitments are often perceived to be reduced by their parental responsibilities (Hall, 1990). Wiley and Eskilson (1988) gave 179 individuals employed in managerial jobs descriptions of either a female or a male junior manager who submitted late and inaccurate work due to a child's serious illness. Both male and female respondents rated a conflict between work and family responsibilities as being more permanent for women than for men. The authors pointed out that such a perception may lead to the belief that women are less dependable in regard to work, and this may interfere with their promotion up the corporate ladder. For this reason, it may be more important for women than men to demonstrate commitment to the organization before promotion will occur. Several studies found that women are more likely to obtain their promotions from within and are less likely to be hired into responsible positions from the outside (Konrad & Cannings, 1993; Konrad & Pfeffer, 1991). Employers are often skeptical about women's commitment to employed work and expect them to leave sooner than men; consequently they hire into management only those women who have proven their commitment to the organization (Konrad & Cannings, 1993, 1994).

Employers may also assume that the performance of employed women with children is reduced by their family responsibilities. As part of their study on how perceptions of women are influenced by marital status, employment, and children, Etaugh and Poertner (1992) had subjects read identical descriptions of an employed woman except that marital status, job performance (outstanding or below average), and whether the woman described had a 1-year-old child were systematically varied. Subjects rated the women on job-performance characteristics such as "dedicated to career" and "successful in job." They found that the outstanding worker who was a mother was rated as less competent than the otherwise identical outstanding worker who had no children.

It is important to realize that research finds women allocate more effort to work than men and when women do put in less time at work because of family responsibilities it typically brings their work effort back to the level of the typical male without family responsibilities (Bielby &

SALLY FORTH By Greg Howard

Reprinted with special permission of King Features Syndicate.

Even when they are qualified and willing to give their work top priority, women may still find they are unable to make it to the top levels of the organization.

Bielby, 1988). Based on their research findings, Bielby and Bielby (1988) noted, the irony is that, given how much harder women work, employers would be better off, statistically speaking, discriminating against men (though the authors did not seriously recommend this). It is also important to note that even women who are not largely responsible for the housework and childcare still experience lower pay and limited work advancement in comparison to men. In other words, even women without children, women whose partners do share family responsibilities equally, or women who can pay for help in the home still face the glass ceiling.

In summary, be aware that the most compelling explanations for women's lower status in the workplace point to situational rather than dispositional factors. In other words, there is little evidence that women possess personality traits or behavior patterns that make them less well-suited for managerial positions. It appears that the major barriers are traditional hiring patterns, stereotypes which suggest women are inappropriate for leadership positions, and organizational barriers such as the lack of mentoring and training of women for leadership positions. This is a very important point. As Geis (1993) noted, if we are under the impression that there is equal opportunity for women and men, then we may falsely conclude that women's lower pay and power are reflections of women's inadequacies. In other words, we will have made the fundamental gender attribution error all over again. Furthermore, such a belief may create self-fulfilling prophecies. If we believe women are less competent or valuable to the organization and treat them accordingly, they will not receive the opportunities which would prove us wrong.

CONCLUDING REMARKS

Working outside the home while remaining responsible for the bulk of the housework and childcare is challenging. Not surprisingly, some women experience *role conflict*, or stress from the competing demands of family and workplace (Crosby, 1991; Valdez & Gutek, 1987). However, you may be surprised to find that the research on employment and women's health does not support the hypothesis that paid employment increases a woman's risk for mental and physical health problems (see Crosby, 1991, Repetti et al., 1989, and Rodin & Ickovics, 1990, for research reviews). Indeed, many studies have found that employed women are less depressed than nonemployed women (e.g., Anseshensel, 1986; Gore & Mangione, 1983; Kandel et al., 1985) and none have found the reverse (Repetti et al., 1989). LaCroix and Haynes (1987) summarized recent studies on women's physical health and noted that in almost all studies employed women were healthier than unemployed women. The health benefits of employment do of course differ depending upon the job and other life circumstances. These things presumably affect one's attitudes and feelings about life, which in turn influence physiological and psychological processes which then lead to or away from mental or physical illness (Sorensen & Verbugge, 1987). For example, Ickovics (1989) found that employed women who felt their skills were underutilized in their jobs were in poorer health than "adequately" employed women. Repetti et al. (1989), in a review of research on employment and women's health, concluded that the health benefits of employment are greater for unmarried women without children, for women whose husbands contribute to household labor, and for those women who work in a supportive work climate. Rodin and Ickovics (1990) noted that it is difficult to establish the direction of causality in these relationships; it could be that less healthy women are less likely to be employed or hold onto demanding jobs. However, they noted that the data so far do not support the view that the stress and strain of employment harms women's health.

If juggling work and family is difficult and stressful, then why isn't there greater physical and mental health fallout for women? The answer, according to *role accumulation theory*, is that the strain from multiple roles may be compensated for by buffers against failure in other roles. In other words, all one's psychological eggs are not in a single basket. For instance, if I give a less than perfect lecture at the university, coming home and playing with my son reminds me of what is right in my life and I get over the work stress much more quickly. Conversely, being successful at work keeps one from being destroyed when the children get on one's nerves or disappoint one in some way, or do not need one as much anymore. Multiple roles provide us with alternate sources of self-esteem, control, and social support (Rodin & Ickovics, 1990). A number of studies are supportive of role accumulation theory (Crosby, 1991; Kibria et al., 1990). For instance, research (e.g., Baruch & Barnett, 1986, 1987) has found that working women report higher levels of rewards than costs for their multiple roles and has indicated that paid employment enhances women's satisfaction with domestic life (Crosby, 1987). Crosby (1991) found that, although employed mothers were stressed by their multiple roles and longed for more time to get everything done, on balance they felt the advantages of multiple roles outweighed the disadvantages. Multiple roles give life variety and buffer the impact of negative events (Crosby, 1991).

Many women work due to economic necessity. According to a special issue of *Time* magazine in the fall of 1990, in 1988 two salaries brought in only 6 percent more than a single salary in 1973. However, while most women who work need the money, research has found that most women who work in jobs such as waitressing or factories are committed to their jobs and would not leave the labor force even if they did not need the money (Hiller & Dyehouse, 1987). As Doyle (1983) said, ". . . a paycheck conveys more than mere monetary value; it also has the symbolic value of giving its bearer a sense of worth and dignity. Women have discovered the lesson that men have known for so long: Our society tends to value people and their activities in proportion to their earned income" (p. 171). In short, many women want and/or need paid work.

For many people who have been brought up with the notion of fairness, exposure to the inequity that women face is uncomfortable. Most of us were raised with the idea that the world is a just and fair one where people get what they deserve and deserve what they get. We are motivated to believe this so that we do not have to change, or deal with the guilt and discomfort that arises when people are unfairly victimized, and so that we can continue to believe that bad things will not happen to us if we behave ourselves. This *just-world thinking*, as it is called by social psychologist M. J. Lerner (1980), may lead both men and women to try to justify existing social arrangements such as those between men and women. It has also led to the development of negative stereotypes of women as the "lesser sex" in order to justify their lower status and lower pay. This tendency to put down the group one is taking economic advantage of so that their exploitation can be rationalized has long been recognized by social psychologists (cf. Allport, 1954). It is a danger to guard against as it may interfere with our acknowledging that change is needed. In Chap. 4 we will see that traditional gender roles are not working that well for men either.

*S*UMMARY

- The majority of women work for wages as well as perform the majority of household and childcare tasks.
- Employed women earn only around 70 percent of what employed men make. The labor force is sex-segregated and most jobs are occupied primarily by one sex or the other. The more women in a job category, the lower the wages associated with that type of job.
- Research does not support the compensating differentials explanation for women's lower pay. This is the idea that women make less money because they choose jobs which pay less because such jobs are more pleasant or conducive to parenting.
- Barriers such as requirements for nonessential training, sexual harassment, early socialization experiences, and social norms limit women's access to higher-status, higher-paying, traditionally male jobs.
- Contrary to the human capital approach, gender pay differentials cannot be entirely explained by differences in job qualifications, time on the job, or work effort.
- Equity theory suggests that, when women in the workplace compare themselves with men, they are likely to experience inequity.

But workplaces in our society are commonly sex-segregated, reducing the opportunity for such comparisons and making it
harder to sue employers for equal pay.

- The majority of society's most prestigious and professional jobs
  are held by men, and women are poorly represented in government and in power positions in the workplace.

- Women often encounter a *glass ceiling* in the organization. According to research it is unlikely that this is due to women's possessing
  fewer leadership abilities or because they bring less "human capital" to the organization.

- Common stereotypes of women suggesting that women are not
  leadership material are partly responsible for the glass ceiling.
  Women are also less likely to be given jobs which lead up the organizational ladder and are less likely to be mentored and groomed
  for promotion.

- Home and family responsibilities may interfere with a woman's
  advancement in the organization by preventing her from putting
  in extra work hours and travel. However, sometimes employers
  mistakenly assume that a woman's responsibilities in the home
  make her less suitable for promotion.

- Many psychological needs of the full-time homemaker may not be
  met and the economic dependence of the homemaker on her male
  partner reduces her power in the marital relationship.

- Employed women perform significantly more of the household labor than their employed male partners, leading to a *gender leisure
  gap.*

- In spite of the strains associated with balancing work and family,
  employed women largely benefit from paid employment.

- Many people engage in *just-world thinking* to justify the differences
  between male and female roles.

4

L imitations of the Traditional M ale R ole

❖

Why It Is Important to Study the Male Role ◆ The Male Gender Role and Its Norms ◆ *The Success/Status Norm* ◆ *The Toughness Norm* ◆ *The Antifemininity Norm* ◆ Male Gender Role Strain, Stress, and Conflict ◆ Concluding Remarks ◆ Summary

"Mommy, why do they say, 'Boys are made of snips and snails and puppy dogs tails,' while girls are 'made of sugar and spice and everything nice?' It's like they're telling boys they shouldn't be nice."

Kane, age 6

*A*t this point female readers may be disturbed by the realization that women receive less pay for their work, do a disproportionate share of housework and childcare, and are low in status in comparison to men. Male readers may feel a bit prickly themselves. They did not personally create inequality in the workplace or the social norms advocating different roles for men and women. Accepting that there is inequity means that they should share more equally in the domestic sphere. But who wants to do laundry, change diapers, do dishes, dust and vacuum, and prepare for and clean up after huge holiday celebrations? Who wants to compete for jobs, power, and career opportunities with thousands of additional people added to the workforce? Changes in gender roles also mean the man loses the helpmate for his professional life—someone to take care of feeding, clothing, appointment scheduling, entertaining, etc. Many men also derive an important part of their identity from being a male, an identity which includes the role of "provider" for the family and one which has emphasized a clear demarcation between what is male and what is female. These thoughts lead many men to be resistant to changes in gender roles and to rationalize existing inequities. However, in this chapter I will make the case that *males also lose from traditional gender roles.*

WHY IT IS IMPORTANT TO STUDY THE MALE ROLE

Some feminists resist exploring the limitations of the male role. They feel that these limitations are trivial in comparison to those of the female role and detract from focusing on the low power of women in comparison to men. For instance, Letty Cottin Pogrebin (1993, p. 96) said: "What troubles me is the overeagerness to weigh in with the male side of every women's issue, and the suggestion that the existence of male victims, no matter how few, balances the suffering of the overwhelming numbers of women." I understand Pogrebin's concerns. However, I think comments like hers are all the more reason to examine the limitations of the male role explicitly. The greater power of men as a group eclipses these limitations and interferes with change in the male role. Furthermore, the interdependent nature of female and male norms means that change in one is tied to change in the other. Kimmel (1987) pointed out that the historically derived definitions of masculinity and femininity encourage a situation where men exert power over women, and to change this a focus on the male role as well as that of the female is needed. Another reason we should care is that as the mothers, fathers, wives, friends, sons, daughters, lovers, etc., of males, it is our loved ones that face the difficulties created by the male role.

Kilmartin (1994) has provided some additional reasons for studying men as gendered beings. Acknowledging the argument that all psychology is essentially based on the psychology of men because it has typically used male subjects and focused on male behavior as the norm, he responded that for the most part psychology has not focused on the *experience* of being male. He says that a study of the psychology of men is needed for the following reasons:

1. While men have customarily had greater power than women, there are many men who are powerless and have been damaged by harsh masculine socialization. Furthermore, because of their greater social power, men are in the position to help bring about change.

2. Many men have trouble dealing with strong women. Because of their upbringing they believe they should be strong and dominant and see strong women as a threat to their masculinity. This issue must be addressed because women are increasingly strong.

3. The quality of men's relationships with others is often impoverished because they are raised in ways which interfere with intimacy, a basic human need.

There is not a lot of scientific research on the limitations of the traditional male role. Research by psychologists on the female role followed a greater social awareness of women's lower status in society, stimulated by the women's movement. In the last several years, greater research attention has been given to the male role. This is an exciting and relatively new area of gender research. Women's critiques of the male role, mostly having to do with male inexpressiveness and their poor contributions to household labor, have drawn attention to problems with the role. Also, as psychologists have gained a better understanding of mental health and adjustment, they have come to realize that there are aspects of the traditional male role which run counter to good mental health. Male psychologists, sensitive to problems with the female role, have begun to look more critically at the male role. Some social problems, such as male violence against women, are also increasingly seen as arising in part from traditional conceptions of masculinity.

THE MALE GENDER ROLE AND ITS NORMS

In earlier chapters we discussed the power of social roles on behavior. The male role is no exception and like other roles its norms are learned through reinforcement, the observation of models, and cultural messengers such as the media. Conformity to the role occurs due to both normative and informational pressure. Males are surrounded by social information communicating what masculinity is all about (informational pressure); they are rewarded for displaying gender-appropriate behavior and punished for exhibiting out-of-role behavior (normative pressure). As Kimmel (1994, p. 120) said, "Manhood does not bubble up to consciousness from our biological makeup; it is created in culture." Like Pleck et al. (1993b), I assert that men act the way they do because of the conception of masculinity they internalize from their culture. These beliefs about what men are like and should do constitute what Pleck et al. (1993a, 1993b) called a *masculinity ideology*. This ideology operates as a set of social norms otherwise known as the male gender role.

Thompson and Pleck (1986, p. 531) defined the male role as "the social norms that prescribe and proscribe what men should feel and do." In their 1986 study of college men, Thompson and Pleck found that the structure of male role norms for college men is threefold. The first factor has to do with the expectation that men achieve status and others' respect (the status norm). This includes the view of men as "success objects," valued insofar as they make lots of money and have high status jobs. The second factor, the toughness norm, reflects the expectation that men be mentally, emotionally, and physically tough (I will discuss each type of toughness as a separate norm). The third factor reflects the expectation that men are to avoid stereotypically feminine activities and occupations (the antifemininity norm).

Recently, masculinity researchers have suggested that it is more accurate to speak of multiple masculinities. In other words, they acknowledge that race, ethnicity, age, class, sexuality, and subculture may all affect how masculinity is defined. The study of masculinity itself is a fairly recent phenomenon and there is even less research examining how masculinities vary based on subgroup. Therefore, I will examine the norms identified by Thompson and Pleck (1986) and, where information is available, I will discuss it in regard to diverse groups of men.

The Success/Status Norm

A woman wrote a letter to "Dear Abby" in which she described herself as a well-paid career woman living with an unemployed man. She said what a great relationship they had, how he did most of the housework, how they were not hurting for money, and how supportive he was of her career. However, she was worried about whether he would ever amount to much financially as he did not seem especially motivated in this area. Abby recommended that the woman end the relationship to avoid being taken advantage of. Do you think she would have given the same response had the situation been reversed in regard to gender? Probably not. In our society, a man's success, and ultimately his masculinity, are based on how well he provides for his family's material needs and wants (Doyle, 1983). Kimmel (1994) called this "marketplace masculinity." Levant (1992) noted that one of the first things most people ask a man is "What do you do? What is your occupation?" Wainrib (1992) discussed how the belief that a man is not a man unless he makes money creates marital problems in those cases where men choose to be househusbands.

Burn and Laver (1994) found overwhelming agreement among both male and female adults that they and their friends expected men to be successful at work. A majority also agreed that men should make lots of money. Davis (1990) analyzed ads placed in the personals of a daily newspaper. He found that women's ads emphasized employment and financial status significantly more than men's. Dating is a good example of how we value men based on their ability to provide financially. Bailey (1988) in her book *From Front Porch to Back Seat* talked about how courtship in

America has always turned on money. Money remains central to dating, and it is the men who are expected to spend the money. If they cannot, they may not be seen as worthwhile relationship material or may not get the opportunity to show that they are.

There are a number of limitations associated with this norm for males. One is that the majority of men are unable to meet it and may experience lowered self-esteem as a result (Pleck, 1981). As Kilmartin (1994, p. 171) put it, "While men as a group retain more economic power than women, the vast majority of men have jobs, not careers." Similarly, Kimmel (1992) wrote that men have constructed the definition of masculinity around wealth, power, and status—whoever has the most toys wins. He added that few men are ever wealthy, powerful, or respected enough to make them feel secure. Someone is always above them on the work or social ladder, making them feel like failures. Kilmartin (1994) pointed out an additional cost when he noted that the traditional man can never get enough and really enjoy what he already has. He must constantly work longer and harder and such a lifestyle often results in stress-related physical and psychological symptoms. Messner (1987) argued that prior to adulthood males must achieve their status through success in sports. The problem, Messner wrote, is that many males are not that good at sports, and that since "you're only as good as your last game," even those who are must constantly reachieve their status.

The societal emphasis on a man's value as determined by how much money he makes may also interfere with self-actualization (the realization of one's unique potential) to the extent that males choose jobs and careers based on how much they pay. I regularly have male students majoring in engineering and other traditionally male majors that lead to potentially high-paying careers who do not enjoy their work and dread the careers they are training for. Some do change majors, but most do not citing reasons such as "my family wouldn't understand," or "the major I'm really interested in doesn't lead to jobs that pay much."

For men whose wives do stay at home, the financial pressure is especially great. It is a lot of pressure to have a group of people totally economically dependent on you. I have a friend who says that he feels like the character Al Bundy on the TV series *Married with Children*. This character is largely perceived by his family as being a bank—everyone, including the family dog, is always "hitting him up" for money. My friend, whose wife does not work outside of the home, says he seems to spend almost all of his time trying to make money for his family. He recently said to me, "Is this it? I had envisioned more for my life." (I am not in any way suggesting that men should abdicate their financial responsibilities to their families for their own individual gain. Nonpayment of child support by divorced fathers is a major social problem.)

The emphasis on men fulfilling their family obligations by bringing home a large paycheck may interfere with a man's parenting since meeting these expectations often requires an extensive time commitment to the workplace (Pleck, 1985). As a father's income increases, his paternal involvement typically decreases (Erickson & Gecas, 1991). Pleck (1993) explained the influence of the breadwinner role on men's use of family-supportive work policies, such as workplace leave, following the birth of a child. He suggested men use these policies less when doing so would decrease earnings, thus weakening the "breadwinner" role, and when their use would lead others to perceive the men as uncommitted to their jobs, or as unmasculine.

In Chap. 6, we will see that since the industrial revolution fathers all over the world have spent relatively little time with their children because their work takes them away from home for most of the day and sometimes for long, extended periods of time. For instance, in Japan, where masculinity is equated with heavy work involvement, Japanese fathers spend, on average, 3 minutes per day on weekdays and 19 minutes a day on the weekends with their children (Ishii-Kuntz, 1993). Kilmartin (1994) pointed out that children may not understand their father is gone from sunup to sundown because he loves them and wants to provide a good standard of living for them. He noted that people often have a deep sense of having been deprived of their father's love. Many men come to regret that they missed out on their children's childhoods and later try to rebuild relationships with their adult children.

Kimmel (1994) pointed out that not all masculinities are perceived as equal, and that the type of masculinity in American society against which all others are compared is a white, middle-class, early middle-aged, heterosexual masculinity. According to Kimmel, only the tiniest fraction of men can live up to these rules of manhood. The majority, he concluded, are disempowered as a result of their race, class, ethnicity, age, or sexual preference. We have already noted that many men are unable to live up to the success/status norm which is typically defined by earning lots of money and being able to financially support a family. Nonwhite men are particularly affected by this. For example, in the United States, black men on average make 72 percent and Hispanic men 65 percent of the income white men make (U.S. Department of Labor, 1993). High unemployment rates for some groups, such as African-American and Native-American males, make living up to the success/status norm especially difficult. In Chap. 3 we discussed how the stereotypes people hold of females interfere with women's success in the workplace. Similarly, stereotypes of African-American males as either athletes or criminals, stereotypes of Native-American men as little more than drunks, and stereotypes of Latino men as manual laborers stymie the economic progress of these men. Such stereotypes interfere with hiring and promotion, and with the dedication of resources to education and training. Furthermore, these stereotypes are widely conveyed through media such as television, and may serve as messages about the masculinity these men are expected to enact. For instance, McAdoo (1983) suggested that the preponderance of negative images of minority men in society is such that the men themselves feel they must imitate or live up to them. In other words, such stereotypes may create self-fulfilling prophecies.

Unemployment rates for black men are among the highest in the United States and are due to poor-quality education, racial discrimination, and technological changes that have eliminated large numbers of decent-paying factory jobs. The area of athletics is one of the only hopes for economic success offered to African-American males, and one that is unlikely to pan out for the majority of them (Majors, 1990; McAdoo, 1983). Majors (1990) pointed out that many black males have accepted the dominant American concept of masculinity (being the breadwinner, having strength, and dominating women) but are denied access to legitimate means to achieve it. Lacking these means, they prove their manhood with a sort of "compulsive masculinity" that involves emotional and physical toughness, domination of women, and risk taking (Majors, 1990; Majors & Billson, 1992). I think of compulsive masculinity as *compensatory masculinity,* an exaggerated masculinity used to compensate for feelings of economic or career failure.

Majors and Billson (1992) talked about how compensatory masculinity often takes the form of being "cool." Coolness is used to enhance masculinity and communicate pride, strength, and control. They wrote, "Presenting to the world an emotionless, fearless, and aloof front counters the low sense of inner control, lack of inner strength, absence of stability, damaged pride, shattered confidence, and fragile social competence that come from living on the edge of society" (p. 8). Note that compensatory masculinity occurs among non-African-American males as well. For instance, Pena (1991) found a high level of male posturing among male Mexican immigrant agricultural workers and concluded that this was a reaction to their poor economic status. Pleck (1981) also suggested that when men "fail" at one aspect of the male gender role, they may exaggerate their masculinity in other areas to compensate. One of those other areas is toughness.

The Toughness Norm

The toughness norm for males comes in several different forms—physical, mental, and emotional.

The Physical Toughness Norm

The physical toughness norm is the expectation that a man be physically strong and masculine. The current popularity of weightlifting is a response to this norm. Gyms are filled with men trying to increase their muscle mass and get "big." Males who feel they are expected to be physically strong and masculine may have lowered self-esteem when they are not, and in the quest for physical toughness, they may engage in unhealthful practices. For instance, they may use steroids to gain muscle mass and strength. Steroid use can lead to mood disorders, joint problems, heart problems, and cancer. Although most users have heard of the dangers, they view steroids as necessary to meet the standards of the physical toughness norm. Perhaps more common than steroid use is refusing to admit pain or seek medical attention for physical problems. There is some reason to believe that this is one reason for the shorter lifespans of men relative to women (Helgeson, 1990). Chances are that you know a number of males who did not back off from physical activities or seek medical attention following an injury and consequently ended up even more badly injured. Indeed, it appears from television commentaries during football games that the player who plays in spite of a serious injury is greatly admired. As my student Mike, his leg encased in a brace after reinjuring his knee skiing, noted, "It seems weak to take time off. The message we get is that real men keep on playing even when injured."

The physical toughness norm sometimes leads to interpersonal violence, especially when the social situation communicates that the male who does not aggress will be viewed as less manly than the one who does, or when a male feels that his masculinity is being threatened or questioned. Males who are unable to achieve in other ways are especially likely to demonstrate their masculinity through violence against others (Toch, 1992). In other words, violence often has its roots in compensatory masculinity. Violence is, after all, a way for an otherwise powerless man to feel powerful, to say, "I am a man, even though I am not economically successful." Majors and Billson (1992) suggested that, for some men without access to mainstream avenues of achievement, violence becomes a form of achievement.

Violence against women may also be related to compensatory masculinity. For example, a man who feels powerless may rape women to reassure himself of his strength, power, and superiority (Kilmartin, 1994). Research finding that male batterers tend to have both low self-esteem and low socioeconomic status is supportive of the idea that violence against women is related to compensatory masculinity (Gondolf, 1988). The greater assault and murder rates sustained by black females from their male partners relative to that of other ethnic and racial groups may be due to some black men feeling that, even though they cannot control the way society treats them, they can control "their women" (Majors & Billson, 1992). Chicano males are also largely denied power, money, and resources, and may compensate by exerting power over women (Blea, 1992). Mary Crow Dog (1993), a Native-American, has maintained that the serious domestic violence problem in Native-American communities is the result of the forced move of Indians to reservations, the consequent destruction of their economies, and the acceptance of a Eurocentric conception of masculinity which Native-American men are unable to meet.

Kimmel (1992) discussed a destructive norm related to the toughness norm: *the "give 'em hell and go for it" norm.* This norm encourages men to engage in daring, risky, and aggressive behaviors to demonstrate their manhood. Kimmel argued that date rape and men's vulnerability to stress-related diseases, drunk driving, accidental death, and AIDS are related to men's obsessive risk taking. Pleck et al. (1993a, 1993b) found the strength of adolescent men's endorsement of traditional masculinity was associated with increased substance abuse, coercive sex, increased numbers of heterosexual partners in a year, and the belief that pregnancy validates masculinity. Males who held traditional attitudes toward masculinity also reported less consistent use of condoms and were less likely to believe that it is the male's responsibility to avoid pregnancy. The authors concluded that traditional masculinity is associated with increased risk of pregnancy and sexually transmitted diseases, including AIDS (Pleck et al., 1993b). Majors and Billson (1992) proposed that young black males are overrepresented in deaths caused by homicide, accident, suicide, and AIDS because self-destructive, risk-taking behaviors are undertaken by some of them to convince others of their masculinity.

The Mental Toughness Norm
Common stereotypes of men suggest that they have a hard time admitting they do not know something and will not even ask for directions. This may be due to the mental toughness norm, which contains the expectation that a male appear highly competent and knowledgeable. For the individual man trying to conform to this model of hypercompetence, the result may be anxiety when he does not know something (especially if he is afraid someone might find out he does not know). In some cases it may interfere with his gaining information since he cannot ask questions that might reveal his lack of knowledge. Interpersonally this norm is a problem because a man who adheres to it demeans others when he refuses to admit he was wrong and they were right or that someone else could possibly know something that he does not.

The Emotional Toughness Norm
This norm suggests that men should be emotionally tough, feeling little and able to solve their own emotional difficulties with no outside help. I believe this norm creates the most problems for men and their loved ones. Kimmel (1992, p. 678) lamented: "Fatherhood, friendship, and partnership all require emotional resources . . . that men have traditionally shunned . . . . The things we thought would make us real men impoverish our relationships with other men and our children." In Chap. 2 we presented research evidence that men are just as emotional as women but may be less emotionally expressive because of the male role, except in the case of anger

which is a socially acceptable emotion for men. A number of studies have found that males are less emotionally expressive than females (Blier & Blier-Wilson, 1989; Brody, 1984; Snell, 1989; Stapley & Haviland, 1989).

One form of emotional expression is "self-disclosure," the communication of personal feelings from one person to another. A comedian once said that men come back from being with their friends and their female partner says, "What did you *talk* about?" The male replies, "Nothing, we were fishing" (or working on the car, etc.). When females come back from being with their friends, the men say, "So what did you *do?*" The female replies, "Nothing, we talked." Several studies have indicated that males self-disclose less than females (Caldwell & Peplau, 1982; Dolgin et al., 1991; Lewis, 1978; Reis et al., 1985; Shaffer et al., 1991). As pointed out by Hacker (1981), self-disclosure is potentially costly: Sharing personal information can result in rejection, ridicule, exploitation, betrayal, and an imbalance of power if the self-disclosure is not reciprocated by the other. To avoid such risks, some males may avoid self-disclosure. This social norm is not unique to white culture. According to Majors and Billson (1992), many black males resist self-disclosure because it is seen as a sign of weakness that may result in a loss of respect.

Of course, not all male-male relationships are characterized by low levels of self-disclosure, and conversely not all female relationships are characterized by high levels. It seems to depend on how sex-typed the individual is (Barth & Kinder, 1988). Winstead et al. (1984) found that men who strongly value traditional masculinity tend to avoid self-disclosure. Lavine and Lombardo (1984) found that androgynous persons, both female and male, exhibit equal levels of disclosure.

According to research, male-male relationships are characterized by more conflict and competitive side-by-side activities and less self-disclosure and emotional sharing than female-female relationships (Aries & Johnson, 1983; Auckett et al., 1988; Carli, 1989; Farr, 1988; Hays, 1988; Maccoby, 1990; Sherrod, 1989; Wright, 1982). Self-disclosure can put the individual at a competitive disadvantage and interferes with the appearance of "toughness" and competence, important components of the male image. Maccoby (1990) suggested that males may need the structure afforded by sports and other such activities to help them safely be close to other men, while women do not. For instance, one of the few times when American men are seen to hug or touch is after a sports win. Messner (1987) suggested that males are attracted to sports because they learn that this is the way for males to be validated and because sports seem to provide a safe way to experience acceptance and attachment to other people. He argued, however, that sports usually do not deliver what is really needed: intimate connection and unity with other human beings.

Men arguably miss out due to this difficulty in self-disclosure. A willingness to self-disclose personal facts and feelings increases intimacy in relationships (Derlega & Berg, 1987), and increases relationship satisfaction for both men and women (Jones, 1991; Siavelis & Lamke, 1992). Majors and Billson (1992) suggested that the label of emotional expressions as "uncool" in the black male community interferes with the establishment of strong bonds with friends, family, and women. Such labeling is not unique to the black male community and may be seen in other ethnic and racial groups as well (including white ones). One of my students, José, wrote about how his tendency to avoid self-disclosure almost ruined his relationship with his girlfriend:

> Although I am usually concerned with others' needs and feelings, I was not comfortable talking about what was going on in my mind. When my girlfriend would ask me what I was thinking about I would change the subject or say some kind of lie. But as she got to know me better she could tell I was not being truthful and would get irritated with my response. Now my error seems obvious: without opening up a little, there is no reason for the other to do so, and the relationship stops growing at a certain point. I have worked hard to change and talking about my feelings has definitely increased the intimacy in our relationship.

Studies consistently find that, at all ages, females rate higher than males in intimacy and have more friendships characterized as intimate (Jones & Dembo, 1989). Both men and women report that their friendships with women are higher in intimacy, enjoyment, and nurturance (Sapadin, 1988). Barth and Kinder (1988) found female same-sex friendships to be of greater involvement, longer duration, and greater depth than relationships where one or both partners were male. A number of studies have found that traditional masculinity in one's partner is associated with reduced relationship satisfaction (Ickes, 1993).

Barbee et al. (1993) suggested that males are not sought out for support because they may respond to disclosures in a logical and unemotional way which may be experienced as a "dismissal." Based on interviews with men about their friendships, Reid and Fine (1992) suggested that it is not that men are overtly negative when other men express their feelings as much as it is that males' disclosures to their male friends do not result in reciprocal disclosures. Men in their study said their friends were externally supportive (e.g., would help them fix a car or move) but felt that they were prevented from self-disclosing by their friends' responses. In general it appeared that their male friends did not respond in ways that reinforced such disclosures. Disclosing behavior is rewarded by concerned and interested responses that acknowledge the feelings involved, including questions that encourage more disclosures. These responses may be less common in the behavioral repertoire of males due to socialization experiences that emphasize competition. It is also possible that males feel less competent in handling the emotions of others than females do and, consequently, discourage others' self-disclosures.

If we look at the availability of the male models in U.S. culture, it is

Copyright 1994 by Ruben Bowing. Distributed by Quaternary Features.

The male role may interfere with opportunities to receive emotional support.

easy to see how emotional inexpressiveness is perpetuated (Kilmartin, 1994). American society prescribes and reinforces a "cool" male image that is tough, emotionally inexpressive, detached, and self-reliant, and many men learn that being "cool" is the key to being socially accepted by their male peers (Majors & Billson, 1992). Males are socialized to compete and maintain individuality at the expense of intimacy (Jones & Dembo, 1989). Hacker (1981) suggested that self-disclosure can be expected to happen least often in male-male relationships since males may be perceived by males to be more stringent upholders of masculine norms than females. The costs of self-disclosure to another male may be greater than the costs of disclosure to a female.

Unfortunately, as noted by Saurer and Eisler (1990), if the expression of tender emotions is experienced as a violation of the male gender role and consequently such expressions are avoided, then the opportunity to receive emotion-focused support may be decreased since others may be unaware that support is needed. Several studies have suggested that females may be better at communicating they need support than males (Gottlieb & Wagner, 1991; Riggio & Zimmerman, 1991; Sarason et al., 1985). According to research, females are more likely than males to seek social support and to get it (Belle, 1987; Shumaker & Hill, 1991). Research also suggests that the female role, which emphasizes nurturance and emotional expressiveness and makes people expect that females will need help, makes it easier for women to obtain social support than does the male role emphasizing achievement, autonomy, and emotional control (Barbee et al., 1993). The female role may also make it easier to ask for help. Barbee et al. (1993) suggested that males may not ask for social support because they do not expect to get it because of negative childhood and adolescent experiences when they asked for help.

Researchers Vredenberg et al. (1986) cited studies suggesting that men's lower incidence of depression is an artifact of the social unacceptability of males' reporting of depressive symptoms. In other words, depression may be considered to be sex-role-inappropriate behavior for males and the lower reported rates of depression for men may occur because male depressives are less likely to seek professional help for their depression. Females are more likely to cope with depression by confiding to a friend or seeking professional help while males try to cope by ignoring the problem, taking drugs, and drinking alcohol (Vredenberg et al., 1986). Social norms may make it harder for men to seek help. For instance, only 23 percent of the males and 4 percent of the females in the Burn and Laver (1994) study agreed that men should take care of their problems without help but the majority of males felt that their male friends expected men to do so. Derlega and Chaiken (1976) found subjects saw a man as less mentally healthy if he shared his personal problems than if he kept them to himself. Majors and Billson (1992) attributed the high rates of suicide among black men to toughness and masculinity norms that interfere with their obtaining help.

Kilmartin (1994) pointed out another serious outcome of the unconnectedness males feel to others when he noted that the lack of feeling close makes men more willing to do physical and psychological harm to others. Males, he wrote, are socialized away from empathy and this enables them to be cruel to those who get in their way. It is, he stated, nearly impossible to understand and experience someone else's emotions when an individual does not understand his or her own. Females are much more likely to be socialized to think about how other people feel and to feel connected to others. The masculine emphasis on competition does not emphasize the consideration of others. He suggests that the disproportionate participation of men in war, violence, damage to the planet, the oppression of marginalized social groups, and psychological cruelty must at least partly be "laid at the doorstep of traditional masculinity" (p. 12).

The Antifemininity Norm

Remember that this norm calls for men to avoid stereotypically female activities, behaviors, and occupations. For example, some men feel that the expression of feelings and self-disclosure "belongs" to women and that they will not appear masculine if they are emotionally expressive. One of my students told how a male friend cried during the last episode of the television show M*A*S*H and his roommate exclaimed: "I just lost all respect for you. What kind of a man are you!" Many of my students have reported that when a man cries or violates a male norm he is derisively called a "woman." A friend said that he remembers feeling like intimacy, emotional sensitivity, and expressivity "belonged" to females. So he felt he was left with only two options: If he was emotionally expressive, he was less than male, but if he was not emotionally expressive, he could not be a complete human being.

We have already discussed how the success/status norm may interfere with fathering. There is reason to believe that the antifemininity norm interferes as well. Psychologists agree that an important part of healthy parenting is being gentle, nurturing, and emotionally supportive, and frequently hugging and telling one's children that one loves them. Many men have difficulty doing these things because they associate them with femininity and have been socialized to avoid the feminine. As a result, many people grow up wondering if their fathers ever really liked or loved them. Unfortunately, the role of the father in our emotional and psychological development and adjustment has received scant research attention from psychologists since the mother is accepted as the primary parent and psychological theories of development emphasize the role of mothers over fathers (Phares, 1992). However, in support of the idea that the traditional male role may interfere with parenting, Russell (1978) found that androgynous fathers were more actively involved with their children on a day-to-day basis. The antifemininity aspect of the male norm may also interfere with equity in the household to the extent that men identify household tasks with women and femininity. One study found that the more masculine husbands were the less likely they were to do housework (Atkinson & Huston, 1984).

O'Neil (1981) suggested that men's *femiphobia*, or fear of femininity, stems from their fears about homosexuality and a social context that has customarily equated femininity in men with homosexuality. This was called the "inversion theory of homosexuality" in Chap. 1, where research finding that deviation from the male role is associated with homosexuality was presented. Kimmel (1994) has claimed that the fear men have of others perceiving them as homosexual propels them to enact all kinds of exaggerated masculine behaviors and attitudes, such as homophobic and sexist remarks, to make sure that no one gets "the wrong idea" about their manliness.

This fear of being labeled as homosexual also interferes with intimacy in male-male relationships (Devlin & Cowan, 1985). For instance, a fear of being labeled homosexual often reduces touching and physical closeness between heterosexual men. Most of us have seen awkwardness between men because of this. As a man greets a special male friend or listens to a male friend's bad news, one can almost see a cartoon-like word bubble above his head with the words "Should I hug him? I don't want him to get the wrong idea and I don't want to be rejected." Both touching and physical closeness are important communicators of liking and caring that some men lose out on. In the United States, females communicate their liking of others by decreasing interpersonal distance (i.e., standing closer) but males only do this with females, not with other males (Aiello, 1987). Women show more variation in the distances they maintain between themselves and others, varying distances based on the level of intimacy they wish to communicate (Forsyth, 1990). It is interesting to note that this is a part of male culture in the United States, while in other countries male-male touching and decreased interpersonal distances between males are not necessarily associated with homosexuality. For instance, my student Alicia traveled to Morocco with a female friend. There, men hold hands and walk arm in arm in public. In Russia it is not uncommon for men to kiss each other in greeting.

MALE GENDER ROLE STRAIN, STRESS, AND CONFLICT

Until relatively recently, American psychology has operated according to what Pleck (1981) called *the theory of male sex-role identity (MSRI)*. This theory holds that males must acquire the proper sex-role identity in or-

SALLY FORTH By Greg Howard and Craig MacIntosh

Reprinted with special permission of King Features Syndicate.

To avoid being perceived as feminine, males may act in ways that run counter to how they feel.

der to possess psychological health. Males without sex-appropriate interests, attitudes, and traits were assumed to be in need of treatment. According to Pleck, this was the dominant psychological theory about masculinity from the 1940s to the early 1970s. As Pleck (1987) put it, the study of the male sex role was preoccupied with the question, "What makes men less masculine and what can we do about it?" Psychologists operating from this perspective focused on "dangers" to the acquisition of male gender identity such as the absence of male role models, feminized environments in the schools, and women's changing roles (Pleck et al., 1993a).

Pleck (1981) proposed a new paradigm based on the idea that aspects of the traditional male role are dysfunctional and contradictory. He called this new paradigm *male gender-role strain*. For example, men are expected to show greater emotional control than women, and are often described as being alienated from their feelings; but at the same time anger and impulsivity are encouraged, especially with other males, and their expression is often seen as validating masculinity. Contradictions are also present when it comes to men's relationships with each other. The traditional male sex role prescribes that men have strong emotional bonds to other men but these male-male bonds often take forms that limit their intimacy (e.g., friends talk about or play sports; their main form of affection is often teasing one another). In the traditional role, men's ties to other men were stronger than with women. Now, there is greater acceptance of tenderness and emotional intimacy, although it is restricted to romantic heterosexual relationships (Pleck, 1976).

Since Pleck's (1976, 1981) groundbreaking work, other psychologists have come to recognize that although there are aspects of masculinity such as assertiveness and confidence which are positive, traditional male socialization may have negative consequences for the individual. For instance Eisler et al. (1988) noted that rather than being a source of identity, the male gender role is often a source of anxiety and strain. They called the stress that arises when a male has difficulty in living up to the male role, or which arises when a situation calls for feminine behaviors (e.g., nurturing and compassion) which are not in his repertoire or are prohibited by the male role, *male gender role stress (MGRS)*. They found MGRS to be significantly correlated with anger and increased anxiety among men. For example, a male friend of mine is out of work and his wife is currently supporting the family. He confesses to feeling great anxiety about not fulfilling his provider role. Saurer and Eisler (1990) found that men who were high on male gender-role stress found situations which elicited the expression of tender emotions to be very difficult and therefore displayed less nonverbal and verbal expressivity than did subjects low in MGRS. I can think of a number of examples of this, many stemming from my brief bout with cancer. Many of my male friends and male relatives were obviously uncomfortable with the news and did not know what to say or do. Most muttered "Sorry," never brought it up again, and were visibly

SALLY FORTH By Greg Howard and Craig MacIntosh

Reprinted with special permission of King Features Syndicate.

Ted experiences gender-role conflict.

uncomfortable in my presence. Sauer and Eisler (1990) also found that high-MGRS male subjects were less satisfied with their social support networks. They saw these two findings as related and suggested that the avoidance of the expression of tender emotions decreases the opportunity to give and receive emotion-focused support.

A similar, but broader, idea comes from O'Neil (1990), who spoke of *gender-role conflict,* a psychological state which occurs when rigid, sexist, or restrictive gender roles have negative consequences or a negative impact on a person or others who come into contact with the individual. For instance, gender-role conflict may occur for a man when he restricts his behavior or the behavior of others which does not fit traditional gender roles, when he is put down by others for violating masculinity norms, or when he puts down himself or others for not living up to the role (O'Neil et al., 1995). Gender-role conflict has both personal and interpersonal effects. Personal effects may include anxiety, depression, low self-esteem, and stress. Interpersonal effects may include reduced intimacy, decreased relationship satisfaction, work conflicts, power and control issues in relationships, and physical and sexual violence (O'Neil et al., 1995).

O'Neil et al. (1986) proposed a model of male gender-role conflict that includes six patterns:

1. Restrictive emotionality—difficulty expressing one's feelings or denying others their right to do so
2. Homophobia—fear of homosexuals, including stereotypes of homosexuals
3. Socialized control, power, and competition—a need to control others and situations and an emphasis on winning
4. Restrictive sexual and affectional behavior—having limited ways of expressing one's sexuality and affection to others
5. Obsession with achievement and success
6. Health care problems—stemming from an unhealthy lifestyle

O'Neil et al. (1986) developed the 37-item *Gender Role Conflict Scale (GRCS-I)* to measure gender-role conflict and fear of femininity. Men indicate how strongly they agree with such items as "Winning is a measure of my value and worth," "I have difficulty telling others how I feel about them," "Expressing my emotions to other men is risky," and "My needs to work or study keep me from my family or leisure time more than I would like." A number of studies have used the GRCS-I to see if the experience of gender-role conflict by men is correlated with psychological distress. Such studies (Davis & Walsh, 1988; Good & Mintz, 1990; Sharpe & Heppner, 1991) have found restrictive emotionality, restrictive affectionate behavior in men, and conflict between work and family relations to be related to lowered self-esteem and intimacy, and heightened anxiety and depression. Gender-role conflict has been documented in both older and younger men, and among black, Hispanic, Asian, and white men (see O'Neil et al., 1995, for a review of these studies). Although the source of the conflict does appear to vary somewhat based on group membership, currently there is not enough research to draw any definitive conclusions regarding differences between these groups.

CONCLUDING REMARKS

Social psychologists have focused much more attention on the female gender role because of its obvious disadvantages (e.g., low power, status, pay). However, there appear to be some significant disadvantages to the male gender role as well. These disadvantages include success norms that stress economic success, sometimes at the cost of personal satisfaction and closeness to family. Because economic success is unattainable for millions of men, they may compensate by exaggerating other aspects of their masculinity at high costs to themselves and others. Majors and Billson (1992), who wrote about the damaging effects of the American criteria for success on black Americans, and Blea (1992), who wrote about its negative effects in the Chicano community, recommended that success be redefined in terms of community, love of family, and good health. Such a redefinition will become increasingly relevant to all men, and to society, as population growth, corporate downsizing, the weakening of unions, and mechanization make "breadwinning" and high economic status increasingly difficult for men to achieve.

Male norms that require restrictive emotionality are also problematic since they increase psychological distress, decrease intimacy in relationships, and make men less sensitive to the harm they cause others. Levant (1992) suggested that there is a high incidence of at least a mild form of *alexithymia* among males. According to Kilmartin (1994), alexithymia occurs when a man who has continually acted as though he has no emotions eventually loses his ability to identify and express emotion. Unfortunately we do not know the percentage of men who are affected by these disadvantages or to what extent they are affected.

Levant (1992) described the male role as being in a state of crisis because of societal change. Men's traditional ways of showing caring (e.g., providing for their families) are no longer valued and men are being asked to do things such as care for children and express intimate feelings that violate the traditional male role and require skills they do not have. Masculinity, according to Levant, needs to be reconstructed so as to save what is good about the role and to eliminate those parts that are obsolete and dysfunctional. The "new" man will:

> . . . be strong, self-reliant and reliable. He will show care by doing for others, looking out for them, and solving their problems. He will be good at solving problems and in being assertive. He will be logical and live by a moral code. But he will no longer be a stranger to emotions. He will have a greater appreciation of his own emotional life, and an ability to express his emotions in words. . . .He will be aware of the emotions of others, and adept at reading their subtle nuances. He will have a better balance in his life between work and love. He will be a better husband and lover because he will be able to experience the true joys of intimacy, and come to prefer that over disconnected lust. He will be the father that he wanted for himself. (p. 387)

It is unclear at this point just how much progress toward a new male role has been made. In some ways there is more latitude for females who stray from their role than males who stray from theirs. For example, Martin (1990) found that people were much more concerned about boys who played girls' games than girls who were "tomboys." Or as Myers (1990) put it, women are freer to become doctors than men to become nurses, married women may choose whether or not to have paid vocations but men who choose to be "househusbands" are viewed as too lazy to work. Because men's roles are typically higher status perhaps, as suggested by Feinman (1981), a female's movement into the highly valued male role is more acceptable than a male's movement into the less valued female role.

There is some reason to believe that people want traditional male norms to change. Thompson and Pleck (1986) found that college-aged men recognized the presence of the traditional male norms but did not strongly agree or disagree with them. Burn and Laver (1994), in a study of people ranging in age from 16 to 88, also found weak endorsement of the norms comprising the traditional male role. They found that the norms receiving the strongest endorsements by both males and females were those regarding success at work, making lots of money, and looking masculine. The norms receiving the weakest endorsements were those suggesting that men should not express their feelings and those advocating a traditional division of labor in the home. Men more strongly endorsed the views that males should be the dominant family decision makers, take care of their personal problems without help, be physically strong and able to fight, and not have to cook and clean house or give up leisure time to care for their children. However, males and females did not differ in their endorsements of statements suggesting that men should make lots of money, focus on success at work, look masculine, choose traditionally male jobs, always act as though they know what they are doing, and stay away from discussions of personal feelings. The only generational difference was an increased endorsement of the emotional/mental toughness component of the traditional male role by older people.

Studies involving female college students asked to describe an ideal person or ideal mate have shown them frequently describing someone with an androgynous rather than a masculine orientation (Cramer et al., 1991). These studies, and others finding weak endorsement of the traditional male norms, suggest that a new set of norms may be evolving. However, it is puzzling that endorsement of the traditional male role seems so weak when it appears that conformity to it is still the rule rather than the exception. There are a number of possible reasons for this, outlined below.

One factor inhibiting change may be the perception that others endorse traditional male norms. Even when men do not strongly endorse those norms, it does not mean that they do not comply with them. Remember that compliance occurs when we conform outwardly in order to avoid social disapproval. O'Leary and Donoghue (1978) pointed out that males may still believe that sex-role deviation will result in negative social consequences. As we discussed in Chap. 1, a number of studies have found that there are social penalties for males who deviate from traditional roles, and gender-inconsistent behavior is especially likely to interfere with the popularity of boys (Berndt & Heller, 1986; Costrich et al., 1975; Huston, 1983; Martin, 1990; Seyfried & Hendrick, 1973; Steriker & Kurdek, 1982). In the Burn and Laver (1994) study, men felt that their male friends endorsed traditional male norms to a larger extent than they did themselves. For instance, both males and females agreed that men should not repress their feelings but men believed their male friends expected them to.

Eisler et al. (1988) found that MGRS (male gender role stress) was not correlated with the endorsement of masculine sex-typed attributes. In other words, even men who were not strongly masculine in their orientation still experienced stress in situations that were appraised as feminine and/or as threatening to male control or competence. Perhaps this occurred because men believe that others expect them to conform to the traditional male role. The perception of these social expectations and the belief that social disapproval may occur if one does not conform to them probably explain a lot of conformity to traditional male roles. To illustrate, here is an excerpt from a paper written by one of my students who was on a university sports team:

> I get along well with just about everyone on the team when we are alone to-
> gether. When they're all together in their male-stereotypical splendor, it's
> something else entirely. Their personalities become more male-extreme. In-
> evitably someone will do something very male (like fart, cuss, burp, insult or
> make sexual comments toward females) and suddenly the group takes that
> tone. I could choose to comply but I would feel untrue to myself. I would be
> hurting people with my insults and treating the women on the team in an un-
> fair way. I could choose to be myself, but that's laden with hurt, embarrass-
> ment, and alienation. My course, then, steers me through the middle. I have
> decided to compromise out of self-interest.

Another reason why behavior changes may lag behind attitude changes is because earlier, more restrictive norms may have resulted in many males not learning relationship and disclosure skills or housework and childcare skills. Because of this, attitude-behavior correspondence may be low. Kilmartin (1994) recommended men's groups, workshops, or therapy where expressive skills can be learned, and Levant (1992) described several such successful projects. Unfortunately, the absence of officially accepted labels interferes with the recognition and treatment of psychological problems arising from the male role. The *Diagnostic and Statistical Manual of Mental Disorders,* 4th ed. (DSM-IV), published by the American Psychiatric Association (1994), has no diagnostic labels corresponding to male gender-role stress, male gender-role conflict, compensatory masculinity, or alexithymia. Caplan (1991) suggested a category for males called *delusional dominating personality disorder,* which includes, among other things, an inability to establish and maintain interpersonal relationships, and an inability to identify a range of feelings in others and express them oneself.

Caplan (1991) offered her "delusional dominating personality disorder" category somewhat sarcastically (revisers of the DSM insisted on including little-researched disorders specific to females but refused to consider corresponding "male" disorders). However, the point remains that clinical psychologists and psychiatrists need to pay more attention to the problems created by traditional gender roles so they may play a part in helping men develop new skills and challenge old roles. Good et al. (1990) advocated "gender-aware" counseling for all clients. Such therapy involves understanding how gender socialization and sexism have impacted on clients. Levant (1992) added that gender-aware therapy requires its own awareness that psychotherapy may require skills and behaviors such as identifying and expressing emotions which conflict with aspects of the traditional male role. O'Neil and Egan (1992) recommended that therapists assist clients in a "gender-role journey" where they explore how gender roles and stereotypes have created negative consequences for themselves and others, and where they eventually change themselves and educate others about sexism. O'Neil and his colleagues have designed and evaluated workshops to facilitate this gender-role journey (O'Neil &

Roberts Carroll, 1987, 1988a, 1988b). Unfortunately, though, most clinical psychologists fail to focus on traditional gender roles as a source of client problems (Kupers, 1993).

Not only may men need help in developing the skills necessary for adapting to changes in the male role, but they may need institutional support as well. In others words, behavioral changes may lag behind attitude changes because organizational norms and policies continue to assume traditional divisions of labor in the home and therefore do not support changes in the role. For instance, Pleck (1985) pointed out that while at a superficial level there is increased verbal support for greater male involvement in the family, there is little institutional support for men to do this (i.e., few policies promoting paternity leave, flextime, time off for children's school events, etc.). Higgins and Duxbury (1992) have also lamented outdated organizational policies that operate on the assumption that a man has a homemaker spouse. They found that dual-career men (men with children and employed wives) experience greater work-family conflict than men with homemaker wives. They suggested that the work environment does not provide the increased flexibility needed by dual-career men to balance the increased role demands associated with their lifestyle. A number of studies have also indicated that work-family conflict for dual-career men is aggravated by the perception that their lifestyle is a violation of those social norms which say a man's top priority should be his "breadwinner" role (Higgins & Duxbury, 1992). Another problem is that the dominant model of career advancement expects and rewards devotion to the company during the first 5 to 10 years of employment, a time that often coincides with the years during which a man has young children (Powell, 1990).

It is possible that men have changed more than we realize, but our stereotypes of men make this difficult to see as we focus on those individuals and behavioral instances which confirm traditional stereotypes. In Chap. 5 we will discuss the social cognition of gender and see that once we have stereotypes of men and women we tend to process information about them in ways that confirm our stereotypes. This idea is important because it suggests that, even once men and women do change, our perceptions of them may not.

SUMMARY

- One component of the male role is the success/status norm. It suggests that a man is valuable to the extent that he makes a lot of money and is successful at work. This norm may interfere with self-actualization, self-esteem, and quality fathering. Compensatory masculinity, an extreme and destructive masculinity, may occur when men are unable to live up to the norm.

- The mental toughness norm communicates that men should always be knowledgeable, competent, and in control. This norm may prevent learning, result in costly mistakes, and create relationship conflicts.

- The physical toughness norm and its sidekick the "give 'em hell and go for it" norm suggest that males should be physically strong and masculine and should embrace danger. It may contribute to aggression and risky behaviors including steroid use, drug and alcohol abuse, physical injuries from overuse or lack of medical attention, driving recklessly, and irresponsible sexual behavior.

- The emotional toughness norm implies that men should show no emotional weakness and should take care of their own problems. Males may receive less emotional support and have less intimate relationships than women because of this prohibition on emotional expression.

- The antifemininity norm conveys the idea that activities and traits associated with women are to be avoided. Like the emotional toughness norm, this may interfere with emotional expression and may keep men from expressing desirable yet stereotypically female behaviors such as tenderness and empathy. It may also interfere with more equitable divisions of household labor.

- Originally, psychologists believed that males were more psychologically healthy if they embodied traditional masculinity. Now it is increasingly believed that the male gender role may be a source of anxiety and strain because of aspects of it that are dysfunctional and contradictory.

- Recent studies have suggested that endorsement of the traditional male role today is relatively weak. However, early socialization, the perception that others still endorse the traditional role, and the absence of institutional support for new ways of behaving all interfere with fundamental changes in the male role. Clinical psychology and psychiatry have also been slow to seriously incorporate the idea that the traditional male role is damaging to mental health.

5

Gender as a Social Category

Gender Differences and Errors in Thinking

❖

Social Cognition ✦ Social Cognition of Gender ✦ *Gender Stereotypes as Schemas That Guide Information Processing* ✦ *The Origin of Gender Schemas* ✦ *The Memorability of Gender Schema-Consistent Information* ✦ *How Gender Schemas May Give Rise to Illusory Correlations regarding the Genders* ✦ *Gender Stereotypes and Self-Fulfilling Prophecies* ✦ Gender Categorization and Ingroup-Outgroup Bias ✦ *Sources of Gender Ingroup Bias* ✦ *Self-Esteem Needs* ✦ The Paradox of Social Identity ✦ Concluding Remarks ✦ Summary

*A*t one time or another we have all encountered someone whose sex was unclear to us. Generally such a situation causes a "double-take" and at least a moment's concerted thought. Recall my male co-worker, Cliff, who wore a skirt, makeup, and nail polish to his restaurant job. Observers were bothered by Cliff's behavior not just because he was violating a norm, but because they were not sure how to process him since his gender was ambiguous. His situation was not unlike Pat's, a character on the television show *Saturday Night Live*. Pat was not clearly male or female and the other characters tried desperately to figure out Pat's gender. For example, when s/he went into a drugstore to buy razors, the clerk offered Pat stereotypically masculine ones (black and silver) and feminine ones (pink) in the hopes that Pat's gender would be revealed, but Pat disappointed the clerk by selecting gender-neutral blades.

As pointed out by psychologists Cross and Markus (1993), the Pat skit is particularly interesting because it reflects the importance of gender as a social category. People who see the Pat segment express discomfort with a person who is not clearly male or female, because they do not know how to process Pat without information about his/her gender. To further illustrate the salience of gender in person processing, note that while we frequently do not notice or remember someone's eye or hair color, or the way the person was dressed, and we frequently forget names, we rarely forget if someone is male or female. Grady (1979), for example, found that people at a subway station, asked to give a description of the person who sold them their token, mentioned the sex of the seller first or second, 100 percent of the time. Most simply, gender is a major social category through which we process people.

SOCIAL COGNITION

This chapter is on the social cognition of gender. *Social cognition* is a social-psychological perspective that focuses on how our natural information-processing strategies, particularly our tendency to categorize, influence how we perceive others. Let us put it this way: The world is full of a potentially overwhelming number of people, situations, and things. We would go crazy if we noticed and processed everything. But we do not go crazy because we do not process everyone and everything in a given situation. Instead we only process those parts of the stimulus situation that are perceptually salient (noticeable). What determines whether something is salient to us? Saliency is due to size, color, loudness, and novelty (unusualness) but it is also greatly affected by past experience and what we have learned is relevant in a given situation.

In order to reduce the world's infinite variety into a cognitively manageable form, we categorize information. These categories are believed to exist in cognitive structures called *schemas*. These schemas influence how information from the environment is perceived, stored, and remembered. In short, they guide information processing. You have cognitive categories for most social situations (event schemas), for individuals you know (person schemas), and for identifiable social groups based on gender, ethnicity, and occupation (role schemas) (Fiske & Taylor, 1984). These categories guide your processing of people and situations. For example, I can go into virtually any grocery store in the United States and find my way around relatively quickly because I have a cognitive category for "grocery store" that tells me what to pay attention to in order to get my needs met.

In 1954 social psychologist Gordon Allport noted that, in order to deal with an overload of information, individuals categorize people as well as objects and situations. Stereotypes are now considered by many social psychologists to be cognitive categorizations (schemas) of particular social groups. *Stereotypes* are generalized beliefs about what members of an identifiable group are like, and operate as schemas when people are perceiving those groups. In other words, like other schemas, they influence perception and memory. Variables, such as race or sex, are used as discriminating variables for grouping and managing person information (Taylor et al., 1978). Salient features of individuals such as gender or ethnicity, accents, etc., "activate" schemas for these groups, which then guide our processing of individual group members. If, for instance, you are not from the Southern United States, and I tell you in a thick Southern accent that I was raised in the Capital of the Confederacy (Richmond, Virginia), this will probably bring to mind certain stereotypes that will influence what you notice and remember about me. Without this information, the same behaviors and qualities might go unnoticed and unremembered.

Research indicates that information that is consistent with our schemas is more likely to be noticed and remembered than is information that is schema-inconsistent (Cantor & Mischel, 1977; Chapman & Chapman, 1969; Cohen, 1981; Hamilton, 1981; Howard & Rothbart, 1980; Rothbart et al., 1979; Snyder, 1981). In one study, subjects watched a videotape of a woman's birthday party. Those told she was a waitress remembered her drinking beer and owning a television, those told she was a librarian remembered her wearing glasses and owning classical records (Cohen, 1981). In other words, "waitress" evoked a different schema than "librarian" and the subjects' processing of the woman's party was guided by their schemas.

The wonderful thing about schematic processing is that it is, as Markus and Zajonc (1985, p. 143) put it, "economical" since it reduces "an enormously complex social environment to a manageable number of meaningful categories. They fill in where there is too little information and allow the perceiver to go beyond the information given." Of course, this is the very shortcoming of schematic processing as well. As Fiske and Taylor (1984, p. 139) put it, "accumulated general knowledge about categories of people does not do justice to the unique qualities of any given individual."

For example, let us say that my telling you that I was raised in the Southern United States activates your "hick" schema, which contains such elements as "ignorant," "culturally backward," and "racist." What would then happen is that your schema would sensitize you to any of my behaviors or qualities that remotely resemble a "hick." Such features would receive your undue attention, they would be central in your processing of me, even if they were not actually representative of my behavior.

Snyder and Uranowitz's (1978) study provides another good research-based illustration. In this study, all subjects read an extensive story about "Betty K." Following the reading, one-third of the subjects were told that Betty K. was a lesbian, one-third were told she was heterosexual, and one-third learned nothing about her sexual preferences. One week after reading the case history, subjects took a 36-item multiple-choice test on the life of Betty K. The results? Subjects told that Betty K. was a lesbian were significantly more likely than the other subjects to choose answers consistent with lesbian stereotypes. In fact, they frequently went beyond the information given in the original story, choosing answers that were not in the story but consistent with lesbian stereotypes. Just as Markus and Zajonc (1985) said, schemas allow us to go beyond the information given.

Schemas, then, influence what we perceive in the first place, and what we remember in the second place. Fiske and Taylor (1984) noted that this is different from the way we normally think of perception. They wrote that to most people it appears that perception is based on a direct copy of the objective data. However, the schema concept is predicated on the idea that organized prior knowledge (schemas) result in the active construction of social reality. While the objective data do shape what you perceive, your existing beliefs and expectations shape how you view the data.

SOCIAL COGNITION OF GENDER

In this section we discuss how our tendency to categorize on the basis of gender guides our information processing, leading us to perceive men and women to be more different than they are. It is remarkable that research does not support the view that men and women are significantly different yet we persist in viewing them as so and in treating them differently based on these perceived differences. We have already discussed at length the research on gender differences and noted that differences, when found, are relatively small. In general, stereotypes suggest that males are agentic, aggressive, and instrumental while females are passive, relational, and emotional (Bergen & Williams, 1991). Hoffman and Hurst (1990) cited research showing that many of the most stereotypical gender differences are too small to lead us to rationally expect such differences. Also, they pointed out, there appears to be little correlation between the size of a sex difference and the degree to which it is emphasized in the stereotypes.

A study by Martin (1987) also demonstrated our tendency to view men and women as more different than they actually are. In this study, males and females circled traits which were descriptive of themselves from a list of thirty traits that included stereotypically masculine, feminine, and neutral traits. Another group of females and males estimated, for each trait, the percentage of men and women in general for whom they believed it was an accurate description. The results: The males and females who rated themselves differed on only five of the forty traits (egotistical, cynical, aware of others' feelings, whiny, fussy), while the other group rated females and males as being significantly different on all forty.

Gender Stereotypes as Schemas that Guide Information Processing

Why do we persist in our perception of males and females as "opposite sexes?" One explanation noted earlier was that the different social roles women and men occupy lead us to assume women and men have different psychological qualities and abilities. We also remarked that a great deal of social information further suggests that males and females are fundamentally different. On top of all this, our natural information-processing strategies may lead us to exaggerate the difference between the genders. This is what the social cognition of gender is all about. Gender stereotypes appear to serve as *gender schemas*. Gender schemas are cognitive categorizations of the genders. These guide our person processing such that we are likely to notice, remember, and interpret information according to our beliefs about the genders. Thus the man who believes that women are ill-suited for management sees the female manager's yelling at her employees as evidence that women are too emotional to be managers, but views the male manager's yelling with tolerance. The woman who thinks men are emotionally stunted jerks easily recalls all those men who fit her stereotype but fails to recall all the men that do not. In one famous study (Condry & Condry, 1976), subjects viewed a film of a 9-month- old child. Half of the subjects were told the film was of a girl, and half it was of a boy. This simple manipulation resulted in different assessments of the same behavior. For example, at one point the child cried after a jack-in-the-box popped out of its box. Those who thought the child was male perceived "him" to be angry; those who thought the child was female perceived "her" to be frightened.

Condry and Ross (1985) also found that children's genders influence adults' perceptions of them. All subjects viewed the same videotape of two children playing in the snow. The children's genders were disguised by snowsuits. One child hit, jumped on, and threw snowballs at the other. One group of subjects was told both children were female, a second group that both were male, a third group that the aggressor was male and the victim female, and a fourth group that the aggressor was female and the victim male. After being told that aggression is "any intentional behavior that could result in harm to the other child," subjects rated the degree of aggression displayed by the hitting, jumping, snow-ball-throwing child. The boy-boy condition was rated by subjects as being significantly less aggressive than the other three conditions. There were no significant differences between the other three conditions on the aggression ratings. In other words, it appears that because rowdy behavior is expected on the part of boys when playing together, it was not perceived as aggressive. The researchers concluded that cognitive social categories such as gender serve to "direct anticipations and expectations along one path rather than another . . . . Believing a child to be a boy sets up one line of anticipations, whereas believing a child to be a girl entrains a different set of expectations" (p. 232).

Several studies by Taylor and her colleagues (Taylor & Falcone, 1982; Taylor et al., 1978) also suggested that gender is an important social categorizer which affects perception. Taylor and Falcone (1982) had subjects listen to a political discussion by three males and three females to see how gender affected subjects' perceptions. The taped discussion was on increasing voter turnout and each speaker made six concrete suggestions. The researchers made sure that all suggestions were equally useful and creative by previously having people rate a number of possible suggestions on these qualities. The researchers then selected thirty-six that had equivalent ratings. After listening to the 13-minute discussion, subjects rated the discussants on how politically "savvy" each was, how influential, how interesting it would be to work with each, how comfortable it would be to work with each, and how effective each person would be running a campaign for a local office. Male discussants were rated significantly more positively on four out of the five dimensions (there was no difference on the "comfortable" issue). In a replication of this study done later by Beauvais and Spence (1987), however, this promale bias was not consistently displayed by the majority of subjects. It is unclear whether this difference was due to attitudinal changes which occurred between 1978 (the year the Taylor and Falcone data were collected) and 1984 (the year the Beauvais and Spence data were collected) or demand characteristics in the later study (because of greater awareness of women's issues, students in 1984 might have guessed the study's hypothesis). Subtle methodological differences between the two studies could also be responsible.

Although the studies differed on the finding of a promale bias, both the Taylor and Falcone (1982) study and the Beauvais and Spence (1987) study found evidence that biological sex is used as a schema to process information about the speakers. In both studies, subjects were significantly more likely to make within-sex errors than between-sex errors. In other words, subjects were more likely to confuse which woman said what than they were to mistakenly think a comment was made by a woman when it was actually made by a man (and vice versa). Similarly, A. P. Fiske et al. (1991) found that subjects were more likely to confuse individuals of the same gender than to confuse individuals of the same age, race, role, or name. Stangor et al. (1992) also found that people were more likely to categorize by sex than by race. These studies clearly suggest that people do categorize by sex.

Research suggests that categorization by gender is especially likely under certain conditions. For instance, any factor that makes an individual's membership in a social group especially salient would tend to engage the stereotype of the group for the individual (Taylor et al., 1978). For instance, gender-stereotypical clothing or appearances probably serve to increase the salience of gender in person processing (Brehm & Kassin, 1992). Gender is also salient when males or females are a numerical minority in a particular role. When a man or a woman is "numerically distinct" in a role, his or her gender is very noticeable and leads to exaggerated perceptions of prominence and exaggerated evaluations (Taylor & Fiske, 1978). If there is only one male in a women's studies class, his gender will be very salient to observers. If there is only one female manager in an organization, her gender will be salient to observers and her behavior is likely to be processed with her gender in mind.

Remember the Ann Hopkins-Price Waterhouse case discussed in the previous chapter? S. T. Fiske et al. (1991) argued that because Hopkins was the only woman out of the eighty-eight people up for partner, her evaluators focused on her sex and processed her behavior according to norms for females. Many psychologists are supportive of affirmative action programs for reasons like these. Such programs are intended to make women and other individuals from traditionally underrepresented groups more common and less numerically distinct in organizations. However, the gender of a female manager may still be salient to observers to the extent that the managerial role calls for behaviors that are not consistent with the female gender role (e.g., being competitive, aggressive, forceful) and if the individual remains a numerical minority in the organization. Fiske and Taylor (1984) noted that out-of-role behavior also attracts our attention and may trigger schematic processing. We will discuss affirmative action in the final chapter.

Fiske and Taylor (1984) pointed out that a schema's activation is based partly on how recently it has been activated and how frequently it is used. The more recently a schema has been activated, the more accessible it is to memory, and the more likely it is to get applied in another context. This is called the *priming effect*. For instance, we might expect that adolescents and young adults, who are intensely preoccupied with sex, might be especially likely to process others on the basis of gender. A frequently used schema is, in a sense, permanently primed (Fiske & Taylor, 1984). We have already discussed the numerous messages in our culture that draw our attention to gender. It is quite possible that such messages serve to keep our gender schemas primed and ready to be activated. As Bem (1981, p. 362) said: "Society's ubiquitous insistence on the functional importance of the gender dichotomy cannot help but render the gender schema even more cognitively available."

Quite a bit of research demonstrates that gender is a potent cognitive category used in person perception (Beauvais & Spence, 1987; Frable &

Bem, 1985; Taylor & Falcone, 1982). However, I occasionally encounter people who insist that they do not process people based on gender. And indeed, there are individual differences in the propensity to use gender as a meaningful piece of information when perceiving others. According to Bem (1981), individuals are *gender-schematic* when they have a readiness to sort attributes and information on the basis of sex, and *gender-aschematic* when they do not. Individuals who are strongly masculine or feminine were expected by Bem (1981) to be especially gender schematic. A study by Hudak (1993) supported this hypothesis.

The Origin of Gender Schemas

Where do our cognitive categorizations of the genders originate? You already know that we have a natural tendency to categorize based on salient features of stimulus persons and situations. This categorization of the world begins in childhood and is the essence of cognitive development. Childhood is a time of rapid schema development and elaboration. Much of our childhood is spent learning and assimilating (incorporating) information about the world.

To aid in the assimilation of vast quantities of information, children categorize. As Serbin et al. (1993) said: "'Male' and 'female' are dichotomous, exhaustive, and perpetually salient 'natural kind' categories emphasized by adults and peers" (p. 1). Gender is a salient categorizer partly because we receive numerous social messages to the effect that the genders are very different. As we discussed earlier, television, literature, and popular humor often present the genders as significantly different. Parents, teachers, and peers also direct our attention to gender and we are raised with the idea that males and females are different in more ways than just genitalia. Children notice that females and males tend to look different and do different things, a perception that is encouraged by socializing agents such as the parents. In Chap. 2 we discussed Eagly's (1987) social roles theory, which suggests that social roles may give rise to social stereotypes (schemas). The fact that most social roles are occupied predominantly by one gender or the other encourages the cognitive dichotomization of the genders. Martin and Halverson (1981) wrote that, because there are so many observable differences between males and females, children find gender category knowledge useful in predicting behavior. The idea that gender segregation in social roles and friendships further contributes to gender stereotyping and, consequently, to gender conflict will be further developed later in this chapter.

As we noted in Chap. 1, gender categorization is at the heart of differential modeling. Martin and Halverson (1981) proposed that, in childhood, we first categorize objects, behaviors, and traits as being for females or for males (they called this an *ingroup-outgroup schema*). Once an object or behavior is classified as belonging to the other sex, there is usually not much attention given to it. Several studies have supported the idea that children are more likely to model and pay more attention to the behaviors specific to their own genders (Leinbach & Fagot, 1986; Perry & Bussey, 1979; Serbin et al., 1993). Biernat (1991) also cited a number of studies suggesting that children's behavioral choices and preferences parallel their knowledge of gender stereotypes.

This categorization into male and female contributes to the development of what Martin and Halverson (1981) called *own-sex schemas,* which consist of scripts and plans of action necessary to carry out gender-appropriate behaviors. Once children identify themselves as female or male, they are motivated to be like others in their own group and this leads them to observe same-sex role models more carefully. This is similar to differential modeling, discussed in Chap. 1. The idea here is quite similar but postulates that this information is stored schematically and guides information processing such that individuals become tuned in to sex-appropriate activities and models. For example, the toy and occupational preferences of children as young as 3 are affected by whether the toys and occupations are labeled as male or female (Huston, 1983; Ruble & Ruble, 1982).

Perhaps these own-sex schemas explain an intriguing comment I have heard from both men and women. The male version goes something like this: "I don't even notice the things that she does. The floor will look filthy to her and I won't even notice it." In other words, it is as if such a male does not possess the same "home cleanliness schema" as his partner. I suspect that many men do not have very detailed home cleanliness schemas because when they were growing up housework was done almost exclusively by women. Therefore they did not pay much attention to it and did not develop the detailed schemas and scripts about it their female counterparts did. Because schemas determine what is noticed in the environment, it is quite possible that some males really do not see the dirty floor. (Of course, many males do notice the dirty floor and many females do not.) Not surprisingly, research indicates that there is quite a bit of individual variation in the acquisition of sex-role information, and that categorization of data as male and female-related is less dramatic in older children and adults (Biernat, 1991; Hort et al., 1991; Huston, 1983). However, it seems likely that there would be less variability in, and more stability of, schemas for roles occupied almost exclusively by men or by women.

In sum, because women and men tend to occupy different social roles, because we see that what counts as appropriate behavior varies in part due to one's biological sex, and because we receive numerous social messages encouraging the perception of the genders as significantly different, we learn that gender is indeed a relevant basis on which to categorize

Cathy and her female friends exhibit detailed home-cleanliness schemas.

people. Therefore, it is not surprising that we come to have gender schemas.

The Memorability of Gender Schema-Consistent Information

There is evidence that we may perceive gender differences to be larger than they are because our memory for schema-consistent behavior is better. This is probably because schemas influence what we notice in the first place and because schema-consistent information is easier to encode into memory (there is less to encode if you are just amending an existing schema rather than creating a new one). For example, both boys and girls recall sex-stereotyped people and activities better than non-stereotyped people and activities, and this memory preference is strongest for those with strong gender stereotypes (Cann & Garnett, 1984; Furnham & Singh, 1986; Hepburn, 1985; Liben & Signorella, 1980; Martin & Halverson, 1983a; Mills, 1983; Ruble & Stangor, 1986; Stangor & Ruble, 1987, 1989).

In general, then, it appears that we have better memory for schema-consistent information. There are, however, some cases in which schema-inconsistent information is likely to be remembered. First, of course, the individual must notice it. Second, the individual must feel motivated to try to explain the inconsistency. Hastie (1981) explained that schema-inconsistent information is likely to be recalled if it competes with the information in the schema and if the cognitive task requires that the person make use of it. Third, the individual must not be able to explain away the inconsistency as being due to the situation or a temporary aberration (Crocker et al., 1983).

Even if individuals remember the schema-inconsistent information, this does not mean that they will alter their stereotypes. The very nature of schemas is such that they persevere even in the face of contradictory evidence. This is called the *perseverance effect*. Fiske and Taylor (1984) pointed out that if people changed their schemas to fit every nuance of every example, the information-processing benefits of schemas would be lost. So what do people do when faced with a schema-contradictory instance? One response is to develop subcategories or subtypes that allow them to maintain the overall stereotype while acknowledging that it does not fit all members of the category (Taylor, 1981). For instance, Deaux et al. (1985) found that people had subcategories for women which included housewives, career women, athletes, feminists, and sex objects, and for men had subcategories of athlete, blue-collar working man, businessman, and macho man. Edwards (1992) found four male subtypes: businessman, athlete, family man, and loser.

Many times people respond to schema-disconfirming instances by developing an *exception to the rule category* for individuals who do not fit. Furthermore, research (Rothbart & Lewis, 1988; Weber & Crocker, 1983) has suggested that, if a schema-disconfirming behavior comes from a group member who is judged to be atypical of the group, then the schema is unlikely to be revised. Fiske and Stevens (1993), for instance, pointed out that the female fighter pilot who also has a husband, two children, and a big kitchen probably does more to counteract stereotypes than the unmarried fighter pilot who hates to cook, because the former individual is more difficult to subtype. Brehm and Kassin (1992) pointed out that members of stereotyped groups face a dilemma. To overcome such stereotypes, they need to portray themselves as exceptions to the rule. Yet to foster change in the group stereotype, they need to seem typical enough of the stereotyped group to affect its image. As an example of this exception-to-the-rule strategy for dealing with schema-inconsistent information, take this case related to me by a female architect who found architecture to be a less-than-friendly profession to women. Once, she said, her male architect boss told her that he did not think women made good architects. She said "What about me? You hired and promoted me. I know you think I'm good." His reply? "You're different from the rest of them."

How Gender Schemas May Give Rise to Illusory Correlations Regarding the Genders

When people expect two things to be related, they tend to overestimate the degree of relationship that exists or impose one when none exists (Fiske & Taylor, 1984). Such a perception is called an *illusory correlation*. In the case of gender, an illusory or exaggerated relationship is often perceived between gender and some trait, skill, or behavior. Meehan and Janik (1990) discussed a number of studies where subjects shown equal numbers of males and females performing traditional and nontraditional behaviors consistently overestimated the number of gender-traditional activities performed.

Another way to put this is to say that perceivers tend to overestimate the frequency of schema-consistent information (Hamilton & Rose, 1980; Martin, 1987). Because our schemas draw our attention to instances that confirm our expectations, we may perceive a stronger relationship between two things than actually exists. For example, Hamilton and Rose (1980) had subjects read sentences about people from six different occupations. Each occupation was paired an equal number of times with a set of twelve traits. However, subjects recalled more instances of pairings that were consistent with their stereotypes of people in the various occupations. As David Myers (1990, p. 359) once said, "to believe is to see." Slusher and Anderson (1987) even found that stereotyped-based imaginings can lead to inflated associations of groups with their stereotypic traits. In other words, people sometimes have stereotypes that lead them to imagine people in an identifiable social group in ways that fit their stereotypes. But, because these imaginings are later not remembered as distinct from actual events, in the stereotype holder's mind they are experienced as additional evidence that the stereotype is correct. The stereotype holder then has the impression that he or she has seen many instances of behavior which confirm the stereotype, although the individual may not be able to recall them.

Illusory correlations occur partly because our schemas draw our attention to cases that confirm our stereotypes but there are several other information-processing tendencies relevant to the formation of illusory correlations as well. Fiske and Taylor (1984) discussed the process by which we form inferences. They noted that research suggests we often draw conclusions based on limited samples (Nisbett & Ross, 1980; Tversky & Kahneman, 1974) and that extreme examples within a sample frequently lead to stronger associations than are warranted (Hamilton & Gifford, 1976; Rothbart et al., 1978; Tversky & Kahneman, 1974).

In regard to gender, then, we may be inclined to generalize traits to all men or all women based on our acquaintance with only a few people possessing them and to overgeneralize one extreme person's behavior to their entire gender (provided it is gender-stereotypical). Thus, we may end up falsely perceiving a strong connection between gender and some behavior, trait, or skill. One student of mine assumed that, because her boyfriend cannot pay attention to more than one thing at a time while she can, that there must be a biological sex difference in attentional abilities. She and her boyfriend differed on this, and the most obvious other difference was their gender; therefore she assumed that the two variables (gender and attentional abilities) were correlated. Furthermore, according to Fiske and Taylor (1984), people are typically unaware that they are drawing conclusions based on limited and extreme samples. And, even when provided with information about the relative frequency of events, people tend to rely more on vivid cases for making estimates of behavior or traits (Hamill et al., 1980). This tendency to underuse information about the relative frequency of events in real life while overusing vivid cases is called the *base-rate fallacy*. For example, take the man who believes that women are bad drivers (we all know someone who insists this is true). This person typically does not notice the 100 women he sees in a day that drive without mishap, but the one that makes a mistake is likely to lead to the exclamation, "See, I told you women can't drive!"

In summary, because gender stereotypes operate as schemas, they guide information processing and we are inclined to notice and remember information that confirms them. In addition, we appear to make generalizations about groups based on information from limited samples and extreme cases. Thus, we may falsely conclude that a particular behavior is associated with one or the other of the genders when statistically it is not.

These tendencies partly explain why people persist in viewing the genders as fundamentally different in spite of the research evidence that they are not.

Gender Stereotypes and Self-Fulfilling Prophecies

People sometimes create evidence that confirms their stereotypes when their stereotypes affect the behavior of others whom they are stereotyping. This can happen because our behavior is influenced by others' expectations of us and their behavior toward us. For example, the man who believes that women cannot drive and states this to a female companion while she is driving may make her so nervous that she does not drive well. Thus, his stereotype is confirmed. You might recognize this as a *self-fulfilling prophecy*, a phenomenon discussed in Chap. 3 in regard to organizations that ensure there are no qualified women for higher managerial positions by their hiring, job assignment, and promotion policies. Definitionally speaking, a self-fulfilling prophecy occurs when a stereotype holder behaves toward a stereotyped person based on the stereotype and by doing so actually elicits behavioral confirmation of the stereotype. Families often do this to family members. Your family may have a stereotype of you based on some early behavior that you feel is no longer valid. Still, they believe it and treat you accordingly. You may then find yourself regressing at the speed of light and behaving in old ways that confirm their stereotype.

Sex stereotype researchers Ashmore and Del Boca (1979) were among the first to suggest that sex stereotypes influence our behavior toward individuals and may elicit behavior in line with our gender-based expectations. Skrypnek and Snyder (1982) also suspected that our stereotypes about women and men influence our interactions with them and elicit confirmatory behaviors from them. To test this hypothesis, they had previously unacquainted female-male pairs seated in different rooms negotiate who was going to do which of a series of tasks, some of the tasks rated as feminine by a set of judges and others rated as masculine. The negotiation was done using a light system so that the females' true sex was anonymous. One-third of the males were told that the person they were interacting with would be an independent, athletic, masculine 20-year-old male. Another third of the subjects were told that they would be interacting with a 20-year-old shy, feminine, conventional female. The remaining third were not told anything. Consistent with the hypothesis, the males behaved differently during the negotiation task depending upon the label of the target person. In particular, when perceivers thought they were interacting with females, they initially chose masculine tasks for themselves and were less likely to change when the targets chose the same task. Furthermore, targets labeled female ended up choosing tasks that were significantly more feminine than did those who were labeled male and those who were not labeled at all.

Self-fulfilling prophecies are of special concern when it comes to the selection of educational programs and occupations by males and females. Eccles et al. (1990) summarized a number of studies suggesting that parents hold gender-differentiated perceptions of, and expectations for, their children's competencies and that through self-fulfilling prophecies parents can socialize gender differences into children's self-perceptions, interests, and skills. First, they cited a number of studies (Eccles, 1984b; Eccles & Jacobs, 1986; Eccles-Parsons et al., 1982) which found that parents hold gender-differentiated perceptions of their children's abilities even when female and male children do equally well as measured by school grades and standardized tests. In particular, girls are seen as being better at English and boys at math. Next, they cited research (Jacobs, 1987) finding that mothers who endorsed the belief that boys were better at math distorted their perceptions of their children's competencies according to their gender-stereotypes. Furthermore, in support of the self-fulfilling prophecy hypothesis, even when the children's actual performance was statistically controlled for, a significant correlation between each mother's perception of her child's math ability and the child's self-perception of his or her own math ability was found.

Eccles et al. (1990) also cited research finding that parents make different attributions for the success of their female and male children depending upon the domain. For instance, Yee and Eccles (1988) found that parents of boys who did well in math attributed it to ability while parents of girls who did well in math were more likely to attribute it to effort. Furthermore, Eccles et al. (1990) found that these beliefs translated into expectations for future course performance and likely career success (talent attributions were related to expectations of success and good course performance).

Based on past research and their ongoing research program, Eccles et al. (1990) proposed a self-fulfilling prophecy model which begins with the parents' gender-role stereotypes. These gender stereotypes are believed to affect the following:

1. Parents' causal attributions for their children's performance (ability or effort)
2. Parents' emotional reactions to their children's performance in various areas
3. The importance parents attach to their children acquiring various skills
4. The advice parents provide their children regarding involvement in various skills
5. The activities and toys parents provide for their children

The above five things are then expected to affect children in the following ways:

1. A child's confidence in his or her abilities
2. A child's interest in mastering various skills
3. A child's affective reactions (feelings) to participating in various activities
4. The amount of time and type of effort that a child devotes to mastering and demonstrating various skills

In the end, then, "these differences in self-perceptions and skills influence the type of jobs and skills that females and males seek out and qualify for" (Eccles et al., 1990, p. 199). This intriguing model is currently undergoing further empirical testing.

GENDER CATEGORIZATION AND INGROUP-OUTGROUP BIAS

In the previous section it was suggested that the use of gender as a social categorizer stems largely from a natural tendency to categorize and from a society that emphasizes that categorization by gender is highly relevant. Social psychologists are also aware that categorization may be motivated in part by identity and self-esteem needs. In this section, the role of such processes in gender categorization is explored. In addition, it is hypothesized that gender categorization may result in an exaggeration of gender differences, and contribute to conflict between the genders.

Sources of Gender Ingroup Bias

People are often biased in favor of their own group (this is called *ingroup bias*) and biased negatively toward groups perceived as being quite different from their own (this is called *outgroup bias*). This phenomenon applies to students at one high school who think they are superior to students at other high schools, to members of fraternities and sororities who think they are superior to members of other fraternities and sororities, to members of families who think they are better than members of other families, to members of ethnic groups who think they are superior to people in other ethnic groups, to citizens of one country who think they are better than those who live in other countries, and so on. It also applies to the genders, a phenomenon I call *gender ingroup bias.*

Research by Williams and Best (1986) found evidence suggestive of gender ingroup bias in college-aged men and women in eleven different countries. In their study, subjects identified the characteristics they associated with women and the characteristics they associated with men. They found that women consistently had a more positive view of women than men had of women, and men consistently had a more positive view of men than women did. Crocker and Major (1989) described a study (Peterson et al., 1988) where men and women completed a measure of a fictional trait and then received bogus feedback. Both the men and the women valued the trait the most when they were told that their sex had more of it than the other sex. This own-sex favoritism appears as early as 2 years old when children ascribe positive characteristics to their own gender and negative ones to the other gender (Kuhn et al., 1978) and similar findings have been found in children aged 5 to 12 (Martin, 1989; McAninch et al., 1993; Powlishta, 1990).

Normal Categorization Processes
Wilder (1981) suggested that ingroup-outgroup bias is a consequence of normal categorization processes (remember, we categorize the world in order to simplify it and make it more cognitively manageable). He noted that such categorization processes often result in the categorization of groups into two mutually exclusive categories, ingroup and outgroup. Due to its physical obviousness and apparent social importance, gender lends itself quite well to this type of categorization of people. Martin and Halverson (1981) suggested that this process begins in childhood when children can identify gender and reliably place themselves in a gender category. Once this is done "they recognize that they belong to one group (in-group) and not the other (out-group) . . . the in-group is then positively evaluated and the out-group negatively evaluated" (p. 1129).

According to Wilder (1981), group categorizations lead people to expect to encounter information which emphasizes the differences between groups. Likewise, gender categorizations operate as schemas which guide our social processing and make us more sensitive to information consistent with our gender categorizations. Many studies find that, once people are separated into identifiable groups, they tend to exaggerate the differences between the groups (e.g., Billig & Tajfel, 1973; see also Brewer, 1979, for a review). Taylor et al. (1978) also noted that, because of this categorization process, within-group differences are minimized and between-group differences are maximized. This tendency, however, may depend on the difference. Eagly and Mladnic (1989) found that men and women perceive large sex differences on dimensions on which their sex is viewed positively, but see the size of sex differences as small on more negative dimensions.

In regard to gender, we tend to overlook how different women are from one another, and how different men are from one another, while we emphasize how different women and men are from each other. Psychologists working in the area of gender differences frequently point out that, even though on some traits males on the average are different from females on the average, there are usually greater differences *among* males and *among* females than there are *between* males as a group and females as a group. This tendency to assume great similarity among outgroup members has been called *outgroup homogeneity bias* (e.g., the "they all look, act, or are alike" bias). Frable and Bem (1985) found that male subjects were more likely to confuse female speakers with each other and females were more likely to confuse male speakers with each other. We are more aware of the differences within our group, but members of the outgroup all seem to be alike.

Gender Segregation
Outgroup homogeneity bias is typically exacerbated by lack of contact between groups and by contact limited to only a few types of situations (Quattrone, 1986). In the case of females and males, it is not that we do not have contact, but that, because of gender segregation in the home, the paid labor force, and in friendships, the contact is such that we may not know the other gender as well as our own. Gender segregation begins in childhood, where we customarily avoid the other gender. Children's tendency to play with same-sex playmates is well-documented, begins as early as 3 years of age, and increases in prevalence until puberty (Serbin et al., 1993). Maccoby and Jacklin (1987) reviewed over twenty research studies on sex-segregated play and friendships in preschoolers to sixth graders and concluded that the segregation of the sexes during these years is quite substantial and does not occur because male and female children have different personalities and are therefore drawn into different groups. They found that children of a wide range of personality types are drawn into same-gender social groups. They suggest that biological sex, social gender labels, and psychological gender identity all come to coincide and draw children toward same-sex associations and away from cross-sex ones.

Cross-sex contact is given a romantic overtone even at the grade school level. In first grade when my son Kane played with his female friend Miriam, the other children taunted them and said that "they were in love" and sang "Kane and Miriam sitting in a tree . . ." (you know the rest because you heard it yourself when you were a kid). Maccoby and Jacklin (1987) suggested that sex segregation in childhood is fueled in part by an avoidance of the implications of sexuality. Normative pressure is apparently operating as well since children are clearly punished by other children, and in some cases by adults, for cross-gender friendships. At one point in first grade, my son's male friends refused to play with him because he played with the girls sometimes as well. Since that time, he has played with girls less and less. Gender segregation is also fostered by differential socialization that leads male and female children to prefer to play different types of games, play with different toys, and be interested in different things.

I think gender segregation in close personal relationships is common throughout the lifespan. Gender-role segregation in adulthood provides us with more opportunities to get to know members of our own gender well and provides us with a pool of experiences we share with members of our own gender. This similarity provides a basis for friendship and intimacy that is often not available for cross-sex adult friendships. Also, because cross-sex contact is given a romantic or sexual overtone in adulthood, it is often not comfortable for males and females to have intimate friendships with one another. Although adults often have cross-sex romantic relationships and on occasion cross-sex friendships, we may not have enough relationships of great enough depth with members of the other gender in order to see the great diversity of individuals within the other sex. The point is that gender segregation may make it such that we know many members of our own gender really well but only a few members of the other gender really well (usually a few family members or romantic partners). When we do not know a large enough sample of an outgroup well, we tend to rely on our stereotypes since we do not have enough experience to see that the stereotypes do not fit the majority of outgroup members. This is especially true when the social context rewards stereotyping of the outgroup (in this case the other gender) which, as we will see in a moment, is often the case.

Self-Esteem Needs

While our natural tendency to categorize people into mutually exclusive groups and gender segregation partly explain our persistence in believing that there are fundamental differences between the genders, it is quite likely that there is more to it than this. Tajfel and Turner (1979) suggested that people are quite resistant to information which contradicts their stereotypes because they are emotionally invested in preserving the differences between their group and an outgroup. This emotional investment is essentially an ego boost from being a member of a "superior" group and from a social context that rewards making such group distinctions. In general, people seem motivated to believe that their group is better than other groups, to put down outgroups, and to emphasize group differences to justify their group's disproportionate share of rewards (Billig & Tajfel, 1973; Brewer, 1979; Burn & Oskamp, 1989; Crocker & Luhtanen, 1990; Turner, 1987). The theory that people are biased in favor of their own group and against members of an outgroup in order to enhance self-esteem is suggested by *social identity theory* (Tajfel, 1981, 1982; Turner, 1987). According to Tajfel (1981, p. 255), social identity is "that part of an individual's self-concept which derives from their knowledge of their membership in a social group (or groups) together with the value and emotional significance of that membership." Crocker and Luhtanen (1990) called this source of self-esteem *collective self-esteem.*

Social Identity Theory
Brewer (1991) proposed that humans simultaneously have a need for validation and similarity to others and a countervailing need for uniqueness and individuation. We want, as Brewer put it, to be both the same as and different from others. Separation into ingroup and outgroup can provide both. The things we have in common with our group members affirm our correctness and provide a sense of belonging while the areas in which our group differs from the outgroup provide evidence of our distinctiveness/uniqueness. Gender identities and the clear demarcation into male/female may serve this function. One of the dynamics of traditional male groups for instance is to avoid the feminine and emphasize activities (such as sports) that are seen as distinctly male. This often has the effect of increasing the cohesiveness of the group and provides males with a unique social identity.

Brewer (1991) noted that ingroup bias is often greater on the part of members of disadvantaged groups and research indicates that this is especially likely when the low status is believed to be illegitimate (Caddick, 1982; Ellemers et al., 1993; Folger, 1987; Turner & Brown, 1978). According to Brewer (1991, p. 481), groups that feel this way turn "what is painful at the individual level" into "a source of pride at the group level—a badge of distinction rather than a mark of shame." For instance, "difference feminists" such as Harding (1986) and Gilligan (1982), have emphasized the desirability of stereotypically feminine qualities and have repudiated stereotypically male ones (in contrast to "similarity feminists" who minimize gender differences and emphasize gender commonalities and androgyny). Difference feminists take what have traditionally been perceived as negative qualities, such as being intuitive, emotional, and other-centered, emphasize their ownership by women, and convert them into sources of pride. Best-selling books like *Women Who Run with the Wolves* (Estes, 1992) also champion women's "feminine instinctive nature" (Estes' term). When women talk about men as the "other," saying things like "a woman would never do that" or "men are so insensitive," they often feel good about their sameness with other women and their separateness from men. It is interesting that according to a Gallup Poll conducted in 1993, only 26 percent of American women surveyed thought that men and women are basically similar in contrast to 43 percent of the men surveyed (Newport, 1993).

Groups often build solidarity by emphasizing the negative qualities of other groups and by having an identifiable outgroup (enemy). Both women and men do this, telling jokes and making derogatory comments at the other sex's expense. See Table 5.1 for a list of "dumb men" jokes and

TABLE 5.1 GENDER JOKES

Dumb Men Jokes

Q: Why do male astronauts need a female astronaut?

A: *So someone will stop and ask for directions.*

Q: Why do men name their penises?

A: *Because people like to know the name of their leaders.*

Q: Did you know that all men are created equal?

A: *Yeah, poor things.*

Q. What's the difference between government bonds and men?

A: *Government bonds mature.*

Q: What did God say after He created man?

A: *"I can do better than this."*

Q: Why are all dumb blonde jokes one-liners?

A: *So men can understand them.*

Q: What's a man's idea of helping with housework?

A: *Lifting his legs so you can vacuum.*

Why Sheep Are Better Than Women Jokes

1. Sheep don't argue.
2. Sheep won't yell at you for leaving the lid up.
3. Sheep don't mind being one of the flock.
4. Sheep won't give your favorite hunting shirt to Goodwill.
5. Sheep will never give you the excuse that they're too hot/cold, too drunk/not drunk enough.
6. Sheep will never break your favorite beer mugs in a fit of pique.
7. The Woolgrower's Association isn't as nasty as the National Organization for Women.

*Note: Jokes made at the other gender's expense may enhance our gender identity and solidarity with members of our gender. However, they may lead to exaggerated perceptions of difference and conflict between the genders.

"why sheep are better than women" jokes. However, while jokes at women's expense have been told for decades, probably to justify their low status, and women have probably always complained about men, the in-group-outgroup nature of the dynamic appears to have escalated since the late 1980s, and antimale jokes and discussions seem much more common than they once were. Sometimes this is popularly called "male-bashing."

The reason for this increase in women's gender ingroup bias is women's awareness of their inequality relative to men. Putting down men is a source of solidarity among women and provides justification for challenging the status quo. Putting down males may also help women to be proud of their gender in a society that seems to value males more. Although such behaviors arise out of a perception of deprivation, they may also stimulate the perception of group deprivation. For instance, a number of the jokes point to men's poor participation in household labor. The jokes arose out of an awareness of inequality but also draw women's attention to this inequality. Because the jokes are told in a social setting, their telling communicates that being angry about such inequalities is an acceptable and even desirable social attitude. Several studies have suggested the perception that one's group is disadvantaged relative to other groups is related to collective action by the oppressed group (Dion 1986; Walker & Mann, 1987). The women's movement in general has worked by emphasizing that women as a group have been discriminated against—that this is what women have in common, and what makes them different from men.

THE PARADOX OF SOCIAL IDENTITY

Although strongly identifying with a group may be a powerful source of identity, and putting down other groups may increase self-esteem and provide the group solidarity necessary to motivate struggles for equality, these behaviors may also lead to exaggerations of group differences, conflicts between groups, and resistance to social change ("backlashes"). I call this the *paradox of social identity*. In the case of gender, strongly identifying with one's maleness or femaleness may be a powerful source of meaning and belonging and in the case of women has formed the basis of a collective movement that has made great strides in increasing women's status. On the other hand, emphasizing gender may also lead to an exaggeration of gender differences that may work against equality since gender stereotypes are often used to justify existing social arrangements. Gender ingroup bias may also foster divisiveness between the genders. For example, male-bashing may enhance males' gender social identity if men feel that the negative stereotypes suggested by male-bashing are unjustified. Men's groups and workshops which encourage men to get in touch with their "wild man" have recently developed in response to perceived attacks on traditional male qualities (see for example Robert Bly's book *Iron John*, 1990). Unfortunately, once men's gender identity is enhanced because of their perception that they have been unfairly villainized, they may also become less supportive of the social changes needed for women's equality.

In research I recently conducted (Burn, 1993), I found support for these ideas. Consistent with gender ingroup bias, in comparison to males, females found a set of male-bashing cartoons to be significantly funnier and more representative of men. Consistent with the idea that ingroup identifications are especially important for members of low-status groups, females were found to more strongly identify with their gender group. Also, as suggested by the social identity paradox, women who strongly

Akbar and Jeff get in touch with their "wild man."

identified with their gender were more supportive of gender-equal policies (e.g., supportive of pay equity programs) while men who strongly
identified with the male gender were less supportive of gender-equal
policies. Because social identities are more important to members of low-
status groups, once gender equality occurs, both the role of gender identification in self-esteem and gender ingroup bias should be reduced. However, it is ironic that, while focusing on gender may very well be the route
to eliminating gender discrimination against women, gender equality
may never occur if women focusing on males as an outgroup creates a
backlash which interferes with attaining male cooperation.

Not only may emphasizing gender lead to an exaggeration of gender
differences and foster divisiveness between the genders, but it may even

lead to greater differences between the genders. Crocker and Major (1989) pointed out that, if a quality possessed by the outgroup is devalued, then individuals of the ingroup will not be motivated to achieve in that domain. For instance, if men devalue emotional sensitivity (a traditionally female quality), they will not aspire to it, and greater gender differences on emotional sensitivity will result. Tavris (1992) also pointed out that the male-female dichotomy and the strong gender identifications it fosters imply that, rather than change, we must simply accept that women and men are inevitably different. This, she noted, distracts us from focusing on what we need to do to have a society based on the qualities we desire in both sexes.

Ingroup-outgroup biases may also foster conflict between groups because they influence the explanations we provide for ingroup and outgroup behaviors. Typically, when the outgroup does something negative, we attribute the behavior to some stable characteristic about members of that group (we make an internal/dispositional attribution). However, when our ingroup does something negative, we attribute it to some temporary situational force (we make an external/situational attribution). Conversely, when the ingroup does something positive, a dispositional attribution is made, and when the outgroup does something positive a situational attribution is made. Pettigrew (1979) called such a tendency the *ultimate attribution error*. The ultimate attribution error is an extension of the fundamental attribution error (the tendency to overemphasize dispositional reasons for others' behavior) and the self-serving bias (the tendency for individuals to make internal attributions for their successes and external ones for their failures) to attributions made regarding group behavior. Hewstone (1990) reviewed the many studies documenting this error.

If you think about it for a moment, you will realize that these types of attributions will lead to increased conflict between groups. For one thing, it means that, in spite of any positive behavior on the part of the outgroup, a negative perception of them will be maintained. For instance, when the husbands of two wives take the children for the afternoon (a positive, desirable behavior), the wives may attribute it to the husbands' guilt, or may believe that the husbands had to be forced to do so, or that the husbands must want something in return. Second, when we are aware of others' negative attributions about us or our group, this is often interpreted as aggression against us or our group. Because we typically respond to aggression with counteraggression, a fight or conflict is the likely result. At the very least, increased psychological distance and dislike between the groups is probable because of *negative affect reciprocity*. Negative affect reciprocity is the tit-for-tat exchange of negative feelings (Brehm & Kassin, 1992). If someone does not like us or says something negative to us, we usually feel inclined to return the favor. Not surprisingly, such interactions can escalate. This is certainly a concern I have about jokes made at the expense of either sex.

Research by Crocker and Luhtanen (1990) has suggested that people who strongly identify with their groups will engage in self- and group-enhancing comparisons following threats. Thus, we might expect that an awareness of the outgroup's negative attitudes or stereotypes of our group may lead us to explain events in ways which allow us to maintain our positive view of our group. Putting down the outgroup is one component of making ourselves feel better in such cases—a critique of our group loses its power if we convince ourselves that those making it are ignorant, evil, or "off the deep end." In sum, when men are aware of women's negative attributions and stereotypes of men, or women are aware of men's negative attributions and stereotypes of women, this makes the other gender even more of an outgroup and the exaggeration of between-group differences is likely to occur and foster even more conflict.

CONCLUDING REMARKS

We began this chapter by pointing out that our perception of the genders as "opposites" is not justified by the research on gender differences and how the social cognition of gender may explain our persistence in believing that they are. In particular, the focus of the chapter was on how our natural information-processing strategies may lead us to exaggerate gender differences. The idea is that once we have expectations about the genders, we are more likely to notice and remember instances that confirm them. This occurs because the expectations operate as schemas. Schemas, of course, are cognitive categorizations that help us selectively attend to what would otherwise be an overwhelming array of stimuli.

The content of group schemas is largely socially determined. In other words, social information based on sex-role segregation suggests to us that certain categorizations are accurate and appropriate. Such is the case with gender schemas. Sandra Bem (1981, p. 362) explained the prevalence of gender-based schematic processing as being due to "society's ubiquitous insistence on the functional importance of the gender dichotomy."

> The typical American child cannot help but observe, for example, that what parents, teachers, and peers consider to be appropriate behavior varies as a function of sex . . . . Society thus teaches the developing child two things about gender. First . . . it teaches the substantive network of sex-related associations that can come to serve as a cognitive schema. Second, it teaches that the dichotomy between male and female has extensive and intensive relevance to virtually every aspect of life.

The conception of the genders as "separate but equal" seems increasingly untenable to me. One of the main points of this chapter was that gender categorization may lead to gender ingroup-outgroup bias and that gender segregation contributes to gender categorization. Most social roles are occupied primarily by members of one or the other gender and from an early age most individuals limit their close friendships to members of the same sex. Once we identify ourselves as female or male and derive part of our self-esteem and identity from our gender, we are motivated to interact primarily with members of our own gender. Ingroup and out-group processes then emerge and foster greater separation and stereotyping of the genders. Women who become aware of their lower social status may foster group pride and solidarity by viewing men as an outgroup. Men may feel attacked and come to see women as an outgroup. Histori-cally, separate ceremonies, rituals, and separate spheres for females and males have been associated with lower power for women (Kimmel & Kaufman, 1994).

Social psychologists often recommend reducing intergroup conflict by emphasizing *superordinate goals,* goals that the conflicted groups have in common and that require cooperation to achieve. Those desiring changes in traditional gender roles may want to broaden support for those changes by emphasizing the benefits that would accrue to both males and females, and that change would be consistent with a democra-tic emphasis on equality. Instead of seeing men or women as the out-group, people should be encouraged to view the social institutions which limit individuals as the "enemy." It is also important that both genders avoid viewing the behaviors suggested by gender stereotypes as in-evitable and dispositionally caused. Instead, people should focus on the situational causes of the differences between the genders such as differen-tial socialization and sex-segregated social roles. This would give us greater hope for change and would direct our change efforts.

Gender schemas are powerful and resistant to change because they draw their power from three sources. First, they are socially rewarded and, as discussed in Chap. 1, there is significant social pressure to comply with them. Second, it appears that we may derive part of our self-esteem from our gender identity. Third, our gender stereotypes operate as schemas and guide information processing such that behaviors are inter-preted in ways consistent with our expectations. It is easy to get discour-aged about the prospects for changing gender stereotypes when we real-ize there are several powerful forces driving their continued use. But there is hope. Devine (1989) found that we can consciously override our stereo-types if we are aware of them. Educating people about their stereotypes and reminding people when they are behaving in a sex-stereotypical fash-ion also has the effect of reducing sex-biased behavior and perceptions (Geis, 1993). The effects of schemas may also be undermined when indi-viduals are aware of the ways in which schemas may bias their thinking and when they are challenged to think of instances that contradict their schemas (Cross & Markus, 1993). The social psychological research on the reduction of racial prejudice is also relevant. Cook (1985) suggested that a number of conditions are necessary before prejudice is reduced. Applying these conditions to gender stereotypes, we can expect that multiple exposures to nonstereotypic persons under equal-status conditions, and social information suggesting that schemas should be changed, are probably necessary before gender schemas will be widely altered. In Chap. 7 we will discuss more specifically how this may be done.

SUMMARY

- Cognitive categorizations called schemas reduce the amount of information we must process. Information that is consistent with our schemas is more easily noticed, stored, and retrieved.

- Gender stereotypes serve as schemas such that we are more likely to notice and remember instances which confirm our existing beliefs about the genders. Gender schemas are "primed" and readily available to guide information processing due to a cultural insistence on the importance of gender distinctions.

- If people notice schema-inconsistent instances, they may develop subcategories that allow maintenance of the overall stereotype or they may simply classify them as exceptions to the rule. In general, schemas are quite resistant to change.

- Because our expectations and stereotypes lead us to notice cases that confirm what we already believe, illusory correlations often occur between gender and particular skills, abilities, or behaviors. People often make these based on very small samples and dramatic cases.

- Our gender stereotypes may affect our behavior toward individuals, which then elicits behavior consistent with our stereotypes. This is called a self-fulfilling prophecy.

- Gender segregation in the social roles and friendships contributes to our seeing the other gender as the opposite sex. Emphasizing gender differences contributes to ingroup-outgroup bias and between-gender conflict.

- Our natural information-processing tendencies, along with a culture that emphasizes gender distinctions, are partly responsible for gender categorization. In addition, individuals often have an emotional investment in seeing the genders as different because they derive part of their social identities from their gender categories.

- Strongly identifying with a group may be a powerful source of identity, and putting down outgroups may boost self-esteem and motivate struggles for social change. However, conflict between groups commonly results from the exaggeration of group differences and the perception of aggression that accompany strong identifications and outgroup putdowns.

6

Gender across Cultures

❖

Pancultural Gender Similarities ✦ *Division of Labor Based on Sex* ✦ *Gender Stereotyping* ✦ *Differential Gender Socialization* ✦ *Females' Lower Status and Power* ✦ Cross-Cultural Gender-Role Ideologies ✦ Concluding Remarks ✦ Summary

C ulture is the set of attitudes, values, beliefs, and behaviors shared by a group of people, and communicated from one generation to the next via language or some other means of communication (Matsumoto, 1994). Are women and men perceived in other countries in the same ways as they are in our culture? Are there gender roles in every culture, and if so, why? Are there pancultural (universal) similarities in gender roles? Early in the book I noted that the study of gender by psychologists has largely been the study of gender in American, middle-class, white society. Social psychologists are increasingly aware of a need for a more cross-cultural social psychology. One reason for this increased awareness is that science aspires to be universal and we need cross-cultural research to find out if our findings are true of other cultures (Moghaddam et al., 1993; Triandis, 1994). Another reason is to avoid ethnocentrism and the assumption that because something is common in our own culture it is "normal" and representative of humankind. A third reason is because culture matters—how we behave and what we think is influenced by our culture, and a cross-cultural psychology can help us determine to what extent psychological processes vary as a result of culture (Williams & Best, 1990b). A cross-cultural study of gender also permits us to further examine the role that culture plays in the creation and maintenance of gender and gender differences.

Some people see the cross-cultural study of gender as important because they assume that cultural universals will indicate the biological bases of gender differences. In other words, if a particular gender difference is consistent across cultures that are otherwise quite different, one can assume that the difference has a biological basis. However, it is difficult to determine whether similarities are indicative of evolutionary factors (and thereby are genetically encoded) or whether they reflect common solutions to survival problems that humans in all cultures face because of the biology of the human species (and thereby are the result of cultural learning). For instance, virtually every society has developed a drinking cup with a handle. This does not mean, however, that there is a "handled cup gene" that was naturally selected for. Rather, it means that humans had a common need for such a cup, and responded by making such items. Similarly, child-rearing is largely delegated to women in virtually every society, whereas hunting and making war are male activities. While these role divisions could have an evolutionary basis, they may have occurred because breast-feeding made these other activities difficult for women (Singleton, 1987).

This chapter explores gender from a broad cross-cultural perspective. This is a relatively new area in the psychological study of gender. The brevity of the chapter is a reflection of this newness, not of its importance. Many of the studies cited here were conducted by psychologists from countries other than the United States, or with their cooperation. To my knowledge, no one has systematically surveyed the psychological study of gender worldwide. Unfortunately, because of language barriers, I have probably left out a number of important studies published in languages other than English.

*P*ANCULTURAL GENDER SIMILARITIES

Cross-cultural psychologists often speak of "etics" and "emics." *Etics* are general, or universal aspects of societies, whereas *emics* are characteristics unique to a culture. As Berry (1980) explained, these terms were coined by Pike (1954) and are derived from the linguistic terms "phonetics" and "phonemics." Phonemics focuses on sounds which are unique to a particular language system whereas phonetics refers to the general or universal aspects of language. If you drop the root (phon-), the two remaining suffixes (-emics and -etics) can be used to represent this local versus universal distinction.

My reading of the cross-cultural gender literature suggests that there are four *gender etics,* or ways in which otherwise diverse cultures tend to be similar in regard to gender. These are (1) a division of labor based on sex (gender roles), (2) beliefs or stereotypes regarding how females and males are different (gender stereotypes), (3) the differential socialization of male and female children, and (4) the lower power and status of females.

These gender etics arose out of all being members of the human species. As mentioned earlier in the book, physical differences between females and males gave rise to gender-based divisions of labor and fostered different behaviors based on gender. As Bem (1993) noted, once upon a time all cultures had no means of birth control, no infant formula, and few instruments that made physical strength less relevant. It appears that gender stereotypes then arose in order to further justify the divisions of labor arising from these conditions (Hoffman & Hurst, 1990), and gender roles became embedded in culture since "socially useful belief systems become incorporated into cultural practices" (Williams & Best, 1990a, p. 240). Children are then differentially socialized in order to prepare them for their different roles (Willams & Best, 1990a).

Division of Labor Based on Sex

Historically, females and males have had different jobs in almost every culture (Almeida Acosta & Sanchez de Almeida, 1983; Davidson & Thomson, 1980; Munroe & Munroe, 1975). According to the United Nations (1991), everywhere in the world the workplace is segregated by sex. Gender-based divisions of labor begin early, in childhood chores (Whiting & Edwards, 1988). For instance, in Mexico, El Salvador, Argentina, South Africa, Peru, the United States, and Pakistan, it is customary for girls to cook, clean, do laundry, and care for younger siblings while boys do more "outside" work such as yard chores. Although gender-based divisions of labor are the rule, the specific kinds of work done by each sex are not necessarily identical from one culture to another. For example, in Senegal women control the rice fields whereas in Sierra Leone males do, and in sub-Saharan Africa women are the chief agriculturalists but in Latin America men are. What men and women do in a culture often changes over time because of technological, ecological, and political change. What does not seem to change much, however, is that women and men are assigned different tasks and, because of this, live to some extent in separate worlds (Bernard, 1987).

Although there are significant cross-cultural variations in the jobs that men and women do, in every society women continue to do most of the household labor (United Nations, 1985) and childcare (Engle & Breaux, 1994). Lower paternal involvement has been documented in such diverse countries as West Africa (Nsamenang, 1992); China (Jankowiak, 1992); Belize, Kenya, Nepal, and Samoa (Munroe & Munroe, 1992); Thailand (Tulananda et al., in press); the United States (Pleck, 1985; Russell & Radin, 1983); Japan (Ishii-Kuntz, 1993); and Puerto Rico (Roopnarine & Ahmeduzzaman, 1993). The general worldwide pattern is that fathers spend approximately one-third of the time mothers do in providing childcare (Engle & Breaux, 1994), although there are a few exceptions such as the hunter-gatherer Aka pygmies of the southern Central African Republic and the northern People's Republic of the Congo (Hewlett, 1992). Lamb (1981) suggested that this sex-based division of childcare labor was aggravated by industrialization, which required fathers to leave the home for large parts of the day in order to work at jobs where children's presence was viewed as inappropriate. Furthermore, labor market changes eliminated the way that fathers traditionally spent time with their children (i.e., training children in family occupations such as farming) (Lamb, 1981). Other writers (Bloom-Fesbach, 1981) have noted that, in societies where labor is such that fathers are more physically present, greater paternal involvement in childrearing occurs.

It is also common all over the world for employed women to do the majority of household labor (United Nations, 1991). In Chap. 3 we discussed how American employed women do a disproportionate share of the household labor. Similar patterns are seen in Japan (Lebra, 1984), the countries making up the former Soviet Union (Kerig et al., 1993), Israel (Anson et al., 1990), Bangladesh (Ilyas, 1990), Greece (Dubisch, 1993), and Switzerland (Charles & Hopflinger, 1992).

Sex-based divisions of labor probably arose because of physical differences related to the childbearing and nursing abilities of women, and the greater size and strength of men (Bloom-Feshbach, 1981). Work that is compatible with the female life course, particularly childrearing, tends to be assigned to women (Bernard, 1987). Sociobiologists such as Tiger and Shepher (1975) often argue that sex-based divisions of labor are biologically destined and hormones make women more naturally suited for childcare. Psychologists like Lamb (1981), however, point out that, in humans, biological predispositions are tendencies, not imperatives, and can be overridden by cultural influences. Observational research, for example, has documented fathers from a number of cultures in nurturant and affectionate interactions with their infants and children (Bronstein, 1984; Lamb et al., 1982; Parke & Neville, 1987; Pedersen et al., 1980; Russell, 1986). However, sex-based divisions of labor and gender norms appear to limit the length and frequency of these interactions. Males in most societies receive little preparation for parenting in comparison to females, who grow up helping with the household labor and caring for younger children. Programs designed to teach fathers about child development and parenting increased the paternal involvement of men in several different countries (Engle & Breaux, 1994; Parke & Tinsley, 1981).

In the next section we discuss the gender stereotyping that may arise from sex-based divisions of labor and contribute to them as well.

Gender Stereotyping

In Chap. 5 we discussed how humans' natural information-processing tendencies lead to gender stereotyping. It seems likely that the tendency to categorize on the basis of group membership is universal because of the universal biology of the human brain. Furthermore, categorization by gender is likely in every culture because of the salience of gender arising from gender-based divisions of labor and cultural information encouraging the gender distinction. Recall also Eagly's (1987) social roles theory. This theory suggests that gender stereotypes arise from the differing roles occupied by females and males. Women are viewed as suited for the roles they typically occupy and men for the roles they typically occupy. The distribution of the sexes into different social roles leads us to expect communal behavior from females (interpersonal sensitivity, emotional expressiveness) and agentic behavior from males (assertive, independent, etc.).

The most definitive work in the area of cross-cultural beliefs regarding differences in the psychological traits of men and women (gender-trait stereotypes) was reported by psychologists John Williams and Deborah Best in their book *Measuring Sex Stereotypes: A Thirty-Nation Study* (1990a). They began with the following:

> Imagine yourself talking with a friend who describes two persons you have not met. One is said to be adventurous, autocratic, coarse, dominant, forceful, independent, and strong, while the other is described as affectionate, dependent, dreamy, emotional, sentimental, submissive, and weak . . . . If you find it easier to imagine the first person as a man and the second as a woman, then you have just demonstrated your knowledge of sex-trait stereotypes . . . . Does it matter what nationality you are? Probably not. You could be Canadian, Peruvian, Nigerian, Pakastani, or Japanese. In all of these countries, the traits in the first group are considered more characteristic of men than women and the traits in the second are considered more characteristic of women than men. (p. 15)

Williams and Best (1990a) were interested in cross-cultural *sex-trait stereotypes,* beliefs about the psychological "makeup" of women and men. In order to ascertain what psychological traits are believed to characterize women more than men, and vice versa, Williams and Best (1990a) had college-aged females and males in twenty-five countries indicate the extent to which 300 adjectives were associated with men relative to women in their cultures. To do this, they had cooperating researchers in each country administer the questionnaire. Subjects received the following instructions (translated when appropriate):

> We are interested in studying what we have termed the typical characteristics of men and typical characteristics of women. It is true that not all men are alike nor are all women alike. However, in our culture some characteristics are more frequently associated with men than with women and some are more frequently associated with women than with men.
>
> The sheet contains a list of 300 adjectives which are sometimes used to describe people . . . . For each adjective, you are to decide whether it is more frequently associated with men rather than women, or more frequently associated with women than men . . . .
>
> You are being asked to serve as an observer and reporter of the charac-

teristics generally said to be associated with men and women in our culture. You are not being asked whether you believe that it is true that men and women differ in these ways and you are not being asked whether you approve of the assignment of different characteristics to men and women. (p. 51)

Of the 300 items, forty-nine were associated with males in at least nineteen of the twenty-five countries (75 percent of the countries) while only twenty-five items were associated with females. See Table 6.1 for a list of these adjectives. The general pattern of these adjectives suggests that men are perceived to be autocratic, independent, aggressive, dominant, active, adventurous, courageous, unemotional, rude, progressive, and wise. In contrast, women are said to be dependent, submissive, fearful, weak, emotional, sensitive, affectionate, dreamy, and superstitious. Williams and Best (1990a) noted, however, that there were a few exceptions to these "rules." For instance, arrogant, lazy, robust, and rude were associated with males in most countries but in Nigeria they were associated with women. Sympathetic was associated with males in Italy and France, and affected with men in Germany. In Malaysia, assertive, ingenious, and humorous were associated with women. In Japan, it was women, not men, who were seen as boastful, disorderly, and obnoxious. Williams and Best (1990a) also found that countries differed in the degrees to which they differentiated between the sexes on the traits. Some, such as Germany and Malaysia, strongly differentiated between the sexes while others, such as India and Scotland, did not.

How do the male- and female-associated items in various countries differ in their relative favorability toward females and males? Williams and Best (1990a) answered this question by first having a group of 100 American subjects rate each of the 300 adjectives using a 5-point index of favorability. For each country, a mean favorability score for the male set of adjectives and the female set was computed. There was considerable variability among the countries in the favorability associated with both the male and female stereotypes. For instance, in Australia, Brazil, Peru, and Italy, male stereotypes were relatively unfavorable while in Japan, Nigeria, South Africa, and Malaysia they were relatively favorable. In contrast, relatively favorable stereotypes of females were held in Italy, Peru, and Scotland, while unfavorable ones were held in South Africa, Nigeria, Japan, and Malaysia. Out of the twenty-five countries, there was no apparent difference between the favorability of the male and female stereotypes in only Finland and Trinidad. Out of the remaining twenty-three countries, there were eleven in which the male stereotypes were to some degree more favorable and twelve in which greater favorability was associated with the female stereotypes. (*Note*: It is important to remember that favorability was assessed by American college students whereas in actuality favorability may depend upon culture, i.e., the same trait may be perceived negatively in one culture but positively in another.)

TABLE 6.1 ITEMS ASSOCIATED WITH MALES OR FEMALES IN AT LEAST NINETEEN OF TWENTY-FIVE COUNTRIES* (NUMBER OF COUNTRIES SHOWN IN PARENTHESES)

Male-Associated Items ($n = 49$)

Active (23)	Ingenious (19)
Adventurous (25)	Initiative (21)
Aggressive (24)	Inventive (22)
Ambitious (22)	Lazy (21)
Arrogant (20)	Logical (22)
Assertive (20)	Loud (21)
Autocratic (24)	Masculine (25)
Boastful (19)	Obnoxious (19)
Clear-thinking (21)	Opportunistic (20)
Coarse (21)	Progressive (23)
Confident (19)	Rational (20)
Courageous (23)	Realistic (20)
Cruel (21)	Reckless (20)
Daring (24)	Robust (24)
Determined (21)	Rude (23)
Disorderly (21)	Self-confident (21)
Dominant (25)	Serious (20)
Egotistical (21)	Severe (23)
Energetic (22)	Stern (24)
Enterprising (24)	Stolid (20)
Forceful (25)	Strong (25)
Hardheaded (21)	Unemotional (23)
Hardhearted (21)	Unkind (19)
Humorous (19)	Wise (23)
Independent (25)	

Female-Associated Items ($n = 25$)

Affected (20)	Meek (19)
Affectionate (24)	Mild (21)
Anxious (19)	Pleasant (19)
Attractive (23)	Sensitive (24)
Charming (20)	Sentimental (25)
Curious (21)	Sexy (22)
Dependent (23)	Shy (19)
Dreamy (24)	Softhearted (23)
Emotional (23)	Submissive (25)
Fearful (23)	Superstitious (25)
Feminine (24)	Talkative (20)
Gentle (21)	Weak (23)
Kind (19)	

*The 25 countries included Australia, Bolivia, Brazil, Canada, England, Finland, France, Germany, Ireland, India, Italy, Israel, Japan, Malaysia, Netherlands, New Zealand, Nigeria, Norway, Pakistan, Peru, Scotland, South Africa, Trinidad, United States, and Venezuela.
SOURCE: From J. E. Williams and D. L. Best, *Measuring Stereotypes: A Multination Study*. Copyright 1990 by Sage Publications, Inc. Reprinted by permission of Sage Publications, Inc.

Williams and Best (1990a) looked at indexes of economic and social development as well as the countries' major religions in order to explain differences between the countries on favorability of the stereotypes. The only variable that seemed to have much explanatory power was religion. Countries with religious traditions in which females were more visible (allowed to participate in religious ceremonies), virtuous, and powerful (i.e., there were major female deities or saints) had more favorable stereotypes of women. For instance, Catholic countries generally had more favorable female stereotypes than Protestant ones (Catholicism has both the Virgin Mary and nuns). Similarly, Pakistan had much more negative stereotypes of females than India. In the Muslim theology of Pakistan, all significant religious figures are male and religious practice is controlled by men. In contrast, the Hindu Indians studied by Williams and Best have a religious tradition which includes female goddesses, and both men and women serve in Hindu temples and are responsible for religious rituals.

Williams and Best (1990a) acknowledged that the finding that female and male stereotypes are similar in favorability is initially surprising in light of the common view that male traits are socially more desirable. They suggested that the greater desirability of the male stereotypes is not as much due to their "goodness" as measured by the favorability index as to the greater strength and activity associated with them. To test this hypothesis, they had 100 American college students rate the 300 adjectives on a 5-point weak/strong scale and another 100 students rate them on a 5-point active/passive scale. They then computed a mean activity score for the female stereotypes for each country, a mean activity score for the male stereotypes for each country, a mean strength score for the female stereotypes for each country, and a mean strength score for the male stereotypes for each country. The findings? In every country the female stereotypes were rated as more passive and weaker than the male stereotypes.

How did the countries differ in terms of representing achievement, nurturance, and other psychological qualities? Earlier in the book we noted that masculinity is typically associated with achievement, autonomy, and striving for control whereas femininity is associated with interpersonal communion, communality, and the awareness and active expression of one's own feelings (Ickes & Barnes, 1978). Researchers such as Bakan (1966) have classified these into two general categories, *agency* and *communion*, where agency is associated with the male, and communion with the female. Williams and Best (1990a) found agentic characteristics were more frequently associated with the male stereotypes while communal characteristics were more frequently associated with the female.

While Williams and Best (1990a) found cross-cultural differences in the extent to which female and male stereotypes differed from country to country and some differences in the content of the stereotypes themselves, the overall pattern of their results suggested a remarkable pancultural similarity in gender stereotypes. Is this pancultural similarity evidence for a fundamental biological difference between men and women?

Williams and Best (1990a) did not think so. They suggested that gender stereotypes are ancient in origin and stem from a division of labor where women are primarily responsible for domestic labor and men for labor outside of the home. Because this division of labor largely persists even today, they reasoned, so do agentic stereotypes of men and communality ones of women. Williams and Best (1990a) predicted that, as these roles change, gender stereotypes should change as well. In support of this, they did find that in countries where economic development had occurred and more women became employed outside the home, gender-role ideology (beliefs about the proper roles of men and women) became more liberal (Williams & Best, 1990b). Seginer et al. (1990) also found differences in gender-role ideology between Israeli Jews and Arabs to mirror gender-role differences in the two cultures.

Differential Gender Socialization

Williams and Best (1990a), Hoffman and Hurst (1990), and Eagly (1987) have all suggested that gender stereotypes arise out of gender roles. Once established, the stereotypes act as norms for females and males and provide models for gender-role socialization (Eagly, 1987; Williams & Best, 1990a). The conditions giving rise to gender socialization in the United States are not unique. There exists a pancultural tendency to teach and learn gender-appropriate behavior, although what is taught varies somewhat from culture to culture. Unfortunately, there is not much high-quality research on this topic and much of that available is based on observations made by anthropologists from the 1950s through the 1970s. These measures were often subjective and because social norms regarding gender have changed in many cultures, they may not accurately reflect current social practices.

Throughout the book we have discussed the variety of ways in which children in the United States learn gender roles, and the dynamics underlying the learning of and conformity to these roles. There is little reason to expect that these processes would not be cross-cultural. For instance, all humans have brains that categorize according to salient features of the environment. Categorization by gender is likely in all cultures because in all cultures men and women look different and occupy different roles, and every culture encourages distinctions by gender. Munroe et al. (1984) found that children in Belize, Kenya, Nepal, and American Samoa exhibited the same patterns of cognitive gender development found in U.S. children. Individuals everywhere rely on others for the satisfaction of physical and social needs, and information to help them understand their social world. Therefore it is not surprising that, once children realize the importance of gender to their culture, they model accordingly. For example, Whiting and Edwards (1988) noted that a cross-cultural concern for gender identity and appropriate sex-role behavior explains a cross-cultural tendency for children to seek out same-sex companions. Whiting and Edwards (1988) found that mothers assigned different chores to boys and girls in the six cultures they studied. Many cultures have initiation ceremonies during childhood or adolescence that further emphasize the importance of gender. Gender is important to society no matter what the society is or where it is located, and so gender is important to every human being.

Societies further increase the salience of gender by directing children's behavior toward gender-appropriate activities and by reinforcing gender-appropriate behavior. For instance, Rogoff (1981) found that five- to six-year-old Guatemalan children were teased by older children if they did not conform to gender roles and consequently became more sex-typed in the chores they would do. In 1994, when Kate O'Neil and I asked people from Argentina, Peru, Ecuador, El Salvador, Mexico, South Africa, and Pakistan, "What happens in your country if a child doesn't do what is expected of his or her sex?" everyone responded that noncomforming individuals were punished through teasing, ridicule, reprimand, and sometimes physical punishment. All of the respondents were able to provide derogatory slang names for children who did not conform to their gender roles. For instance, girls who act like boys in Ecuador are called "huevona," or "girls with balls." In Mexico, Ecuador, and Argentina boys who show femininity are called "maricon," which respondents translated into English as "fag."

Remember that the purpose of gender-role socialization is to teach our children what is socially appropriate for their gender and to prepare them for adult roles. To the extent that sexual divisions of labor are similar across cultures, we could expect gender-role socialization to be similar as well. One early study of 110 cultures (Barry et al., 1957) found clear pan-cultural similarity in the differential socialization of boys and girls. In particular, Barry et al. (1957, 1967, 1976) found that there was a greater emphasis on nurturance, obedience, and responsibility for girls, and achievement and self-reliance for boys.

A 1981 reanalysis of the Barry et al. (1957) data by Welch and Page compared gender socialization patterns in African countries with other countries in the sample. They found that African societies closely resembled non-African societies in the communication of different values and behaviors to male and female children (although male children in African societies encountered greater pressure to conform to male norms than did children in the other societies). A reanalysis of the Barry et al. (1976) data by Low (1989) found that girls were more likely to be encouraged to be industrious, responsible, and obedient in contrast to boys who were encouraged to be more self-reliant, competitive, aggressive, and tough (show fortitude). Low (1989), however, noted significant cultural variations in the extent to which this was the case. Her analysis indicated that males were encouraged to be more achievement-oriented in polygamous societies (where success buys one the opportunity to have more wives and children). Also, in societies where women had greater control over resources there was less of a tendency to socialize girls to be obedient.

Whiting and Edwards (1988) examined anthropological data from Kenya, Liberia, India, Mexico, the Philippines, Okinawa, Guatemala, Peru, and two small communities in the United States in order to examine the cross-cultural role of gender in socialization (data were collected by different researchers in different years ranging from 1954 to 1975). They suggested that the main way gender socialization occurs is through the assignment of males and females to different settings where they interact with different categories of individuals and, consequently, learn different things. Across all the cultures studied, boys had greater access to the wider community than did girls, were more likely to be given responsibilities that took them further away from home, and had more free play and idle time and consequently greater access to the wider community. Girls were found more often with their mothers than were boys, and boys more often with their fathers than girls. Of the communities studied, this gender difference was smallest in the Philippine and Okinawa communities. These two had the most egalitarian relations between wives and husbands. Conversely, the difference was largest in the two communities that most greatly stressed gender differences beginning in early childhood (a community in Mexico and one in India). The researchers also noted early sexual divisions of labor where parents assigned different chores based on sex and where girls generally did more work than boys. They suggested that this occurred because the fathers were usually off working and the work which remained at home was considered female work. Mothers, they wrote, were therefore more likely to recruit the girls to help them. In the majority of the cultures studied by Whiting and Edwards (1988), girls also received earlier social pressure for proper social behavior and received more practice in the development of nurturance. Kerig et al. (1993) also noted that in Russia there were almost no household chores considered appropriate for boys.

Females' Lower Status and Power

Another pancultural gender similarity is that in every society women have lower status and less power than men. The United Nations' (1985) report titled *The State of the World's Women* concluded the following:

1. Women do almost all the domestic work.
2. Women grow half the food of the world but own hardly any land.
3. Women make up one-third of the world's official labor force but are concentrated in the lowest-paid occupations.

TABLE 6.2 WOMEN'S AVERAGE WAGES AS A PERCENTAGE OF MEN'S

Developed regions*	Africa	Asia and the Pacific
Iceland (90)	United Republic of	Jordan (79)
France (89)	Tanzania (92)	Sri Lanka (75)
Australia (87)	Kenya (76)	Hong Kong (74)
Denmark (82)	Swaziland (73)	Singapore (69)
New Zealand (79)	Egypt (64)	Cyprus (59)
Netherlands (77)		Republic of Korea (50)
Belgium (74)		
Germany (73)		
United Kingdom (70)		
Czechoslovakia (68)		
Switzerland (67)		
Luxembourg (65)		
Japan (52)		

*For Latin America and the Caribbean there were no data available. The United States is not included, although you may recall from Chap. 3 that the figure is approximately 70 percent.
SOURCE: From United Nations, *The World's Women: Trends and Statistics 1970-1990* (New York), based on International Labour Office, *Yearbook of Labour Statistics* 1989 (Geneva).

4. Women earn less than three-quarters of the wages that men earn for doing similar work.

5. Ninety percent of all countries have organizations that promote the advancement of women but women are still dramatically underrepresented in the decision-making bodies of their countries.

In Chap. 3 we discussed the existence of a "glass ceiling" for women in the United States. This pattern is repeated throughout the world, albeit with considerable variation. For instance, in Bangladesh and Indonesia, women hold only 1 percent of managerial jobs, while in Norway and Australia the rate is about 33 percent (French, 1992). In Russia, women earn less than men for equivalent jobs and jobs held predominantly by women are low in prestige and poorly paid (Kerig et al., 1993). According to the United Nations, women worldwide are almost always in less prestigious and lower-paid jobs than men. As the level, prestige, and pay increase for types of jobs, so do the numbers of men in those job categories (United Nations, 1991). Everywhere women are paid less than men (on average 30 to 40 percent less) although this varies considerably from region to region (see Table 6.2).

Also according to the United Nations (1991), women make up less than 5 percent of the world's heads of state, heads of major corporations, and top positions in international organizations. Only six of the 159 U.N. member states were headed by women in 1990: Iceland, Ireland, Nicaragua, Norway, Dominica, and the Philippines (United Nations, 1991). In 1987 only 10 percent of parliamentary positions were held by women worldwide (United Nations, 1991). In nonindustrial and developing nations, women hold about 6 percent of government posts in comparison to about 5 to 11 percent in European nations (French, 1992). Women, however, have long been leaders in their communities and at grass roots' levels, and women are leaders of many important environmental protection and peace organizations (United Nations, 1991). Involvement in such organizations may be more consistent with a female role that takes responsibility for family health and well-being. It is also the case that such organizations are often begun by women and women do not have to run for office in order to assume leadership positions in them.

One major barrier to women's equal status worldwide is education. Poor education and training limit many women to menial low-paying jobs that are becoming increasingly rare because of mechanization. Mechanization has created greater opportunities for those with administrative and technical skills—skills that men are overwhelmingly more likely to learn through their greater educational opportunities (United Nations, 1991). There are more illiterate women than men in all parts of the world—about 597 million women in 1985 in comparison to 352 million men (United Nations, 1991). Major gains in education have been made and in most developed countries there is near universal literacy among young people. But this is not the case in rural areas and in many developing countries. For instance, in Africa about 55 percent of women and 35 percent of men are illiterate. In southern Asia, almost 60 percent of women and 35 percent of men are illiterate. In many countries the picture for higher education is bright. In most developed countries the number of women in college is at least equal to that of men and in some cases is higher (United Nations, 1991). There is, however, more to changing women's lower status and power than education. Even when educated, women worldwide still face hiring biases, the "glass ceiling," and pay differentials.

Some social scientists have questioned the assumption that women are lower in status and power. For instance, Rogers (1985) argued that male dominance in peasant societies is a myth to which both men and women acquiesce, men because they want to give the appearance of power, and women because the myth satisfies men such that they leave the domestic realm to women, which in peasant societies is the real source of power. Triandis (1994) wondered if our definitions of power and status have not led us to overlook the power and status that women have in the household and the possibility that in some cultures women enjoy a "separate but equal" relationship. He discussed extensively the case of today's Japan, where, he wrote, wives manage the household finances and are free to work, go to school, or "write poetry" while husbands are "slaves to the corporation." Upper middle-class women in the United States may be perceived similarly. However, these are not the lives of the majority of women worldwide, nor even in the United States or Japan. For example, women make up half of Japan's employed workforce, but are concentrated in low level jobs and earn less than men (Sugisaki, 1986), and are expected to maintain their domestic duties even when employed full time (Lebra, 1984).

While there may be cases where the absence of women in politics or power positions in the workforce belie their power in the home, studies (Lips, 1991; Stroh et al., 1992; Weller, 1968) have found that, the larger a woman's monetary contribution to household income, the greater her decision-making power within it. In other words, men often have significant power even in what we think of as traditionally female domains. Engle (1993), for example, found that, in Guatemalan families, the greater a woman's income in comparison to the total family income, the greater her role in family decision-making (the only exception was food purchasing, which was her decision regardless). Triandis (1994) noted that wife-beating occurs in approximately 84 percent of societies, that adult women are most likely to be the victims and adult men the perpetrators of violence, and that wife-beating occurs most frequently in those societies where the husband has more economic and decision-making power than the wife.

Why are women usually lower in status and why do they have less power than men across the globe? Like a sex-based division of labor, this too may also originate in physical differences between the sexes. At one time, women were dependent on men for physical protection and economic help because of child-bearing and child-nursing. The smaller physical size of females also undoubtedly contributed to their domination as well. Triandis (1994) suggested that dangerous activities such as hunting and fighting were inappropriate for women and were glorified in order to get men to do them. According to him, the continued tradition of glorifying men's activities over women's is a remnant of what was once a functional cultural belief. Bem (1993) suggested that females may have been so preoccupied with babies and children and other responsibilities that they had fewer opportunities to institutionalize their power. Worldwide, women continue to be overwhelmingly responsible for housework and childcare and this limits both their economic and their political power.

CROSS-CULTURAL GENDER-ROLE IDEOLOGIES

Although there is remarkable similarity in pancultural gender stereotypes, divisions of labor by sex, and women's status globally, cultures do differ in beliefs about the proper role relationships between men and women (called *gender-* or *sex-role ideologies*). Some societies are more *traditional*, believing that men are more important than women and have the right to dominate them, while others are more modern and *egalitarian* and assume that men and women are equally important and men should not dominate women (Williams & Best, 1990b).

Women are consistently found to be more egalitarian than men when it comes to gender-role ideology. This finding has been found with Americans (Spence & Helmrich, 1978), Lebanese (Spence & Helmrich, 1978), Israeli Jews and Arabs (Seginer et al., 1990), Northern Irish (Kremer & Curry, 1987), British, Irish, and Canadian subjects (Kalin et al., 1982), Fijians (Basow, 1986a), Brazilians (Spence & Helmrich, 1978), in eight of fourteen cultures studied by Williams and Best (1990b), and in a study of international students representing forty-six countries (Gibbons et al., 1991). This gender difference probably occurs because the advantages of greater gender equality are more obvious to females, who, as we have already noted, generally experience a lower status due to their sex.

Williams and Best (1990b) studied gender-role ideology in fourteen countries (Netherlands, Germany, Finland, England, Italy, Venezuela, United States, Canada, Singapore, Malaysia, Japan, India, Pakistan, Nigeria) using the SRI (Sex-Role Ideology Scale) developed by Kalin and Tilby (1978). The SRI requires that respondents indicate how strongly they agree with each of thirty items such as: "The first duty of a woman with young children is to home and family," "For the good of the family, a wife should have sexual relations with her husband whether she wants to or not," and "Woman's work and men's work should not be fundamentally different in nature." Williams and Best (1990b) found significant cross-cultural variations in the extent to which respondents held traditional or modern ideologies. The order of the fourteen countries in the first sentence of this paragraph reflects their findings. The first country, Netherlands, had the most egalitarian gender-role ideology of the fourteen countries studied and the last, Nigeria, had the most traditional and least egalitarian views.

Williams and Best (1990b) then correlated the SRI scores with economic development, religion, the percentage of women employed outside the home, and the percentage of women attending universities in each country. The results from these analyses indicated that gender-role ideology shifts toward being more egalitarian with economic development, that Muslim countries have more traditional ideologies than Christian countries, and that higher numbers of employed women, and women in the university, are associated with more egalitarian gender-role ideologies. Significant variations in gender-role ideology may also occur within a culture based on education, generation, and acculturation into other societies. This point is well illustrated in a review of the research literature on gender role ideology in Hispanic women by Vazquez-Nuttall et al. (1987). That review found that Hispanic women having greater contact with Anglo-American society had more egalitarian conceptions of gender roles (Canino, 1982; Espin & Warner, 1982; Kranau et al., 1982; Torres-Matrullo, 1980); better-educated Hispanic women had more liberal ideologies (Pacheco, 1981; Soto & Shaver, 1982); and older generations held more conservative ideologies than younger ones (Rosario, 1982; Soto & Shaver, 1982).

CONCLUDING REMARKS

This chapter has largely focused on *gender etics* (cultural universals) but *gender emics* (cultural specifics) are important, especially when considering the process of gender role change. There are several issues here. One is that culture affects the extent to which the individual is willing not to conform. Social change may occur more quickly in those countries where obedience to authority and allegiance to group norms are not as great as in those where they are. Western cultures, such as that in the United States, are characterized by cross-cultural psychologists as "individualistic" societies. In individualistic societies there is greater interest in self-promotion, individual rights, and independence (Hofstede, 1984; Hui & Triandis, 1986), and this may make it easier to go against prevailing social norms. Collectivistic societies, such as that in Japan, emphasize the subordination of individual goals to the goals of the collective as evidenced in a greater concern for the needs of others and interdependence (Hui & Triandis, 1986). Conformity and obedience in such societies is socially encouraged and valued to a greater extent than in American culture. Moghaddam et al. (1993) also suggested that cultures which encourage obedience to elders may be more resistant to social change because people may become more resistant to change as they age.

Another issue affecting gender-role change has to do with a culture's beliefs regarding equality. Goffman (1977) predicted that gender roles will shift as societies shift from a belief that these roles are based on biological differences to a belief in general social equality. However, social equality is not a dominant value in many cultures. For instance, in India, the caste system results in differential treatment based on the social group into which one is born. This system is grounded in Hindu religious beliefs suggesting that one is born into a caste based upon his/her behavior in past lives. Thus stratification, or wide variations in social class, is accepted in India to a large extent. Although the United States is more socially stratified than most Americans like to admit, U.S. culture is based on an ideology that stratification is undesirable (e.g., "All men are created equal"). Perhaps, then, it is not surprising that the women's movement originated in the United States and has taken greater hold there and in other individualistically oriented societies than elsewhere. Countries that are more openly stratified and accepting of class differences may foster a greater acceptance of inequality. Women's movements in these countries may have to rely on a different rationale than those in Western countries in order to garner support.

These factors suggest that the journey to gender equality may be different for different cultures. We have spoken a great deal in this chapter of pancultural gender similarities, but the specific changes needed, and how those may be brought about, vary depending upon culture. For instance, in the United States, a country based on individuality and personal freedom, it makes sense to motivate change by emphasizing how traditional gender roles interfere with personal freedom and equality. However, in Japan, a society that emphasizes the obligations of the individual to the social group, this emphasis is unlikely to be as effective.

Margolis (1993) remarked that specific issues often have very different connotations depending upon culture, and that the issue which galvanizes a particular movement in one country may hurt it in another. She gives the example of family planning. In the West, family planning and abortion have served as major mobilizing issues for women's movements, but such programs often arouse suspicion and opposition from Third World women who may see them as attempts to limit the population of their ethnic groups. This approach may also not make sense to women in countries where women's status is enhanced by having lots of children or where women need lots of children to help with agricultural labor. Similarly, Soh (1993) discussed how gender equality is incompatible with the widespread Korean Confucian worldview of yin/yang gender complementarity. She pointed out that women legislators in Korea owe their participation to being women, as they are almost always elected or appointed as representatives of the interests of women and children and are successful to the extent that they continue to behave in traditional ways in social situations and with regard to their families. In other words, the process by which gender equality is attained in Korea depends upon Korean culture.

Margolis (1993) examined women's movements for equality around the world. She focused on how these movements take different forms and center around different issues depending upon political, economic, and cultural differences. She cautioned us to guard against the "ethnocentric assumption that women's movements follow an evolutionary path that leads toward a movement similar to the one that has developed in the United States" (p. 386). In regard to politics, Bouchier (1984) suggested that egalitarian and liberal social movements do best where political culture is more liberal and egalitarian. He wrote that this is why Scandinavian countries and Holland have the largest and most integrated feminist organizations. Siemienska (1986) noted that gender reform is more likely in political systems based on pluralism (formal representation of a variety of group interests as opposed to one-party or one-class rule). Margolis (1993) noted that, while it may seem obvious that conservative governments who see the subordination of women as central to their platform may interfere with gender equality, the same can be said of leftist governments that tend to subordinate women's issues to the more general issues of worker exploitation.

Struggles for gender equality may also be subordinated to other political issues, particularly those involving economic and ethnic survival (Margolis, 1993). This is especially likely in Third World and developing nations, where basic survival is an issue or where ethnic conflict is present. For instance, Canadian psychologist Patricia Kerig and Russian psychologists Yulya Alyoshina and Alla Volovich said in a 1993 article that in modern Russia feminism is considered to be somewhat utopian and less important than more basic economic concerns. It is probably no coincidence that the women's movement in the United States took off during a time of relative economic prosperity and social calm following the civil rights movement and the Vietnam War, and was largely the work of middle-class white women. For women of color in the United States and women in the Third World, the most pressing concerns may be freedom from starvation and ethnic discrimination (Bulbeck, 1988). LaFromboise et al. (1990) noted that Native-American women are at least as concerned with the preservation of their race and culture as they are with women's equality. Furthermore, they suggested that Native-American gender equality movements will differ from other feminist movements as Native-American women seek a feminism that works within the context of Native-American families, their nations, and their views of Sacred Mother Earth.

There is an increasing awareness of the cultural issues discussed above and how Western feminism is often inapplicable to non-Western cultures. Some feel that cultural diversity is so great as to make impossible a common worldwide gender equality movement. In spite of these concerns, there is an increasing acceptance of human rights as a matter of international concern, and a current trend toward the legitimacy of international law, and this may help pave the way toward greater gender equality worldwide. In 1979 the United Nations' General Assembly adopted a convention stating that "discrimination against women is incompatible with human dignity and the welfare of society" and that "it is necessary to ensure the universal recognition in law and in fact of the principle equality of men and women" (Defeis, 1991). Nations that ratify the convention are required to eliminate discrimination against women in employment, education, and politics. One hundred and four of the UN member nations have ratified the convention. Unfortunately, the United States is not yet one of them, as ratification has been bogged down by various constitutional concerns (see Defeis, 1991, for a description). The United Nations also declared 1975–1985 as the "Decade of the Woman" and had three international conferences on women's issues in 1975, 1980, and 1985 (a brief history of the three conferences appears in Bernard, 1987). The Fourth International United Nations Conference on Women will be held in Beijing, China, in 1995. The work of the United Nations appears to have stimulated plans for the advancement of women in many countries as well as the collection of statistical information about the relative status of men and women. This enabled the UN to write a 1985 statistical report on the international status of women, something that had not been possible before.

A discussion of gender across cultures raises another issue: cherishing cultural diversity. A Mexican-American student, Lucilla, came to speak with me after a class discussion on gender roles. She said that she was conflicted because on the one hand she was a champion of her culture and wanted to promote its appreciation in the United States, but on the other she had a hard time accepting the treatment of women in her culture. Can we cherish cultural diversity and yet advocate that non-American cultures adopt the goals of gender equality? The question is an important one.

Katzenstein (1989) remarked that feminist values may conflict with traditional customs and it is a legitimate question to ask which should be privileged when this occurs. El-Bakri and Kameir (1983) objected to holding the role of women in the Middle East and Third World countries to the standards of Western democracies. We certainly do not want to be so presumptuous as to impose our Western worldview on others. Just because a culture is different from our own does not mean that it is wrong.

On the other hand, as Nussbaum (1992) pointed out, we can go too far in the worship of cultural difference. She cited a number of examples of scholars who have defended disturbing cultural practices out of reverence for the culture at hand. Doing so sounds dangerously close to what philosophers call "cultural relativism," the belief that something is morally right (or wrong) if the culture says it is right or wrong. As philosopher J. Rachels (1993) pointed out, it does not stand to reason that, just because cultures differ, right and wrong are matters of opinion. If we were to take cultural relativism seriously, we would have to agree that all sorts of questionable behaviors were not immoral because those countries in which they occur do not define them as immoral. Is wife-beating okay because it is an accepted cultural practice in Kuwait? What about the genital mutilation of females in some African countries? It is true that we should not reject cultural practices just because they are not our own and that we should not presume to understand fully the experiences of those in a different culture. And it is true that many cultural practices are nothing more than what Rachels (1986) called "social conventions" which, objectively speaking, are neither right nor wrong, and about which we should keep an open mind. But should we accept cultural practices that obviously result in serious harm to large segments of a society out of respect for an existing culture? If we had done so in the United States, we would not have abolished slavery, allowed women to vote, or passed civil rights legislation. As Rachels (1986) noted, moral progress cannot occur if we take cultural relativism too far. To say that cultural practices are right because a culture says they are does not permit us to call cultural practices into question and to change them when change is called for.

I agree with Rachels (1986) when he argued that some values transcend culture—that is, that some values are desirable regardless of culture. A little reflection will lead you to the same conclusion. For instance, you will surely agree that prohibitions on slavery are universally desirable. Rachels (1986) noted that another such value should be the impartial promotion of the interests of everyone alike, except when individuals deserve particular responses as a result of their own past behavior. Such a principle rules out racism and sexism. It is not defensible to treat individuals differently solely on the basis of their sex or race. This is not a universal value because I say so or because it is currently valued by Westerners. It should be a universal moral value because, as Rachels (1993) argued, it remains valid even after intense scrutiny. The bottom line is that gender equality and cultural diversity may sometimes clash, but respecting cultural diversity need not require unquestioned acceptance of all cultural practices. There are some universal values, such as gender and racial equality, that should lead us to be critical of some cultural practices and to promote their change.

SUMMARY

- It is often assumed that cultural universals (etics)—practices found in many societies around the world—indicate a biological basis underlying gender differences. However, it is difficult to say whether similarities occur because of evolutionary factors or whether they are common solutions to problems faced by humans the world over.
- Sex-based divisions of labor are common to all cultures, as are gender stereotypes, the differential socialization of male and female children, and the lower status and lower power of women in comparison to men.
- Sex-based divisions of labor begin in childhood. Overall, worldwide, fathers spend about one-third the time mothers do with children. All over the world, women do the majority of household labor, even when employed outside the home.
- There is evidence of pancultural similarity in gender stereotypes. In a twenty-five nation study, males were generally perceived as more agentic and females as more communal, although there were cultural differences in the degree to which countries differentiated between the sexes on these traits. In every country female stereotypes portrayed women as more weak and passive than men. Countries with religions where females play a prominent role had more favorable stereotypes of females than countries where all significant religious figures are male and religious practices are controlled by males.
- There are significant cross-cultural variations in how strongly different societies advocate traditional gender roles. However, in general all over the world, women are more egalitarian than men when it comes to gender-role ideology.

- Emics (cultural specifics) are particularly important in regard to changing gender roles. Change may occur more quickly in individualistic versus collectivistic cultures, and cultures where the political and cultural ideologies emphasize equality and minimal social stratification. Furthermore, the journey to gender equality is different depending upon the particular culture and those issues which have led to change in the United States may not be the ones that lead to change in other countries.
- We should not assume a cultural practice is wrong just because it is different from our own. However, we should not go so far in our championing of cultural diversity that we accept cultural practices involving ethnic or gender discrimination.

7

Changing Gender Roles

————— ❖ —————

The times are changing. Change may be occurring too quickly for some, but change is not occurring fast enough for many boys and girls limited by their gender roles to less than full lives.

Carol Nagy Jacklin, 1989

T his final chapter concentrates on the ways in which gender roles have changed, the changes still needed, and how to bring about change. Chapters 3 and 4 were intended to make the case that traditional gender roles need changing. Problems associated with the female role include low pay, low status and little power, and heavy workloads in the home. Limitations of the male role include impoverished relationships, lack of social support, and physical problems from overwork, overexercise, and risky behavior. These limitations point to changes needed in the roles. In this chapter we will also consider additional reasons for changing traditional gender roles.

157

CHANGES IN ATTITUDES

One of my favorite novels is *Woman on the Edge of Time* by Marge Piercy (1976). In it Piercy describes a genderless society in the year 2137. In this future, it is difficult at times to tell whether individuals are male or female. The language is gender-neutral—the words "she" and "he" are not even used. There is great individual freedom—individuals choose jobs and hobbies based on their individual gifts, regardless of their biological sex. Females and males parent equally, and are all called "mothers." The dominant values of Piercy's futuristic society are love, tenderness, independence, strength, and community, and these are not considered to be male or female values, but human values.

We are a long way off from such a future but there is evidence that things have changed in the direction of gender equality. You can easily get a sense of this from talking with your parents or grandparents. Oskamp (1991) traced trends in gender-role attitudes over a 50-year period. Using data from Gallup Polls conducted from 1937 to 1987, he noted that only 33 percent of the people surveyed in 1937 agreed that if their party nominated a woman for President they would vote for her if she was qualified. By 1987, 82 percent agreed. In 1988, public support for the Equal Rights Amendment, which states simply that "Equality of rights under the law shall not be denied or abridged by the United States or by any state on account of sex," rose to an all-time high of 73 percent from a low of 57 percent in 1976. Oskamp (1991) also noted that in the last 20 years there has been evidence of increased support for the women's movement. In 1985, 73 percent of women and 69 percent of men said they were in favor of "efforts to strengthen and change women's status in society" in comparison to 40 percent of women and 44 percent of men in 1970. A Gallup Poll conducted in 1993 and reported in *The Gallup Poll Monthly* by Newport, also showed how much attitudes have changed, and suggested that many Americans are supportive of changes in gender roles. In 1975, 48 percent of those polled said that women did not have equal job opportunities to men; in 1993, that percentage rose to 60 percent. In 1975, 68 percent of those polled approved of wives working even when they had a husband who could economically support them; in 1993, this figure rose to 86 percent. Ninety-nine percent of those polled in 1993 agreed that women should be paid the same salaries as men when doing the same work.

These are changes in attitudes but we know that attitudes are imperfect predictors of behavior. Has behavior changed? Yes, some. Women are entering management and other male-dominated jobs in record numbers and the gender pay gap has been reduced slightly over the last 10 years. In the United States, more women than ever hold elected political offices. Men are doing slightly more housework and many are spending more time with their children than their own fathers did. However, it is apparent from the information presented in earlier chapters that we still have a long way to go. In the next section, specific areas in which changes are needed and how to encourage those changes are discussed.

CHANGING THE WORKPLACE

Increasing the Compatibility of Work and Family

The behavior of individuals is influenced by the structure and norms of the environments in which they find themselves, as well as their own personal attitudes. For instance, in Chap. 3 we mentioned that women may want to work for pay, or husbands may want to stay home with the kids, but because of women's lower pay, these choices may not be economically feasible. Currently, the structure of the workplace inhibits gender-role change. Work organizations are still structured as if employees have a wife at home to assume total responsibility for family life (Biernat & Wortman, 1991). Powell (1990) wrote that we need to abandon the model of a successful career as an uninterrupted sequence of promotions and stop seeing any request to take time out from career for family reasons, either by a woman or a man, as evidence of a lack of career commitment. Both men and women should be able to temporarily leave the "fast track" in an organization and return to it later.

Family-Supportive Workplace Policies

According to Pleck (1993), the three most important family-supportive workplace policies are childcare supports, flexible schedules, and parental leave. Childcare supports include work-site childcare centers, purchasing or subsidizing childcare centers, providing information and referral services, and dependent-care reimbursement programs that allow employees to pay for childcare with pretax income. Flexible work schedules, which allow workers to begin and end their workdays as needed as long as they put in a required number of hours, have been found to increase the amount of time parents are able to spend with their children (Pleck, 1993). Okin (1989) suggested that both parents should be entitled to more flexible hours ("flextime") without career penalties for the first 7 years of a child's life. Finally, parental leave permits parents to take off work for the birth of a child. Parental leave policies vary widely, both in the length of time parents are allowed to take off and whether they are paid or unpaid. Unfortunately, family-supportive policies, particularly childcare supports and flexible work schedules, are currently the exception rather than the rule in most organizations.

The need for childcare is a reality for two-thirds of American families, and childcare must be shaped into an effective social institution that supports families in their responsibilities and serves the developmental needs of children (Zigler & Lang, 1990). Affordable, high-quality childcare is working parents' greatest need (Pleck, 1993). Admittedly, an employed mother goes against conventional wisdom regarding what is best for children. However, the majority of mothers have no choice but to work for pay, and, furthermore, a society that professes to be democratic cannot require mothers to stay home with their children (Zigler & Lang, 1990). The good news is that research finds school achievement, IQ scores, and the emotional and social development of working mothers' children are comparable to what is found in children whose mothers do not work (for example, see Clarke-Stewart, 1989; Scarr, 1984; Scarr et al., 1989). After reviewing research on the effects of maternal employment on children, Scarr et al. (1989) concluded that our fears about the effects of maternal employment on child development have more to do with socially determined theories about what is best for children than they do with scientific fact. They further pointed out that working parents are with their children for half of the children's waking hours and spend the same total amount of time in direct interaction with their children as do parents in families where only the father is employed. Crosby (1991) listed a number of benefits that children reap from having an employed mother including: increased contact with the work world, interpersonal resourcefulness and resilience, a decrease in sexist ideas about the genders, a higher standard of living, and positive self-regard and initiative.

The effects of daycare on children obviously depend upon the quality

©Anne Gibbons

Many people believe that daycare is harmful to children although there is little evidence to that effect.

of that care and research has identified those features of childcare supportive of children's development (see National Research Council, 1990; Zigler & Lang, 1990, for discussions). Unfortunately in America, financially advantaged families can afford adequate environments for their children while poor and middle-class families often cannot (Zigler & Lang, 1990). Also, because of a large pool of potential workers available to replace those who leave their jobs, there is currently little incentive for organizations to provide on-site childcare, paid parental leave, or flextime. Most employers do not believe they need new, expensive benefits to attract and keep employees, and many organizations cannot afford such benefits anyway. This means that government must play an important role. For instance, subsidies or tax breaks could be given to companies who develop on-site childcare programs. Zigler and Lang (1990) suggested many creative and tenable ways to provide quality (developmentally appropriate) childcare for the nation's children. The National Research Council's *Who Cares for America's Children: Child Care Policy for the 1990's* (1990) also has a good discussion of national objectives and alternative childcare policies.

The development of policies supportive of children with employed parents has not been a priority of our government. There are a number of reasons for this. One is that these are not difficulties most top government representatives have personally faced. There is also a continuing belief that women belong home with their children, and consequently there is a reluctance to do anything to discourage this arrangement (Zigler & Lang, 1990). Last, legislators pay the most attention to organized political groups and there is no organized "parents lobby." Crosby (1991) noted that working parents have not really rallied for reform because, deep down, they too believe that to share responsibility for childrearing with others is a shirking of their responsibilities. Parents are also reluctant to draw their employers' attention to their dual commitment to home and family because of the perception that they will be seen as less committed to the workplace. The employed parent also has little time for political organizing and involvement.

Increasing Gender Diversity in Organizations

Chapter 3 discussed a number of organizational factors that lead to women's lower pay and status. It was apparent from that discussion that pay equity programs and hiring and promotion policies to break the glass ceiling are needed. Powell (1990), in a review of research on sex differences in management, concluded that there is not much difference between the needs, values, and leadership styles of male and female managers. He suggested that it is important for the facts about sex differences in management to be disseminated to key decision makers in organizations. According to him, the implications of the research for organizations are clear: If there are no differences between female and male managers, companies should not act as though there are. They should become gender-blind in their decisions and should try to minimize differences in the job experiences of their male and female managers so that artificial sex differences in career success do not arise.

Affirmative action programs (AAPs) are one way to increase the number of individuals from traditionally underrepresented groups in organizations. Affirmative action programs or policies are intended to increase the number of women and other traditionally underrepresented groups, such as African-Americans, in jobs customarily held by Euroamerican males. As noted by Geis (1993), affirmative action is one way to provide multiple, socially supported female authority models so that people will see high status as acceptable and possible for women. Although affirmative action programs may involve targeted recruitment efforts, preferential selection on the basis of race or sex, special training programs, or race or gender as a "plus" factor for hiring or promotion, they are forbidden [by Supreme Court decisions such as *Johnson vs. Santa Clara County* (1987)] to involve strict "quotas" or the disregard of applicant qualifications. As mentioned in Chap. 4, such programs are one way to reduce gender segregation in the workplace. They encourage employers to widen the applicant field to include women and other underrepresented groups. Because common stereotypes of women and minorities lead employers to perceive them as inappropriate for jobs customarily held by white males, qualified minority and female applicants may not be seriously considered for a job without affirmative action policies in place. There are, however, a number of barriers to the effectiveness of such policies, to which we now turn.

One major problem plaguing affirmative action is *the assumption that affirmative action recipients are not qualified.* Heilman et al. (1992) found that there is a "stigma of incompetence" associated with affirmative action. When it is believed that a woman is an affirmative action hiree, both males and females rate her as less competent than women not associated with affirmative action. It appears that people assume that qualifications are not considered in the affirmative action hire, and that hirees are not well qualified. People also seem to reason that, if the affirmative action hiree was really competent, she would not have needed help from affirmative action (Heilman et al., 1992; Pettigrew & Martin, 1987). Such reasoning may occur because the traditionally lower status of women and minorities leads to the development of stereotypes to justify their lower status. When individuals from traditionally powerful groups achieve, their achievement is assumed to be based on merit, while the achievements of those from less powerful groups are played down (Eberhardt & Fiske, 1994). Affirmative action can even feed into stereotypes of women and minorities to the extent that they are seen as needing extra help because of their inferiority. As Eberhardt and Fiske (1994) pointed out, some people see blacks or women as needing help to advance because their stereotyped perceptions are that blacks are lazy and women dependent.

If others assume you are not qualified, your suggestions will go unheeded, your performance will be selectively processed, and you may encounter a noncooperative job climate. For instance, in a study of African-American female firefighters, 82 percent agreed that "it is not uncommon for a woman to present an idea and get no response, then a man will present the same idea and get praised," and 82 percent felt their mistakes were noticed more than the mistakes of others (Yoder & Aniakudo, 1994). The good news is that research indicates when observers are provided with information documenting the qualifications of an affirmative action recipient, they are less resistant and hostile to the hiring (Major et al., 1994; Murrell et al., 1994). Eberhardt and Fiske (1994) recommend that employers provide unambiguous information regarding the qualifications of newly hired or promoted women or minorities to other employees, to reduce their fears and suspicions.

Researchers and policy analysts have also wondered whether the stigmatization of affirmative action affects recipients' self-perceived competence. Indeed, some critics of affirmative action claim that it leads beneficiaries to doubt their skills and abilities and is thus harmful (Nacoste, 1990). Experimental studies have generally found that female subjects, led to believe they were selected for a task only because of their sex, devalue their performance (Heilman et al., 1987; Turner & Pratkanis, 1994; Turner et al., 1991). However, as pointed out earlier, in reality, affirmative action rarely involves a lack of consideration of qualifications and recipients know this. Also, most recipients probably do not feel as though they are not qualified. For instance, 77 percent of the African-American women firefighters studied by Yoder and Aniakudo (1994) reported that they were affirmative action hires, but none of these women thought that this undermined their own feelings of competence. Heilman et al. (1990) found that sex-based preferential selection produced negative self-perceptions of competence only when individuals already lacked confidence in their abilities. Furthermore, there is evidence that explicit, positive performance feedback and telling affirmative action recipients they are perceived as qualified may prevent the self-doubt and self-deprecation that may occur with selection by sex alone (Heilman et al., 1991; Turner & Pratkanis, 1994; Turner et al., 1991).

Another problem with AAPs is that *recipients are usually still statistically rare enough in organizations such that gender- or race-based processing of them still occurs.* It is ironic that affirmative action programs are intended to reduce gender- or race-segregated employment roles but may trigger gender-stereotyped processing of affirmative action recipients. This occurs because the woman or minority individual typically remains a minority in the role because affirmative action programs often do not result in the hiring of more than a few individuals from traditionally underrepresented groups. The numerical rarity of the stereotyped group in the organization makes the woman or person's minority group membership (e.g., race or sex) highly salient, thus triggering the processing of them according to gender or race stereotypes. This high visibility also creates significant performance pressures for the token individual who may feel as though she or he is constantly being "watched" (Powell, 1987). Also, stereotypes tend to persevere in spite of contradictory evidence, so stereotype holders must have numerous contacts with nonstereotypical individuals before they will revise their stereotypes (Mackie et al., 1992a, 1992b). The hiring of only a few individuals from traditionally underrepresented groups is often not enough to override "exception-to-the-rule" thinking (the creation of a subcategory for individuals who disconfirm the stereotype). The number of women and minorities in all job categories must be increased such that individual variations within each group are apparent and it is obvious that nonstereotypical individuals are not simply exceptions to the rule.

Lack of support is yet another barrier to the effectiveness of affirmative action programs. Kravitz and Platania (1993) found that a lot of people's dislike of affirmative action is based on misconceptions about what it entails. For instance, their respondents thought that affirmative action programs were likely to include the use of quotas and forced hiring of unqualified applicants. They suggested that support would be greater if people were better informed. For instance, people should be made aware that affirmative action does not permit attention to applicants' demographic membership until applicants are screened for competence. Media coverage given to white males who may have been hired or promoted were it not for AAPs may also contribute to the disproportionate sense of deprivation attributed by white males to affirmative action and the perception that affirmative action is largely a matter of quotas and reverse discrimination. I suspect that cases which seem particularly unjust to whites are likely to receive more media attention and are therefore more available to memory as examples of affirmative action. According to the *availability heuristic* (Kahneman et al., 1982) the more available to memory something is, the more frequent we judge it to be. The images of affirmative action that most people have available to them are not representative of the majority of AAPs and may lead them to overestimate the frequency of more controversial AAP practices.

Lack of support for affirmative action is also due to the zero-sum thinking that occurs because of job and promotion scarcity. A zero-sum conflict is one in which the perception is that for one to win the other must lose. White males often believe that if women and minorities are hired, they will not be. Zero-sum thinking is recognized by social psychologists as a contributor to intergroup conflict (Rubin et al., 1994). White males have the most negative attitudes toward affirmative action (Kravitz & Platania, 1993), and frequently believe that affirmative action is unjust reverse discrimination. They feel that they have been denied something they deserve and feel themselves to be victims of an unjust selection procedure (Heilman, 1994; Nacoste, 1990). It is true that in today's scarce job climate employers sometimes try to redress past discrimination by giving those few openings to individuals from traditionally discriminated-against groups. Perhaps better economic times will reduce the perception of affirmative action as a zero-sum situation. However, I suspect that white males overattribute affirmative action as the cause of their joblessness or lack of advancement (as demonstrated in Chap. 3, white males still have significant employment advantages). They do this because this attribution works on many levels—it serves impression management purposes by protecting the white male's public image (i.e., it can be used to convince others that the failure was caused by the situation and not by the person himself), it protects his ego (i.e., he does not have to make an ability attribution for the failure), and it is a socially reinforced and available attribution (i.e., others in the social group agree with and encourage it).

The attitudes of top management are also important and commitment from an organization's higher administration is apparently one of the most important factors affecting AAP effectiveness (Hitt & Keats, 1984). Konrad and Linnehan (1993) found that the more positive top management's attitudes were toward affirmative action, the greater the implementation of affirmative action policies and the greater the number of women and people of color in management. In some cases, employers are required to demonstrate adequate representation of women and minorities in order to receive government contracts. Konrad and Linnehan (1993) found that AAPs were more likely under these circumstances. However, even when required, some employers and managers may implement AAPs only minimally and may react negatively to affirmative action recipients because of psychological reactance. Psychological reactance occurs when we react to attempts to control our behavior because we resent behavioral control being taken away from us (Brehm, 1966).

When does affirmative action work? Affirmative action is obviously no panacea and by itself cannot be expected to change gender roles or eliminate gender inequality. However, if certain conditions are met, affirmative action can be an important part of movements toward gender equality. Without it, gender and ethnic stereotypes may prevent qualified women and members of traditionally underrepresented groups from being seriously considered for positions customarily held by white males. Konrad and Linnehan (1993) found that AAPs resulted in greater numbers of women and people of color in management.

In the discussion of affirmative action above, several suggestions for enhancing the success of affirmative action programs were made. It appears that employers should provide unambiguous information regarding the qualifications of newly hired or promoted women or minorities to other employees to reduce their fears and suspicions. People should also be better informed about what affirmative action entails. In particular, they should understand that by law applicants must first be screened for competence. The Equal Employment Opportunity Commission (EEOC) guidelines explicitly state that selection under affirmative action plans should be based on the ability of the applicant to do the work and that such plans should not require the selection of the unqualified. As mentioned previously, several Supreme Court decisions have also emphasized that strict quotas and disregard of applicant qualifications are not allowed. Turner and Pratkanis (1994) also suggested emphasizing to employees that affirmative action can result in a diversity of skills and perspectives useful to the organization. Sufficient numbers of women and minorities must also be hired such that individual variations within each group are apparent and make it obvious that nonstereotypical individuals are not simply exceptions to the rule.

I recall hearing my white father-in-law tell about a federal government job where he had to work closely with the other employees, all African-American women, including his boss. He said that at first he could not believe they could be competent and scoffed at the idea of a female manager. He now admits that the experience of working with these women changed his mind. Cook (1985), in discussing racial desegregation, outlined the conditions under which contact will produce favorable attitude changes. The first condition is that the status of the participants in which the contact occurs must be equal. The second is that the contact must be such that it becomes apparent that negative stereotypes are incorrect. The third is that there needs to be a mutual goal for which individuals from the traditionally oppressed group and traditionally dominant group must cooperate to achieve. Fourth is that the contact must be such that there is high acquaintance potential, that is, that individuals from the traditionally oppressed group can be seen as individuals rather than simply as members of the stereotyped group. And fifth is that social norms must favor the concept of equality and intergroup contact. As my father-in-law's experience illustrates, affirmative action programs, like school desegregation, probably work best under these conditions. Organizations with AAPs should maximize these conditions in order to increase the effectiveness of their programs.

CHANGING THE HOME
Why Household Divisions of Labor Should Change

Gender roles are unlikely to change until the division of labor in the home changes. Current gender-based divisions of labor in the household are symptomatic of continuing gender inequality and gender-role socialization (Blair & Lichter, 1991). As Braverman (1991, p. 26) pointed out, "the allocation of housework and childcare reflects in microcosm the power inequities between men and women in society at large." Traditional divisions of household labor may also perpetuate the lower status of females. It is apparent to the child that the person who works all day and who must then come home and cook and clean is of lower status than the one who works all day and does not have these duties when he returns home. Children may then infer that females must really be inferior or they wouldn't have this lower status.

Traditional divisions of household labor lead children to develop gender stereotypes and learn different skills based on their gender. When children see women and men in different roles, they assume that males and females have different qualities that make them better suited for these differing roles. These gender stereotypes then act as social norms, or prescriptions, for behavior. In other words, children come to believe that men and women should occupy different roles and have different psychological qualities. They are then motivated to learn different skills depending upon their gender, and consequently may be ill-prepared for the variety of roles they are likely to occupy in later life. My female dorm-residing students frequently tell me of teaching male "dormies" how to iron or do laundry. Or, as Jacklin (1989) noted, gender roles and sex-based divisions of labor encourage the development of nurturance in females but not in males: "Why," she asks, "should nurturance be encouraged in only one sex? Nurturing may be an antidote to violence" (p. 132).

Placing the burden of childcare and housework on women also interferes with their gaining organizational and political power. You may recall from Chap. 3 that women in management are less likely to be married and to have children than women not in managerial positions. This may be the case because employed women may be unable to work late or on weekends or to travel, and may miss more work due to childcare problems and children's illnesses. Furthermore, senior managers are often reluctant to promote women because of the assumption that women's familial responsibilities make them less committed to the organization (even when this is not the case). In short, it is well-known that women are largely responsible for the domestic sphere, and if this were to change this would not be used against them in the workplace. To paraphrase Tavris and Wade (1984), in regards to political power, the hand that rocks the cradle and works outside the home may be too tired to rule the world, and too busy with other responsibilities to institutionalize her power.

Another reason for changing traditional distributions of labor in the home is that conflicts over household responsibilities and childcare are a major source of marital and relationship tension. In one study of 600 couples filing for divorce, researcher George Levinger (cited in Hochschild,

1989) found that the second most common reason women cited for divorce was their husbands' neglect of home or children. A 1984 study by Booth et al. found that, as the number of disagreements over household labor increased, marital satisfaction and stability decreased. In their study of dual-career couples, Steil and Turetsky (1987) found that the more responsibility a husband assumed for childcare and household tasks, the more satisfied his wife was with the marriage. Pleck (1985) examined available research on husbands' childcare and housework participation and concluded that husbands' participation had a positive effect on husbands' and wives' ratings of satisfaction and happiness with their family life. He suggested that this is because wives are less resentful, actively participating in the household may provide a husband with an increased sense of control, and some tasks, such as childcare, may be gratifying to both husbands and wives. Male partners who participate equally in household labor may also experience positive mental health benefits from a reduction of guilt.

Household Labor as a Case of Attitude-Behavior Inconsistency

Although men and women often agree that when both partners are employed there ought to be more egalitarian distributions of labor in the home, research has found relatively little evidence of behavioral change in this direction (Demo & Acock, 1993; Hardesty & Bokemeier, 1989; Hilton & Haldeman, 1991; Lawrence et al., 1987). Pleck (1985) concluded that available data suggest men are more psychologically involved with their families than with their jobs, and he suggested that this involvement provides a foundation for enlarging men's performance of housework and childcare. However, he acknowledged that men perform relatively little housework and childcare.

How can people be so inconsistent? We normally think of people's attitudes and behaviors as being consistent with each other. Indeed, one very popular theory in social psychology during the 1960s and early 1970s, called *cognitive dissonance theory* (Festinger & Carlsmith, 1959), is based on the idea that inconsistency is so psychologically uncomfortable that, once aware of it, we are strongly motivated to remedy it by either changing our behavior or rationalizing the inconsistency. One way to rationalize the woman's larger contribution in the home is by focusing on her smaller economic contribution to the household. Ross et al. (1983) found that the higher the husband's earnings the less likely he was to share housework and childcare, and the higher the wife's earnings, the more likely he was to share these responsibilities. Steil and Turetsky (1987), in a study of 815 dual-career couples, found that the more the wife earned relative to the husband the greater her share in the making of major decisions and the less the responsibility she had for household tasks (other than childcare, which was unaffected by this variable). Of course, as we noted earlier, women tend to be concentrated in low-paying, low-status jobs, which means that most women will earn less than their husbands. The irony is that women's larger contributions in the home are sometimes used to justify their lower status and pay in the workplace, while their lower status and pay in the workplace are used to justify their doing more work in the home.

Sex-based household labor differentials are common even when they are difficult to justify. One woman told me her husband initially argued that his smaller contribution to the household labor and childcare was justified by his higher salary. She then pointed out to him that with her benefits (insurance, etc.) her financial contribution was equal to his. At this point, then, we would expect him to agree to help more with the household chores because the rationalization that her financial contribution to the household was smaller than his was no longer available as a justification for his lack of help at home (there is now what social psychologists call "insufficient external justification" for the discrepancy). Yet this is not what happened: He still will not help. Fishbein and Ajzen (1975) and Wicker (1969) identified a number of situations in which people exhibit attitude-behavior inconsistency without seeming motivated to change. Many of the explanations offered can be used to explain why males and females verbally advocate more egalitarian divisions of labor, yet display traditional divisions of labor in the way they live.

One reason for attitude-behavior inconsistency is that *the individual may not know how to perform the consistent behavior.* Some people argue that it is not that men are trying to get rid of sharing the second shift, so much as it is that because of socialization, men do not really know how to thoroughly clean, cook, or mind the children. Early socialization experiences may not have provided men with the skills needed to notice and perform household tasks. Consequently, behavior changes may lag behind attitude change. Etaugh and Liss (1992) found that girls were asked to do more at home than boys, and were significantly more likely to have kitchen, laundry, and vacuuming/dusting tasks. Also, because children pay more attention to same-sex models, male children do not pay close attention to, nor model, the behavior of their mothers. As a result, they do not develop the more detailed home cleanliness schemas that females do. Braverman (1991) suggested that if men's early experiences do not provide them with home cleanliness skills, men should allow themselves to be tutored and mentored by women. Humorist Dave Barry (1987) suggested that women spend many hours patiently going over basic cleaning concepts (such as where clean dishes come from) which remain baffling mysteries to the "cleaning impaired" person (which he says is about 85 percent of all men).

Another reason given for poor attitude-behavior correspondence is that *broad general attitudes often do not predict specific behaviors.* In other words, broad general questions about whether household labor should be shared more equitably by males may not predict how much a specific male contributes. If you really want to know whether a man will help in the home, ask him his attitude toward his performance of specific household tasks.

A third reason for attitude-behavior inconsistency is that *other attitudes may specify competing behaviors.* For instance, equality in dual-wage earning households often requires that men give up some of their leisure time to do more at home. Men's proleisure attitudes and behaviors may interfere with their performing behaviors consistent with the attitude of equity. Men's hatred of boring housetasks may override their proequity attitudes. A male friend of mine once said, "I'm all for women's rights. I don't expect her to do the housework and I don't think it's 'women's work.' I just don't want to do it." Men's attitudes toward career success may also override their proequity attitudes since doing more at home may mean doing less at the workplace.

Like men, women may have an attitude that suggests men should do more at home but have competing beliefs that "good" women take care of the home. Therefore they may not be very assertive about their need for more help. Biernat and Wortman (1991) found that professional women were critical of their own performance as wives and mothers, and when evaluating themselves seemed to use nonemployed wives and mothers as the standards of comparison. Many women feel very conflicted: On the one hand, they have been raised to believe that "good" women do these things for their families as expressions of love, while on the other, they are truly overwhelmed and need help (especially those with children and/or those with demanding jobs or careers). They feel angry when men don't help, but feel like "bad" women when they ask their male partners for that help. This experience may be less likely for African-American women. Because of their longer history of participation in the labor force, black women do not see employment and being a wife and mother as mutually exclusive (Dugger, 1988). One study found that black women saw employment as more compatible with motherhood than white women did (Murrell et al., 1991).

Attitude-behavior correspondence also depends in part on social norms, and *social norms may call for behaviors which are inconsistent with one's attitude.* For instance, it may be that men perceive social norms as saying their masculinity is based in part on avoiding feminine activities such as housework and childcare and fear their relatives or male friends will give them a hard time for engaging in such work. He may anticipate derisive remarks from others such as "Man, are you whipped," "I can tell who wears the pants in the family and it ain't you," and "*My,* aren't we womanly." Such reactions from others communicate to males that doing housework is socially inappropriate for males. Gunter and Gunter (1990) found that in marriages where husbands were sex-typed masculine (as measured by the Bem Sex Role Inventory), wives performed the greatest number of household chores and husbands the least. Fowlkes (1987) points out that while a woman's status is often enhanced by adding paid employment to her domestic responsibilities, a man's status is often diminished if he does "women's work." Social norms surrounding housework become apparent to us during childhood (we already mentioned how parents assign boys and girls different chores and how these reflect traditional divisions of labor in the home).

Women may also perceive that social norms support more traditional divisions of labor in the home. Most of us were raised in households where the labor was sex-segregated and it is clear when we look around us that these norms persist. It is difficult to violate social norms, and many women feel less guilt and discomfort regarding their paid work if they do the majority of the housework and childcare. Of course, as we pointed out earlier, social norms even within the same society are not uniform. In some social groups, a woman is not negatively perceived when she does not satisfy her homemaker role or if her male partner contributes equally to the household labor.

Equity and Household Labor Differentials

How do women deal with the inequitable distribution of household labor? *Equity theory*, discussed in Chap. 3, is relevant here. Remember that according to equity theory, the person perceiving underpayment inequity usually attempts to achieve equity. Women typically try to do this in household chores by decreasing their own inputs, which includes lowering their standards (e.g., not making the bed every day, allowing the kitchen floor to stay dirty longer), trying to get their male partners to increase their inputs (e.g., to take over some of the household tasks), or, more commonly, both. According to Hochschild's (1989) research, most women lose the battle for greater household participation from their husbands. Equity theory suggests that once one loses this battle the choices for resolving the inequity are to leave the relationship or change one's perception of the situation. While some women do end their relationships over these issues, cognitive adjustments are probably more common. These could include emphasizing that one's partner does more than most men, or that he's "good with the children" (if true), or learning to enjoy one's status as "superwoman."

Attempts to increase the husband's household inputs sometimes result in additional conflict when the man makes what the woman perceives as half-hearted attempts at sharing household responsibilities. I have a friend who left her children with her husband, who forgot to feed them, change their clothes, and brush their hair. His response to her alarm at the way he cared for them was to say: "Hey, they survived, didn't they?" Similarly, conflict occurs when women have to ask repeatedly for help and end up feeling like "nags" (Crosby, 1991). Often women just stop asking, do all the household tasks themselves, and feel resentful.

Often men claim their attempts are adequate but are just not up to the unnecessarily high standards of women. They feel as though their female partners discourage their participation by requiring that tasks be done in particular ways, at particular times, and up to certain standards (Hawkins & Roberts, 1992). One problem is that employed women often learned their standards from women who were not employed outside of the home like their mothers and grandmothers or even television moms. Biernat and Wortman (1991) found that employed wives were significantly more bothered by the house being dirty, the meals not being good, and household projects not getting done than were their husbands. They suggested that wives' relatively harsh standards in evaluating the home environment occur because women are taught to derive their self-worth from how well the household is running. Similarly, others (Hochschild, 1989; Pleck, 1983) have suggested that women are reluctant to relinquish control over household duties because the domestic sphere remains a wife's primary source of identity. It also seems plausible that women might be reluctant to give up control over the one area in which they are acknowledged to be more competent than men. Dovidio et al. (1988), in an experimental study using mixed-sex dyads discussing feminine tasks, masculine tasks, or gender-neutral tasks, found that the only time female subjects displayed more verbal and nonverbal power behaviors was when a feminine task unfamiliar to males (sewing) was being discussed. Males exhibited more power behaviors than females for both a masculine task (changing car oil) and a non-gender-linked task (vegetable gardening).

What can be done to reduce this inequity in divisions of household labor? I have a number of suggestions. One suggestion is that reducing the gender pay gap would help to increase men's participation. This would get rid of the rationalization that women should do more household labor to offset their smaller financial contributions to the household. Another suggestion is that in some cases, women should consider lowering their standards. A third suggestion is that parents teach their male children how to perform household tasks. Similarly, men should allow themselves to be tutored or mentored by women.

Finally, women should be clear in their requests for men's participation in the home. Because women are often ambivalent about asking men to contribute more, they are not always direct in their requests for help. They may, for example, say something like "Boy, this laundry really piles

Some gender conflict regarding household chores could be reduced by women lowering their standards.

up quickly. I'm having a hard time staying on top of it," when what they really mean is, "Please do a couple of loads of laundry this week." This non-assertiveness is aggravated by the fact that they don't want to have to ask. There are two reasons for this. One is that they don't want to be a "nag." It doesn't feel good. Second is that they use their male partner's unsolicited participation as an indication of his love for them. In other words, women often feel: "If you really loved me, you would want to ease my burden by helping." Consequently, they keep waiting and hoping to see this sign of his love. When this doesn't happen, they feel angry, resentful, and hurt. Their anger is aggravated when they see men's lack of participation as communicating that men think they are higher in status and power than women. In other words, they feel as though men's lack of participation in the household labor is another way of saying: "I deserve more privileges than you. I should not have to come home and do more work, but you, because you are female, are not so privileged." Not surprisingly, this upsets women who want to be equal partners. I think that many men are unaware of these often unstated dynamics and would be motivated to participate at a greater rate in the household labor if they realized what damage their lack of participation does to their relationships with women.

CHANGING PARENT AND TEACHER BEHAVIOR

Parents and teachers need to learn to treat children on the basis of their individual differences rather than presumed gender differences. It is apparent from Chaps. 1, 2, 5, and 6 that children's genders may influence the expectations parents and teachers have of them, and this may lead to differential treatment of children based on gender. Children may then develop gender-differentiated skills and self-perceptions that limit them later on.

Teachers could be encouraged to attend workshops that describe gender bias in teaching and how to combat it. Bem (1981) suggested that in educational settings seemingly innocuous gender distinctions are nonetheless quite important to gender-based schematic processing. For example, Bem (1981) noted that boys and girls are often told to line up separately, they learn songs where fingers are "ladies" and thumbs "men," and they see girl silhouettes and boy silhouettes placed alternately on calendars. In my son's classroom in 1993 it was girl bears and boy bears on the calendar and songs like "little girls are made of sugar and spice and everything nice . . . boys are made of snips and snails and puppy dogs' tails." It seems to me that even gender distinctions such as these, which appear harmless, do not belong in the classroom because they lead children to make gender distinctions about things that do matter such as whether it is appropriate for members of their own gender to excel at a particular subject. Gender distinctions also contribute to gender segregation in childhood relationships by suggesting that boys and girls are and should remain separate. Parents and teachers often encourage gender segregation in schools and home and this leads to further categorization by gender. Maccoby and Jacklin (1987) recommended that teachers and parents deliberately create gender-free environments for children which encourage mixed-gender play, equal-status interactions, and participation in cross-gender games (e.g., girls playing soccer; boys learning to hopscotch). Because spatial and mathematical skills and empathy are desirable qualities to possess regardless of gender, parents and teachers should encourage all children to play games and with toys that foster the development of these attributes.

Jacklin (1989) suggested that national organizations such as the Parent-Teacher Association (PTA) educate parents about the role of sex-based expectations in mathematics learning. Books on child development read by parents could discuss differential socialization and how it may limit the development of their child's unique potential. Unfortunately, as noted by Jacklin (1989), the media often misinform the public about research on gender differences, suggesting to parents that differences between their male and female children are natural and to be expected.

In Chap. 1 we noted that one way children learn about gender roles is through observation. In Chap. 4 we noted that cognitive categorizations of the genders originate in childhood, where we see men and women in different social roles and find gender to be a useful category for guiding our behavior. This suggests that in our homes equal divisions of labor and not designating particular tasks as appropriate for males or females would reduce the significance of gender distinctions to children. Serbin et al. (1993), in a discussion of sex typing in childhood, suggested that stereotyping is natural but not inevitable—"environmental factors have a major effect on the extent to which children learn and accept the stereotypes defined by their culture" (p. 55). Martin (1993) suggested that it is inevitable, given the abundance of gender-related cues in our culture, that children learn our culture's stereotypes of the sexes. However, she noted that the application and adoption of such stereotypes are not inevitable, especially if children are exposed to non-sex-typed role models. When parents step outside of traditional gender-role arrangements, it may have the result of altering their children's attitudes about gender roles. For instance, in an 11-year longitudinal study, paternal involvement in children's preschool years predicted adolescents' support for nontraditional employment, and paternal involvement from 7 to 9 years of age predicted support for nontraditional childrearing arrangements (Williams et al., 1992).

Parents, however, are not the only agents of gender socialization. Gender-neutral language in children's literature and the portrayal of both females and males in domestic and agentic (action) roles in children's media would go a long way toward reducing children's categorization by gender. Some research has suggested that the media can alter sex-stereotyped perceptions (Johnson & Ettema, 1982; Roberts & Bachen, 1981) and we cited some evidence in Chap. 1 that there has been some improvement in gender portrayals in the media. Unfortunately, traditional gender portrayals will predominate as long as they are believed to sell products and gain viewers or readers. Consumers can sometimes influence media portrayals by writing letters and refusing to purchase the products of companies that participate in stereotypical gender portrayals. In the meantime, parents should critically evaluate the books, movies, and television shows their children watch to reduce children's exposure to sex-stereotypical imagery. For instance, Junn et al. (1994) found that Disney's children's films available for purchase and rental portray the genders in remarkably sex-stereotypical ways. Furthermore, because these are often viewed repeatedly (children will happily watch the same film over and over again), they may be especially potent in implanting such views.

CHANGING FAULTY BELIEFS ABOUT GENDER

Philosopher James Rachels (1986) wrote that when we feel strongly about something it is tempting to believe that we know what the truth is without fully examining our beliefs in the light of reason. The problem, Rachels noted, is that, if we want to discover the truth, we must be guided by reason. Such is the case with gender. We are surrounded by a culture which communicates that men and women are different and should occupy different social roles. We are used to and comfortable with the idea that the genders are opposites. These ideas are so pervasive in our culture that they assume the status of truth and prevent change. Reason and research, though, suggest that many cultural beliefs regarding gender are erroneous.

Faulty Beliefs about Gender

Faulty Belief 1: Gender Differences Are Large

The widely used expression "opposite sexes" is just one example of the widespread belief that the genders are significantly different. In a Gallup Poll conducted in 1993, 65 percent of those polled said that, not including purely physical differences, men and women are basically different (Newport, 1993). One of the points of this book, however, is that gender differences are not nearly as large as our culture leads us to believe. They are not found in important areas such as memory, intelligence, creativity, analytic ability, leadership ability, and personality. Small differences are found on some verbal, math, and spatial abilities but even when gender differences relating to cognitive abilities are found, they are small—on average about 5 to 10 percent. Research on gender differences in emotion, empathy, aggression, altruism, and influencability has found that not only are differences small, they are highly dependent upon the gender norms of the situation being studied.

There are three related reasons why we perceive gender differences to be larger than they are. The first is that our culture draws our attention to gender and communicates in a myriad of ways that the genders are different. Second, our culture's emphasis on gender gives rise to the development of gender schemas. These cognitive categorizations influence information processing such that we are more likely to notice, remember, and process in ways that are consistent with our gender expectations.

Thus we are inclined to notice and explain behavior in ways that confirm our beliefs about gender differences. Third, most social roles are occupied predominantly by one sex or the other. Female roles typically call for different behaviors and skills than male roles. Consequently, the genders seem very different.

Faulty Belief 2: Gender Differences Are Due to Fundamental Biological Differences between the Sexes
At the end of Chap. 2, we called this belief the fundamental gender attribution error. The belief that gender differences are fundamental biological differences is not surprising given the cultural messages we receive to this effect. This, combined with a preoccupation with sexual relations that draws our attention to the anatomical/biological differences between the genders, makes a biological attribution for gender differences more cognitively available and likely. Social accounts of gender differences are less cognitively available to most people. However, an important theme of this book is that differences between the sexes are often due to sex-segregated social roles and differential socialization rather than to biology. We begin socializing our female and male children differently in infancy and communicate different expectations to males and females throughout the lifespan. The fact that gender differences in areas such as aggression, altruism, emotion, and empathy depend on the gender norms of the social situation, and that gender differences are becoming smaller as social institutions change, also suggests the large role that social factors play in the creation of gender differences.

Faulty Belief 3: Biological Gender Differences Make Males and Females Better Suited for Different Social Roles
While it is true that gender roles may have originally arisen because of sex differences in physical strength and women's ability to nurse infants, these differences do not justify the differential treatment males and females receive in modern society. For instance, in comparison to men, women are seldom found in positions of power in our society yet there is no evidence that men are better leaders than women. Gender differences in cognitive abilities are also not large enough to justify directing males and females toward different career paths. To paraphrase Hubbard (1990), people's capacities to work at socially useful tasks and to nurture children and form nonexploitative and mutually satisfying relationships are not limited by biology, but by discriminatory economic and social practices.

Bem (1993) wrote that, even if it should turn out that females and males differ biologically with respect to abilities or predispositions, those differences are unlikely to justify the different roles currently occupied by men and women. If, for example, she noted, women are found to be more biologically nurturant than men, this should make them psychiatrists, not secretaries. And even if men have a higher aptitude for math than women, she pointed out, it does not explain why so many women having a high math aptitude do not have careers reflecting that aptitude. Even those who believe that some gender differences are due to biological differences between the sexes admit that it is a mistake to then conclude that differences are unavoidable. For instance, Halpern (1992) noted that attributing sex differences to biology often leads people to conclude that differences are unavoidable when in fact it does not mean that the differences are large, that they cannot be eliminated with instruction, or that psychosocial variables do not still play a role.

The issue of childrearing is more complex because the fact that women bear and can breastfeed children makes it seem that, in comparison to men, they are naturally suited for childcare. However, while having mammaries may make one capable of nursing an infant, it does not give one an intimate knowledge of how to care for or nurture children (we all know plenty of individuals who can attest to this). Childcare behaviors are learned and men as well as women can learn them. Although giving birth and nursing an infant foster the attachment between the infant and the mother, infants can and will attach to fathers who share in their care and fathers who share in the care of their infants form stronger attachments to their children as well.

Philosopher Rachels (1993) defended a simple and intuitively plausible principle of equality or equal treatment: Individuals are to be treated in the same way unless there is a difference between them that justifies the difference in treatment. Rachels' ideas fit in quite well with one of the main points of this book. That point is that we are not justified in our differential treatment of the genders, and the gender stereotypes which we use to justify doing so do not hold up under scrutiny. Rachels (1986) argued, however, that it is morally justifiable to treat people differently when there are real differences between them, and I acknowledge that some minor differences in treatment would be justified based on real differences between the sexes. For example, I think we can justify having separate public restrooms and we can justify women being able to go on disability leave from work when they are pregnant. But the fact remains that we cannot justify many of the other ways in which we treat males and females differently.

At the end of Chap. 1, I cautioned that just because sexual divisions of labor contributed to survival at one time does not mean that these divisions are genetically encoded in some way, nor does it mean that these arrangements make survival sense in the modern world. I also pointed out that even if there is a biological basis for human behavior we do not have to let it dictate our values. These are important points since they imply that gender inequality, gender differences, and sex-linked social roles are not inescapable biological facts and, indeed, may be changed by altering the social context.

Faulty Belief 4: The Genders Are Separate But Equal
Chapters 3 and 6 highlighted the ways in which the genders are separate but not equal. Gender separateness stems from sex-based divisions of labor, beliefs that gender differences make females and males better suited for different activities, and the different lives males and females lead because of gender roles. Gender inequality is evident in women's lower pay, lower status, and disproportionate share of household labor and childcare even when they are employed outside the home. A gender-just society requires that we give up the belief that the traditional division of labor between the sexes is natural and unchangeable (Okin, 1989).

Faulty Belief 5: The Needs of Society Are Best Served by Traditional Gender Roles
When the Gallup Poll asked Americans in 1993 whether they agreed that "it is generally better for society if the man is the achiever outside the home, and the woman takes care of the home and family," 43 percent agreed and 56 percent disagreed (Newport, 1993). While people frequently maintain that many social problems such as teen pregnancy and gangs are caused by changes in traditional gender roles such as women working outside of the home, it appears unrealistic to expect a return to traditional roles. Although some people will offer the persistence of these roles as evidence of their usefulness (i.e., "This is the way it's always been done, so it must be right."), this reasoning is faulty. Tradition alone is not a good justification for continuing to do something and close examination of the traditional roles suggests that they are no longer serving us well. Furthermore, what many people think of as the traditional division of labor in the United States (e.g., man as breadwinner, woman as stay-at-home mother and helpmate) is actually a fairly recent development (Lips, 1991).

As we have already discussed, economic realities, along with the desires of many women to work outside the home, mean that the majority of women with children are employed full time. In 1987 only 34 percent of women said that their ideal lifestyle was to be married without a full-time job (Gallup Report, 1987). Indeed, in spite of the strain that may come with occupying multiple social roles (employee, wife, mother) women's working outside the home is likely to continue since women need the money, the social contacts, and/or the sense of accomplishment that comes from a job outside the home. At this point women's employment is a given rather than an unusual occurrence (Crosby, 1987; 1991; Zigler & Lang, 1990). As discussed earlier in this chapter, an insistence on traditional roles in the home creates problems for male-female relationships, reduces paternal involvement in the home and with children, and may contribute to the "glass ceiling." In Chap. 4 problems created by the traditional male role were discussed. These included impoverished relationships, reduced social support, physical problems from overwork and overexercise, violence, and risky behavior. Population growth, mechanization of the workplace, and economic downturns make it increasingly risky for males' worth to be defined in terms of their economic worth. To insist on this definition of manhood is to set most men up for failure, and to set up society for the compensatory masculinity fallout. In short, traditional roles do not seem to be working very well in modern society.

Another way in which traditional roles are outdated is marital divorce. About 40 percent of children under age 10 live in a divorced household. As we noted earlier, most children do not see their fathers at all by the time the divorce is 3 years old. The standard of living for children and their mothers drops dramatically following divorce (by 73 percent) while the standard of living for divorced men typically increases (by 42 percent) (Clarke-Stewart & Bailey, 1990). This occurs because the legal system does not require that child support be high enough to enable children or their mothers to enjoy a standard of living equal to that of the noncustodial parent. Women usually cannot make up the difference because women's work pays less, and they often gave up wage-earning and educational pursuits to be primary parents and therefore cannot get good-paying jobs following divorce. The lack of affordable quality childcare is another problem. Okin (1989) argued that it is unjust for women and children to suffer economically vastly more than men because of a division of labor that was mutually agreed upon by both parents (e.g., the mother staying at home full time while the father worked for pay). She suggested that one benefit of a more gender-equal society would be that separated and divorced fathers who had shared equally in the nurturance of their children would be more likely to see them and contribute financially to their support. Also, if women did not give up their educational and career pursuits just because they got married or had children, they would be in better economic shape should divorce occur. Divorce may even be reduced to the extent that husbands and wives have more in common and consequently have stronger, more interesting relationships.

Raising our female and male children differently also does them a great disservice by not preparing them for the different roles they are likely to occupy and by unnecessarily limiting their career choices. I remember a comedian who said at least girl's toys and games taught you something useful—he had never as an adult had much use for being able to bunt a baseball. The world also would be a better place if both males and females possessed the traditional female qualities of empathy and interpersonal sensitivity and the traditional male qualities of confidence and independence—in other words, if individuals were socialized to be more androgynous. We discussed androgyny in Chap. 1. Recall that Bem (1975) suggested that the androgynous person could function more effectively in a wider variety of settings than a person who was more traditionally male or female. In later writings, Bem (1981) cautioned that the androgyny concept still presupposes some desirable qualities are "masculine" and some "feminine" and it is this distinction that creates gender schemas and perpetuates the projection of gender into situations which have nothing to do with gender. The ideal situation then, is one in which empathy, interpersonal sensitivity, confidence, and independence are valued traits but are not associated with femininity or masculinity, but rather with humanity.

How Can These Faulty Beliefs Be Changed?

We began in Chap. 1 by exploring the idea that the main sources of gender differences are the social norms and stereotypes communicated by our culture. Such norms and stereotypes are embedded in our culture and are easily seen in literature, movies, television, popular humor, and in the different activities performed by females and males. Because of our desire to be both socially correct and socially liked, individuals' compliance with gender norms is virtually automatic. Furthermore, as Bussey and Bandura (1992, p. 1249) once said:

> Pressure from parents alone is unlikely to achieve egalitarian standards and conduct in children unless the peer group and other significant elements in the culture endorse them (Weisner & Wilson-Mitchell, 1990). Because of the overwhelming sex segregation of children and strong pressures for conformity from the peer group, stereotypic gender-linked standards may be particularly stable and resistant to modification in the absence of sweeping social changes.

Sweeping social changes? How can these occur? How can we bring about the changes in social norms needed to move toward a gender equal society? What role can individuals play in changing social roles? Thoits (1987) noted that human beings are not just robots programmed by society; they are willful actors capable of choosing noncomformity and altering the social structure if they so wish. Social psychologists have found that minorities can influence majorities to change when the minority is consistent and confident (Forsyth, 1990).

Remember that just as you look to others for information about what is socially appropriate, they look to you. And, if public opinion polls are any indication, the majority of people are sympathetic to gender equality. This suggests that a lot of conformity to gender norms is compliance (public rather than private conformity). This means that you may be able to influence change more than you might think. If you challenge the norms verbally or behaviorally, this could influence others who secretly agree with you to do the same. As social psychologists will tell you, several dissenters can seriously challenge and change a majority (Latane, 1981; Moscovici, 1985). Consequently, if you believe in gender equality, you should be ready to talk about it to others, and you should be a role model for gender equality. You should also support organizations and political candidates who work to develop, enact, and enforce gender-equal laws and national childcare and working-parent policies.

CONCLUDING REMARKS

To sum up, a social psychology of gender emphasizes that gender is a social norm to which we conform due to normative pressure (a desire for social approval) and informational pressure (the use of social information to help us define reality). Although research has not found men and women to be significantly different on most traits, we perceive them to be very different. Part of this is due to the fact that women and men occupy different social roles and so we assume they differ in ways which justify these roles. Our culture also communicates to us that men and women are different and should be different. Furthermore, our natural cognitive tendency to categorize and process on the basis of those categorizations additionally contributes to the perception that gender differences are large and relevant. We are further motivated to see the genders as different to the extent that we derive part of our identity from our gender. A social psychology of gender shifts our attention away from biology and to the situational and social forces underlying the separation into female and male and, by doing so, provides us with suggestions for change toward gender equality. At the same time, social psychology explains why changes in gender roles and stereotypes will be slow and uncertain without concerted effort. This effort usually comes from women but change may occur more quickly if we acknowledge that traditional roles are unjust, ill-suited for modern society, and limiting to males as well as females.

SUMMARY

- Opinion polls suggest that things have changed in the direction of gender equality but research on pay differentials, women in management, the division of household labor, the portrayal of the sexes in the media, etc., indicate that more change is needed.
- Flextime, paid maternity and paternity leave, on-site and subsidized quality childcare, pay equity programs, and affirmative action are all recommended as ways to restructure the workplace to eliminate sex discrimination and increase the compatibility of employment and family life.

- Quality, affordable daycare is necessary for gender equality. Most research has found that the intellectual, social, and emotional development of children whose mothers are employed outside the home is comparable to that of children whose mothers are not so employed.

- The effectiveness of affirmative action programs is hindered by assumptions that recipients are not qualified for their jobs, and by a lack of social support. In addition, the number of women and minorities in organizations is often not large enough to combat "exception-to-the-rule" thinking. There are ways to increase the effectiveness of AAPs such as better education about what affirmative action entails, providing employees with information about the qualifications of affirmative action hirees, and providing opportunities for equal-status, personal contact between such hirees and other employees.

- Traditional divisions of labor in the home are symptomatic of gender inequality and contribute to sex-stereotyped thinking in children as well as relationship conflict. People advocate more equitable divisions of labor, but for a number of reasons (e.g., social norms, competing attitudes, not knowing how to perform household tasks) attitude-behavior inconsistency remains.

- Teachers and parents should create gender-free environments for children, model egalitarian gender-role arrangements, and monitor children's consumption of gender-stereotyped portrayals in the media.

- Five faulty beliefs about gender inhibit change. These are the belief that gender differences are large, the belief that gender differences are fundamental biological differences, the belief that biological roles make females and males better suited for different roles, the belief that the genders are separate but equal, and the belief that society is best served by traditional gender roles.

References

ADAMS, J. S. (1965). Inequity in social exchange. In L. Berkowitz (Ed.), *Advances in experimental social psychology* (Vol. 2, pp. 267–299). New York: Academic Press.

AIELLO, J. R. (1987). Human spatial behavior. In D. Stokols & I. Altman (Eds.), *The handbook of environmental psychology* (Vol. 1, pp. 389–504). New York: John Wiley.

ALLPORT, G. (1954). *The nature of prejudice.* Cambridge, MA: Addison-Wesley.

ALMEIDA ACOSTA, E., & SANCHEZ DE ALMEIDA, M. E. (1983). Psychological factors affecting change in women's role and status: A cross-cultural study. *International Journal of Psychology, 18,* 3–35.

AMERICAN ASSOCIATION OF UNIVERSITY WOMEN. (1991). *The AAUW report: How schools shortchange girls.* Washington, DC: AAUW.

AMERICAN PSYCHIATRIC ASSOCIATION. (1994). *Diagnostic and statistical manual of mental disorders* (4th ed.). Washington, DC: American Psychiatric Press.

ANESHENSEL, C. S. (1986). Marital and employment role-strain, social support, and depression among adult women. In S. E. Hobfoll (Ed.), *Stress, social support, and women* (pp. 99–114). New York: Hemisphere.

ANSON, O., LEVENSON, A., & BONNEH, D. Y. (1990). Gender and health on the kibbutz. *Sex Roles, 22,* 213–236.

ARCHER, D., IRITANI, B., KIMES, D. D., & BARRIOS, M. (1983). Face-ism: Five studies of sex differences in facial prominence. *Journal of Personality and Social Psychology, 45,* 725–735.

ARIES, E. J., & JOHNSON, E. L. (1983). Close friendship in adulthood: Conversational content between same-sex friends. *Sex Roles, 9,* 1183–1196.

ARONSON, E. (1992). *The social animal* (6th ed.). San Francisco, CA: Freeman.

ASCH, S. E. (1956). Studies of independence and conformity: A minority of one against a unanimous majority. *Psychological Monographs, 70* (9, Whole No. 416).

ASHMORE, R. D. (1990). Sex, gender, and the individual. In L. A. Pervin (Ed.), *Handbook of personality theory and research.* New York: Guilford Press.

ASHMORE, R. D., & DEL BOCA, F. K. (1979). Sex stereotypes and implicit personality theory: Toward a cognitive-social psychological conceptualization. *Sex Roles, 5,* 219–248.

ASHTON, E. (1983). Measures of play behavior. The influence of sex-role stereotyped children's books. *Sex Roles, 9,* 43–47.

ATKIN, D. J., MOORMAN, J., & LINN, C. A. (1991). Ready for prime-time: Network series devoted to working women in the 1980's. *Sex Roles, 25,* 677–685.

ATKINSON, J., & HUSTON, T. L. (1984). Sex role orientation and division of labor early in marriage. *Journal of Personality and Social Psychology, 46*, 330–345.

AUCKETT, R., RITCHIE, J., & MILL, K. (1988). Gender differences in friendship patterns. *Sex Roles, 19*, 57–66.

AVERILL, J. R. (1982). *Anger and aggression.* New York: Springer-Verlag.

BAILEY, B. L. (1988). *From front porch to back seat: Courtship in twentieth century America.* Baltimore, MD: Johns Hopkins University Press.

BAKAN, D. (1966). *The duality of human existence.* Chicago: Rand McNally.

BAKER, D. P., & JONES, D. P. (1993). Creating gender equality: Cross-national gender stratification and mathematical performance. *Sociology of Education, 66*, 91–103.

BALDWIN, A. C., CRITELLI, J. W., STEVENS, L. C., & RUSSELL, S. (1986). Androgyny and sex role measurement: A personal construct approach. *Journal of Personality and Social Psychology, 51*, 1081–1088.

BANDURA, A. (1969). Social learning theory of identificatory process. In D. A. Goslin (Ed.), *Handbook of socialization theory and research.* Chicago: Rand McNally.

BANDURA, A. (1977). *Social learning theory.* Englewood Cliffs, NJ: Prentice-Hall.

BARBEE, A. P., CUNNINGHAM, M. R., WINSTEAD, B. A., DERLEGA, V. J., GULLEY, M. R., YANKEELOV, P. A., & DRUEN, P. B. (1993). Effects of gender role expectations on the social support process. *Journal of Social Issues, 49*, 175–190.

BARON, J. N., & BIELBY, W. T. (1984). The organization of work in a segmented economy. *American Sociological Review, 49*, 454–473.

BARON, J. N., DAVIS-BLAKE, A., & BIELBY, W. T. (1986). The structure of opportunity: How promotion ladders vary within and among organizations. *Administrative Science Quarterly, 31*, 248–273.

BARRY, D. (1987). *Dave Barry's guide to love and/or sex.* Emmaus, PA: Rodale Press.

BARRY, D. (1991). *Dave Barry talks back.* New York: Crown.

BARRY, H., BACON, M. K., & CHILD, I. L. (1957). A cross-cultural survey of some sex differences in socialization. *Journal of Abnormal and Social Psychology, 55*, 327–332.

BARRY, H., BACON, M. K., & CHILD, I. L. (1967). Definitions, ratings, and bibliographic sources for child training practices of 110 cultures. In C. Ford (Ed.), *Cross-cultural approaches* (pp. 293–331). New Haven, CT: Human Relations Areas Files Press.

BARRY, H., JOSEPHSON, L., LAUER, E., & MARSHALL, C. (1976). Traits inculcated in childhood: Five cross-cultural codes. *Ethnology, 15*, 83–114.

BARTH, R. J., & KINDER, B. N. (1988). A theoretical analysis of sex differences in same-sex friendships. *Sex Roles, 19*, 349–363.

BARUCH, G. K., & BARNETT, R. C. (1986). Role quality, multiple role involvement, and psychological well-being in midlife women. *Journal of Personality and Social Psychology, 51*, 578–585.

BARUCH, G. K., & BARNETT, R. C. (1987). Role quality and psychological well-being. In F. J. Crosby (Ed.), *Spouse, parent, and worker: On gender and multiple gender roles* (pp. 63–73). New Haven, CT: Yale University Press.

BASOW, S. A. (1986a). Correlates of sex-typing in Fiji. *Psychology Women Quarterly, 10*, 429–442.

BASOW, S. A. (1986b). *Gender stereotypes* (2nd ed.). Monterey, CA: Basic Books.

BASS, B. M. (1981). *Stogdill's handbook of leadership.* New York: Free Press.

BAUMRIND, D. (1982). Are androgynous individuals more effective persons and parents? *Child Development, 53,* 44–75.

BEAUVAIS, C., & SPENCE, J. (1987). Gender, prejudice, and categorization. *Sex Roles, 16,* 89–100.

BECKER, B. J., & HEDGES, L. V. (1984). Meta-analysis of cognitive gender differences: A comment on analysis by Rosenthal and Rubin. *Journal of Educational Psychology, 76,* 583–587.

BECKER, J. R. (1981). Differential treatment of females and males in mathematics classes. *Journal for Research in Mathematics Education, 12,* 40–53.

BECKMAN, L. J., & HOUSER, B. B. (1979). The more you have, the more you do: The relationship between wife's employment, sex-role attitudes, and household behavior. *Psychology of Women Quarterly, 4,* 160–174.

BELL, E. L., DENTON, T. C., & NKOMO, S. (1993). Women of color in management: Toward an inclusive analysis. In E. A. Fagenson (Ed.), *Women in management: Trends, issues, and challenges in managerial diversity* (pp. 105–130). Newbury Park, CA: Sage.

BELL, L. A. (1989). Something's wrong here and it's not me: Challenging the dilemmas that block girls' success. *Journal for the Education of the Gifted, 12,* 118–130.

BELL, N. J., & CARVER, W. A. (1980). A reevaluation of gender label effects: Expectant mothers' responses to infants. *Child Development, 51,* 925–927.

BELLE, D. (1987). Gender differences in the social moderators of stress. In R. C. Barnett, L. Biener, & G. K. Baruch (Eds.), *Gender and stress* (pp. 257–277). New York: Free Press.

BEM, S. L. (1974). The measurement of psychological androgyny. *Journal of Consulting and Clinical Psychology, 42,* 155–162.

BEM, S. L. (1975). Sex-role adaptability: One consequence of psychological androgyny. *Journal of Personality and Social Psychology, 31,* 634–643.

BEM, S. L. (1979). Theory and measurement of androgyny: A reply to Pedhazur-Tetenbaum and Locksley-Colten critiques. *Journal of Personality and Social Psychology, 37,* 1047–1054.

BEM, S. L. (1981). Gender schema theory: A cognitive account of sex typing. *Psychological Review, 88,* 354–364.

BEM, S. L. (1989). Genital knowledge and gender constancy in preschool children. *Child Development, 60,* 649–662.

BEM, S. L. (1993). *The lenses of gender: Transforming the debate on sexual inequality.* New Haven, CT: Yale University Press.

BENBOW, C. P., & STANLEY, J. C. (1980). Sex differences in mathematical ability: Fact or artifact? *Science, 210,* 1262–1264.

BENBOW, C. P., & STANLEY, J. C. (1982). Consequences in high school and college of sex differences in mathematical reasoning ability: A longitudinal perspective. *American Educational Research Journal, 19,* 598–622.

BERARDO, D. H., SHEHAN, C. L., & LESLIE, G. (1987). A residue of tradition: Jobs, careers, and spouses' time in housework. *Journal of Marriage and the Family, 49,* 381–390.

BERGEN, D. J., & WILLIAMS, J. E. (1991). Sex stereotypes in the United States revisited: 1972–1988. *Sex Roles, 24,* 413–423.

BERGMANN, B. R. (1989). Does the market for women's labor need fixing? *Journal of Economic Perspectives, 3,* 43–60.

BERNARD, J. (1987). *The female world from a global perspective.* Bloomington, IN: Indiana University Press.

BERNDT, T. J., & HELLER, K. A. (1986). Gender stereotypes and social influences: A developmental study. *Journal of Personality and Social Psychology, 50,* 889–898.

BERRY, J. W. (1980). Introduction to methodology. In H. C. Triandis & J. W. Berry (Eds.), *Handbook of cross-cultural psychology: Methodology* (Vol. 2, pp. 1–14). Boston: Allyn & Bacon.

BERZINS, J. I., WELLING, M. A., & WETTER, R. E. (1978). A new measure of psychological androgyny based on the Personality Research Form. *Journal of Consulting and Clinical Psychology, 46,* 126–138.

BEST, B. J., & SPECTOR, P. E. (1984, March). *The effects of applicant attractiveness, managerial attributes and gender on executive employment decisions.* Paper presented at the 30th annual meeting of the Southeastern Psychological Association, New Orleans.

BETZ, N. (1993). Women's career development. In F. L. Denmark & M. A. Paludi (Eds.), *Psychology of women: A handbook of issues and theories* (pp. 627–684). Westport, CT: Greenwood Press.

BHATNAGAR, D. (1988). Professional women in organizations: New paradigms for research and action. *Sex Roles, 18,* 343–355.

BIELBY, D. D., & BIELBY, W. T. (1988). She works hard for the money: Household responsibilities and the allocation of work effort. *American Journal of Sociology, 93,* 1031–59.

BIELBY, W. T., & BIELBY, D. D. (1989). Family ties: Balancing commitments to work and family in dual earner households. *American Sociological Review, 54,* 776–789.

BIELBY, W. T., & BIELBY, D. D. (1992). I will follow him: Family ties, gender-role beliefs, and reluctance to relocate for a better job. *American Journal of Sociology, 97,* 1241–1267.

BIERNAT, M. (1991). Gender stereotypes and the relationship between masculinity and femininity: A developmental analysis: *Journal of Personality and Social Psychology, 61,* 351–365.

BIERNAT, M., & WORTMAN, C. B. (1991). Sharing of home responsibilities between professionally employed women and their husbands. *Journal of Personality and Social Psychology, 60,* 844–860.

BILLIG, M., & TAJFEL, H. (1973). Social categorization and similarity in intergroup behavior. *European Journal of Social Psychology, 3,* 27–52.

BINION, V. J. (1990). Psychological androgyny: A black female perspective. *Sex Roles, 22,* 487–506.

BIRNBAUM, D. W., NOSANCHUK, T. A., & CROLL, W. L. (1980). Children's stereotypes about sex differences in emotionality. *Sex Roles, 6,* 435–443.

BJORKQVIST, K. (1994). Sex differences in physical, verbal, and indirect aggression: A review of recent research. *Sex Roles, 30,* 177–188.

BJORKQVIST, K., LAGERSPETZ, K.M.J., & KAUKIANEN, A. (1992). Do girls manipulate and boys fight? Developmental trends regarding direct and indirect aggression. *Aggressive Behavior, 18,* 117–127.

BJORKQVIST, K., & NIEMELA, P. (1992). New trends in the study of female aggression. In K. Bjorkqvist & P. Niemela (Eds.), *Of mice and women: Aspects of female aggression.* San Diego, CA: Academic Press.

BJORKQVIST, K., OSTERMAN, K., & LAGERSPETZ, K.M.J. (1994). Sex differences in covert aggression among adults. *Aggressive Behavior, 20,* 27–33.

BLACK, K. N., & STEVENSON, M. R. (1984). The relationship of self-reported sex-role characteristics and attitudes toward homosexuality. *Journal of Homosexuality, 10,* 83–93.

BLAIR, S. L., & LICHTER, D. T. (1991). Measuring the division of household labor: Gender segregation of housework among American couples. *Journal of Family Issues, 12,* 91–113.

BLAU, F. D., & FERBER, M. A. (1987). Occupations and earnings of women workers. In K. S. Koziara, M. H. Moskow, & L. D. Tanner (Eds.), *Working women: Past, present, future* (pp. 37–68). Washington, DC: BNA Books.

BLEA, I. I. (1992). *La chicana and the intersection of race, class, and gender.* New York: Praeger.

BLIER, M. J., & BLIER-WILSON, L. A. (1989). Gender differences in self-rated emotional expressiveness. *Sex Roles, 21,* 287–295.

BLOCK, J. H. (1973). Conceptions of sex-role: Some cross-cultural and longitudinal perspectives. *American Psychologist, 28,* 512–526.

BLOCK, J. H. (1979, September). *Personality development in males and females: The influence of differential socialization.* Paper presented as part of the master Lecture Series at the meeting of the American Psychological Association, New York.

BLOOM-FESHBACH, J. (1981). Historical perspectives on the father's role. In M. E. Lamb (Ed.), *The role of the father in child development* (pp. 71–112). New York: Wiley.

BLUMSTEIN, P., & SCHWARTZ, P. (1983). *American couples.* New York: William Morrow.

BLY, R. (1990). *Iron John: A book about men.* Reading, MA: Addison-Wesley.

BOOTH, A., JOHNSON, D. R., WHITE, L., & EDWARDS, J. N. (1984). Women, outside employment, and marital instability. *American Journal of Sociology, 90,* 567–583.

BOUCHIER, D. (1984). *The feminist challenge.* New York: Schocken.

Bowers v. Hardwick, 478 U.S. Supreme Court (1986).

BRADBARD, M. R. (1985). Sex differences in adults' gifts and children's toy requests at Christmas. *Psychological Reports, 56,* 969–970.

BRAVERMAN, L. (1991). The dilemma of housework: A feminist response to Gottman, Napier, and Pittman. *Journal of Marital and Family Therapy, 17,* 25–28.

BREHM, J. W. (1966). *A theory of psychological reactance.* New York: Academic Press.

BREHM, S. S., & KASSIN, S. M. (1992). *Social psychology* (2nd ed.). Boston, MA: Houghton-Mifflin.

BRENNER, O. C., TOMKIEWICZ, J., & SCHEIN, V. E. (1989). The relationship between sex role stereotypes and requisite management characteristics revisited. *Academy of Management Journal, 32,* 662–669.

BRETL, D. J., & CANTOR, J. (1988). The portrayal of men and women in U.S. television commercials: A recent content analysis and trends over 15 years. *Sex Roles, 18,* 595–609.

BREWER, M. B. (1979). Ingroup bias in the minimal intergroup situation: A cognitive-motivational analysis. *Psychological Bulletin, 86,* 207–324.

BREWER, M. B. (1991). The social self: On being the same and different at the same time. *Personality and Social Psychology Bulletin, 17,* 475–482.

BRIERE, J., & LANKTREE, C. (1983). Sex-role related effects of bias in language. *Sex Roles, 9,* 625–632.

BRODY, L. R. (1984). Sex and age variations in the quality and intensity of children's emotional attributions to hypothetical situations. *Sex Roles, 11,* 51–59.

BRODY, L. R. (1985). Gender differences in emotional development: A review of theories and research. *Journal of Personality, 53,* 102–149.

BRONSTEIN, P. (1984). Differences in mothers' and fathers' behaviors toward children: A cross-cultural comparison. *Developmental Psychology, 6,* 995–1003.

BROPHY, J. (1985). Interactions of male and female students with male and female teachers. In L. C. Wilkenson & C. B. Marrett (Eds.), *Gender influences in classroom interaction.* Hillsdale, NJ: Erlbaum.

BULBECK, C. (1988). *One world women's movement.* London: Pluto Press.

BURBANK, V. K. (1994). Cross-cultural perspectives on aggression in women and girls: An introduction. *Sex Roles, 30,* 169–176.

BURKE, R., & McKEEN, C. (1988). Work and family: What we know and what we need to know. *Canadian Journal of Administrative Sciences, 5,* 30–40.

BURN, S. M. (1993). *The social identity paradox and the effects of male-bashing on collective self-esteem.* Paper submitted for publication.

BURN, S. M., & LAVER, G. D. (1994). *Normative and informational pressure in conformity to the male role: Males', females', and friends' masculinity ideologies.* Paper submitted for publication.

BURN, S. M., NEDEREND, S., & O'NEIL, A. K. (1994, August). *Childhood tomboyism and adult androgyny.* Paper presented at the 102nd Annual Convention of the American Psychological Association, Los Angeles.

BURN, S. M., & OSKAMP, S. (1989). Ingroup biases and the U.S.-Soviet conflict. *Journal of Social Issues, 45,* 73–89.

BUSS, D. M. (1989). Sex differences in human mate preferences: Evolutionary hypothesis tested in 37 cultures. *Behavioral and Brain Sciences, 12,* 1–49.

BUSS, D. M., & BARNES, M. (1986). Preferences in human mate selection. *Journal of Personality and Social Psychology, 50,* 559–570.

BUSSEY, K., & BANDURA, A. (1992). Self-regulatory mechanisms governing gender development. *Child Development, 63,* 1236–1250.

BYLSMA, W. H., & MAJOR, B. (1992). Two routes to eliminating gender differences in personal entitlement. *Psychology of Women Quarterly, 16,* 193–200.

CADDICK, B. (1982). Perceived illegitimacy and intergroup relations. In H. Tajfel (Ed.), *Social identity and intergroup relations* (pp. 137–154). Cambridge, England: Cambridge University Press.

CAIN, R. (1991). Stigma management and gay identity development. *Social Work, 36,* 67–73.

CALDERA, Y. M., HUSTON, A. C., & O'BRIEN, M. (1989). Social interactions and play patterns of parents and toddlers with feminine, masculine, and neutral toys. *Child Development, 60,* 70–76.

CALDWELL, M. A., & PEPLAU, L. A. (1982). Sex differences in same-sex friendship. *Sex Roles, 8,* 721–731.

CALLAHAN, L. G., & CLEMENTS, D. H. (1984). Sex differences in rote-counting ability on entry to the first grade: Some observations. *Journal for Research in Mathematics Education, 15,* 378–382.

CAMPBELL, A., & MUNCER, S. (1987). Models of anger and aggression in the social talk of women and men. *Journal for the Theory of Social Behavior, 17,* 489–512.

CAMPBELL, A., MUNCER, S., & COYLE, E. (1992). Social representation of aggression as an explanation for gender differences: A preliminary study. *Aggressive Behavior, 18,* 95–108.

CANINO, G. (1982). Transactional family patterns: A preliminary exploration of Puerto Rican female adolescents. In R. E. Zambrana (Ed.), *Work, family, and health: Latina women in transition* (pp. 27–36). New York: Hispanic Research Center.

CANN, A., & GARNETT, A. K. (1984). Sex stereotype impact on competence ratings by children. *Sex Roles, 11,* 333–343.

CANN, A., & SIEGFRIED, W. D. (1990). Gender stereotypes and dimensions of effective leader behavior. *Sex Roles, 23,* 413–419.

CANTOR, N., & MISCHEL, W. (1977). Traits as prototypes: Effects on recognition memory. *Journal of Personality and Social Psychology, 35,* 38–48.

CAPLAN, P. J. (1991). Delusional dominating personality disorder (DDPD). *Feminism and Psychology, 1,* 171–174.

CARLI, L. L. (1989). Gender differences in interaction style and influence. *Journal of Personality and Social Psychology, 59,* 941–951.

CARTER, D. B., & MCCLOSKEY, L. A. (1984). Peers and the maintenance of sex-typed behavior: The development of children's conceptions of cross-gender behavior in their peers. *Social Cognition, 2,* 294–314.

CATALYST. (1990). *Catalyst's study of women in corporate management.* New York: Catalyst.

CHAPMAN, L. J., & CHAPMAN, J. P. (1969). Illusory correlations as an obstacle to the use of valid diagnostic signs. *Journal of Abnormal Psychology, 74,* 271–280.

CHARLES, M., & HOPFLINGER, F. (1992). Gender, culture, and the division of household labor: A replication of U.S. studies for the case of Switzerland. *Journal of Comparative Family Studies, 23,* 375–387.

CHESSLER, P., & GOODMAN, E. J. (1976). *Women, money, and power.* New York: Morrow.

CIALDINI, R. B. (1993). *Influence: Science and practice* (3rd ed.). New York: HarperCollins.

CLARKE-STEWART, K. A. (1989). Infant day care: Maligned or malignant? *American Psychologist, 44,* 266–273.

CLARKE-STEWART, K. A., & BAILEY, B. L. (1990). Adjusting to divorce: Why do men have it easier? *Journal of Divorce, 13,* 75–94.

COBB, N. J., STEVENS-LONG, J., & GOLDSTEIN, S. (1982). The influence of televised models on toy preference in children. *Sex Roles, 8,* 1075–1080.

COHEN, C. E. (1981). Person categories and social perception: Testing some boundaries of the processing effects of prior knowledge. *Journal of Personality and Social Psychology, 40,* 441–452.

COHEN, J. (1969). *Statistical power analysis for the behavioral sciences.* New York: Academic Press.

CONDRY, J., & CONDRY, S. (1976). Sex differences: A study of the eye of the beholder. *Child Development, 47,* 812–819.

CONDRY, J., & DYER, S. (1976). Fear of success: Attribution of cause to the victim. *Journal of Social Issues, 32,* 63–83.

CONDRY, J. C., & ROSS, D. F. (1985). Sex and aggression: The influence of gender label on the perception of aggression in children. *Child Development, 56,* 225–233.

CONNOR, J. M., SCHACKMAN, M., & SERBIN, L. A. (1978). Sex-related differences in response to practice on a visual-spatial test and generalization to a related test. *Child Development, 49,* 24–29.

CONNOR, J. M., & SERBIN, L. A. (1985). Visual-spatial skill: Is it important for mathematics? Can it be taught? In S. F. Chipman, L. R. Brush, & D. M. Wilson (Eds.), *Women and mathematics: Balancing the equation* (pp. 151–174). Hillsdale, NJ: Erlbaum.

COOK, S. W. (1985). Experimenting on social issues: The case of school desegregation. *American Psychologist, 40,* 452–460.

COSTRICH, N., FEINSTEIN, J., KIDDER, L., MARACEK, J., & PASCALE, L. (1975). When stereotypes hurt: Three studies of penalties for sex-role reversals. *Journal of Experimental Social Psychology, 11,* 520–530.

CRABB, P. B., & BIELAWSKI, D. (1994). The social representation of material culture and gender in children's books. *Sex Roles, 30,* 69–79.

CRAMER, R. E., DRAGNA, M., CUPP, R. G., & STEWART, P. (1991). Contrast effects in the evaluation of the male sex role. *Sex Roles, 24,* 181–193.

CROCKER, J., HANNA, D. B., & WEBER, R. (1983). Person memory and causal attributions. *Journal of Personality and Social Psychology, 44,* 55–66.

CROCKER, J., & LUHTANEN, R. (1990). Collective self-esteem and ingroup bias. *Journal of Personality and Social Psychology, 58,* 60–67.

CROCKER, J., & MAJOR, B. (1989). Social stigma and self-esteem: The self-protective properties of stigma. *Psychological Review, 96,* 608–630.

CROSBY, F. J. (1982). *Relative deprivation and working women.* New York: Oxford University Press.

CROSBY, F. J. (1987). Job satisfaction and domestic life. In M. D. Lee and R. N. Kunango (Eds.), *Management of work and personal life.* New York: Praeger.

CROSBY, F. J. (1991). *Juggling: The unexpected advantages of balancing career and home for women and their families.* New York: Free Press.

CROSS, S. E., & MARKUS, H. R. (1993). Gender in thought, belief, and action: A cognitive approach. In A. E. Beall & R. J. Sternberg (Eds.), *The psychology of gender* (pp. 55–98). New York: Guilford Press.

CROW DOG, M. (1993). *Ohitika woman.* New York: Grove Press.

CULP, R. E., COOK, A. S., & HOUSELY, P. C. (1983). A comparison of observed and reported adult-infant interactions: Effects of perceived sex. *Sex Roles, 9,* 475–479.

DARLEY, S. A. (1976). Big-time careers for the little woman: A dual-role dilemma. *Journal of Social Issues, 32,* 85–98.

DAVIDSON, A. R., & THOMSON, E. (1980). Cross-cultural studies of attitudes and beliefs. In H. C. Triandis & W. W. Lambert (Eds.), *Handbook of cross-cultural psychology* (Vol. 5, pp. 25–72). Boston: Allyn & Bacon.

DAVIS, D. M. (1991). Portrayals of women in prime-time network television: Some demographic characteristics. *Sex Roles, 23,* 325–332.

DAVIS, F., & WALSH, W. B. (1988, August). *Antecedents and consequents of gender role conflict: An empirical test of sex role strain analysis.* Paper presented at the 96th Annual Convention of the American Psychological Association, Atlanta.

DAVIS, S. (1990). Men as success objects and women as sex objects: A study of personal advertisements. *Sex Roles, 23,* 43–51.

DEAUX, K. (1985). Sex and gender. *Annual Review of Psychology, 36,* 49–81.

DEAUX, K. (1993). Sorry, wrong number—A reply to Gentile's call. *Psychological Science, 4,* 125–126.

DEAUX, K., & EMSWHILLER, T. (1974). Explanations of successful performance on sex-linked tasks: What is skill for the male is luck for the female. *Journal of Personality and Social Psychology, 29,* 80–85.

DEAUX, K., & LEWIS, L. L. (1984). Structure of gender stereotypes: Interrelationships among components and gender label. *Journal of Personality and Social Psychology, 46,* 991–1004.

DEAUX, K., WINTON, W., CROWLEY, M., & LEWIS, L. L. (1985). Level of categorization and content of sex stereotypes. *Social Cognition, 3,* 145–167.

DEFEIS, E. F. (1991). An international human right: Gender equality. *Journal of Women's History, 3,* 90–107.

DEGLER, C. N. (1990). Darwinians confront gender; or, There is more to it than history. In D. L. Rhode (Ed.), *Theoretical perspectives on sexual difference* (pp. 33–46). New Haven, CT: Yale University Press.

DeLEON, B. (1993). Sex role identity among college students: A cross-cultural analysis. *Hispanic Journal of Behavioral Sciences, 15,* 476–489.

DEMO, D. H., & ACOCK, A. C. (1993). Family diversity and the division of domestic labor. *Family Relations, 42,* 323–331.

DENMARK, F. L., & FERNANDEZ, L. C. (1993). Historical development of the psychology of women. In F. L. Denmark & M. A. Paludi (Eds.), *Psychology of women: A handbook of issues and theories* (pp. 3–22). Westport, CT: Greenwood Press.

DERLEGA, V. J., & BERG, J. H. (1987). *Self-disclosure: Theory, research, and therapy.* New York: Plenum Press.

DERLEGA, V. J., & CHAIKEN, A. L. (1976). Norms affecting self-disclosure in men and women. *Journal of Consulting and Clinical Psychology, 44,* 376–380.

DEUTSCH, M., & GERARD, H. B. (1955). A study of normative and informational social influence on social judgment. *Journal of Abnormal and Social Psychology, 51,* 629–636.

DEVINE, P. G. (1989). Stereotypes and prejudice: Their automatic and controlled components. *Journal of Personality and Social Psychology, 56,* 5–18.

DEVLIN, P. K., & COWAN, G. A. (1985). Homophobia, perceived fathering, and male intimate relationships. *Journal of Personality Assessment, 49,* 467–473.

DEW, M. A. (1985). The effect of attitudes on inferences of homosexuality and perceived physical attractiveness in women. *Sex Roles, 12,* 143–155.

DION, K. L. (1986). Responses to perceived discrimination and relative deprivation. In J. M. Olson, C. P. Herman, & M. P. Zanna (Eds.), *Relative deprivation and social comparison: The Ontario Symposium* (Vol. 4, pp. 159–179). Hillsdale, NJ: Erlbaum.

DION, K. L., & SCHULLER, R. A. (1990). Ms. and the manager: A tale of two stereotypes. *Sex Roles, 22,* 569–577.

DOBBINS, H. G., CARDY, L. R., TRUXILLO, M. D. (1988). The effects of purpose of appraisal and individual differences in stereotypes of women on sex differences in performance ratings: A laboratory and field study. *Journal of Applied Psychology, 3,* 331–558.

DOLGIN, K. G., MEYER, L., & SCHWARTZ, J. (1991). Effects of gender, target's gender, topic, and self-esteem on disclosure to best and middling friends. *Sex Roles, 25,* 311–329.

DONNELL, S. M., & HALL, J. (1980). Men and women as managers: A significant case of no significant difference. *Organizational Dynamics, 8,* 60–76.

DOSSEY, J. A., MULLIS, I. V. S., LINDQUIST, M. M., & CHAMBERS, D. L. (1988). *The math-*

ematics report card: Are we measuring up? Trends and achievement based on the 1986 National Assessment. Princeton, NJ: Educational Testing Service.

DOVIDIO, J. F., BROWN, C. E., HELTMAN, K., ELLYSON, S. L., & KEATING, C. F. (1988). Power displays between men and women in discussions of gender-linked tasks: A multichannel study. *Journal of Personality and Social Psychology, 55,* 580–587.

DOYLE, J. A. (1983). *The male experience.* Dubuque, IA: Wm. C. Brown.

DUANE, M. J. (1989). Sex differences in styles of conflict management. *Psychological Reports, 65,* 1033–1034.

DUBISCH, J. (1993). 'Foreign chickens' and other outsiders: Gender and community in Greece. *American Ethnologist, 20,* 272–287.

DUGGER, K. (1988). Social location and gender role attitudes: A comparison of black and white women. *Gender and Society, 2,* 425–448.

DUXBURY, L. A., & HIGGINS, C. A. (1991). Gender differences in work-family conflict. *Journal of Applied Psychology, 76,* 60–74.

DWECK, C. S., & BUSH, E. S. (1978). Sex differences in learned helplessness: I. Differential debilitation with peer and adult evaluators. *Developmental Psychology, 12,* 147–156.

DWECK, C. S., DAVIDSON, W., NELSON, S., & ENNA, B. (1978). Sex differences in learned helplessness: II. The contingencies of evaluative feedback in the classroom and III. An experimental analysis. *Developmental Psychology, 14,* 268–276.

DWECK, C. S., GOETZ, T. E., & STRAUSS, N. L. (1980). Sex differences in learned helplessness: IV. An experimental and naturalistic study of failure generalization and its mediators. *Journal of Personality and Social Psychology, 38,* 441–452.

EAGLY, A. H. (1978). Sex differences in influenceability. *Psychological Bulletin, 85,* 86–116.

EAGLY, A. H. (1983). Gender and social influence: A social psychological analysis. *American Psychologist, 38,* 971–995.

EAGLY, A. H. (1987). *Sex differences in social behavior: A social-role interpretation.* Hillsdale, NJ: Erlbaum.

EAGLY, A. H., & CARLI, L. L. (1981). Sex of researchers and sex-typed communications as determinants of sex differences in influenceability: A meta-analysis of social influence studies. *Psychological Bulletin, 90,* 1–20.

EAGLY, A. H., & CROWLEY, M. (1986). Gender and helping behavior: A meta-analytic review of the social psychological literature. *Psychological Bulletin, 100,* 283–308.

EAGLY, A. H., & JOHNSON, B. T. (1990). Gender and leadership style: A meta-analysis. *Psychological Bulletin, 108,* 233–256.

EAGLY, A. H., MAKHIJANI, M. G., & KLONSKY, B. G. (1992). Gender and the evaluation of leaders: A meta-analysis. *Psychological Bulletin, 111,* 3–22.

EAGLY, A. H., & MLADNIC, A. (1989). Gender stereotypes and attitudes toward men and women. *Personality and Social Psychology Bulletin, 15,* 543–548.

EAGLY, A. H., & STEFFEN, V. J. (1984). Gender stereotypes stem from the distribution of women and men into social roles. *Journal of Personality and Social Psychology, 46,* 735–754.

EAGLY, A. H., & STEFFEN, V. J. (1986). Gender and aggressive behavior: A meta-analytic review of the social-psychological literature. *Psychological Bulletin, 100,* 309–330.

EAGLY, A. H., & WOOD, W. (1982). Inferred sex differences in status as a determinant of gender stereotypes about social influence. *Journal of Personality and Social Psychology, 43,* 915–928.

EAGLY, A. H., & WOOD, W. (1985). Gender and influenceability: Stereotype versus behavior. In V. E. O'Leary, R. K. Unger, & B. S. Wallston (Eds.), *Women, gender, and social psychology* (pp. 225–256). Hillsdale, NJ: Erlbaum.

EAGLY, A. H., & WOOD, W. (1991). Explaining sex differences in social behavior: A meta-analytic perspective. *Personality and Social Psychology Bulletin, 17,* 306–315.

EAGLY, A. H., WOOD, W., & FISHBAUGH, L. (1981). Sex differences in conformity: Surveillance by the group as a determinant of male nonconformity. *Journal of Personality and Social Psychology, 40,* 384–394.

EBERHARDT, J. L., & FISKE, S. T. (1994). Affirmative action in theory and implementation: Issues of power, ambiguity, and gender versus race. *Basic and Applied Social Psychology, 15,* 201–220.

ECCLES, J. S. (1984a). Sex differences in achievement patterns. In T. Sonderegger (Ed.), *Nebraska Symposium on Motivation, 32.* Lincoln, NE: University of Nebraska Press.

ECCLES (PARSONS), J. S. (1984b). Sex differences in mathematics participation. In M. L. Maehr & M. W. Steinkamp (Eds.), *Women in science: Advances in motivation and achievement* (Vol. 2). Greenwich, CT: JAI Press.

ECCLES, J. S. (1989). Bringing young women to math and science. In M. Crawford & M. Gentry (Eds.), *Gender and thought: Psychological perspectives* (pp. 36–58). New York: Springer-Verlag.

ECCLES (PARSONS), J. S. (1990). Gender-role socialization. In R. M. Baron & W. G. Graziano (Eds.), *Social psychology* (pp. 160–191). Fort Worth, TX: Holt Rinehart and Winston.

ECCLES, J. S., & BLUMENFELD, P. (1985). Classroom experiences and student gender: Are there differences and do they matter? In L. C. Wilkenson & C. Marrett (Eds.), *Gender influences in classroom interaction.* Hillsdale, NJ: Erlbaum.

ECCLES, J. S., & JACOBS, J. (1986). Social forces shape math attitudes and performance. *Signs, 11,* 367–380.

ECCLES, J. S., JACOBS, J., & HAROLD, R. D. (1990). Gender role stereotypes, expectancy effects, and parents' socialization of gender differences. *Journal of Social Issues, 46,* 183–201.

ECCLES-PARSONS, J., ADLER, T., & KACZALA, C. (1982). Socialization of achievement attitudes and beliefs: Parental influences. *Child Development, 53,* 310–321.

EDWARDS, G. H. (1992). The structure and content of the male gender role stereotype: An exploration of subtypes. *Sex Roles, 27,* 533–551.

EISENBERG, N., FABES, R. A., SCHALLER, M., & MILLER, P. A. (1989). Sympathy and personal distress: Development, gender differences, and interrelations of indexes. In N. Eisenberg (Ed.), *Empathy and Related Emotional Responses: New Directions for Child Development, 44,* 107–127.

EISENBERG, N., & LENNON, R. (1983). Sex differences in empathy and related capacities. *Psychology Bulletin, 94,* 100–131.

EISLER, R. M., SKIDMORE, J. R., & WARD, C. H. (1988). Masculine gender-role stress: Predictor of anger, anxiety, and health-risk behaviors. *Journal of Personality Assessment, 52,* 133–141.

EL-BAKRI, Z. B., & KAMEIR, E. M. (1983). Aspects of women's political participation in Sudan. *International Social Science Journal, 35,* 605–623.

ELLEMERS, N., WILKE, H., & VAN KNIPPENBERG, A. (1993). Effects of legitimacy of low group or individual status on individual and collective status-enhancement strategies. *Journal of Personality and Social Psychology, 64*, 766–788.

EMMERICH, W., GOLDMAN, K. S., KIRSH, B., & SHARBANY, R. (1977). Evidence for a transitional phase in the development of gender constancy. *Child Development, 48*, 930–936.

EMMOT, S. (1985). Sex differences in children's play: Implications for cognition. Special issue: Sex roles, sex differences, and androgyny. *International Journal of Women's Studies, 8*, 449–456.

ENGLE, P. L. (1993). Influences of mothers' and fathers' income on children's nutritional status in Guatemala. *Social Science & Medicine, 37*, 1303–1312.

ENGLE, P. L., & BREAUX, C. (1994). *Is there a father instinct? Fathers' responsibility for children.* Report for The Population Council (New York) and the International Center for Research on Women (Washington, DC).

ERICKSEN, J. A., YANCEY, W. L., & ERICKSEN, E. P. (1979). The division of family roles. *Journal of Marriage and the Family, 41*, 301–313.

ERICKSON, R. J., & GECAS, V. (1991). Social class and fatherhood. In F. W. Bozett & S.M.H. Hanson (Eds.), *Fatherhood and families in cultural context* (pp. 114–137). New York: Springer-Verlage.

ERLICH, H. J. (1973). *The social psychology of prejudice: A systematic theoretical review and propositional inventory of the American social psychological study of prejudice.* New York: Wiley.

ESPIN, O., & WARNER, B. (1982). Attitudes toward the role of women attending a community college. *International Journal of Social Psychiatry, 28*, 233–239.

ESTES, C. P. (1992). *Women who run with the wolves.* New York: Ballantine.

ETAUGH, C., & LISS, M. B. (1992). Home, school, and playroom: Training grounds for adult gender roles. *Sex Roles, 26*, 129–147.

ETAUGH, C., & POERTNER, P. (1992). Perceptions of women: Influence of performance, marital and parental variables. *Sex Roles, 26*, 311–321.

FABES, R. A., & MARTIN, C. L. (1991). Gender and age stereotypes of emotionality. *Personality and Social Psychology Bulletin, 17*, 532–540.

FAGOT, B. I. (1978). The influence of sex of child on parental reactions to toddler children. *Child Development, 49*, 459–465.

FAGOT, B. I., & LEINBACH, M. D. (1989). The young child's gender schema: Environmental input, internal organization. *Child Development, 60*, 663–672.

FAIRCHILD, B., & HAYWARD, N. (1989). *Now that you know: What every parent should know about homosexuality.* New York: Harcourt Brace Jovanovich.

FARR, K. (1988). Dominance bonding through the good old boys sociability group. *Sex Roles, 18*, 259–277.

FAUSTO-STERLING, A. (1985). *Myths of gender.* New York: Basic Books.

FEINGOLD, A. (1988). Cognitive gender differences are disappearing. *American Psychologist, 43*, 95–103.

FEINMAN, S. (1981). Why is cross-sex-role behavior more approved for girls than for boys? A status characteristic approach. *Sex Roles, 7*, 289–299.

FENNEMA, E., & SHERMAN, J. A. (1977). Sex-related differences in mathematics achievement, spatial visualization, and affective factors. *American Educational Research Journal, 14*, 51–71.

FENNEMA, E., & SHERMAN, J. A. (1978). Sex related factors: A further study. *Journal for Research in Mathematics Education, 9*, 189–203.

FERREE, M. M. (1980). Satisfaction with housework. In S. F. Berk (Ed.), *Women and household labor* (pp. 89–112). Beverly Hills: Sage.

FERREE, M. M. (1987). Family and job for working-class women: Gender and class systems seen from below. In N. Gerstel & H. E. Gross (Eds.), *Families and work* (pp. 289–301). Philadelphia: Temple University Press.

FESTINGER, L., & CARLSMITH, J. M. (1959). Cognitive consequences of forced compliance. *Journal of Abnormal and Social Psychology, 58,* 203–210.

FIERMAN, J. (1990, July 30). Why women still don't hit the top. *Fortune,* p. 42.

FILER, R. (1985). Male-female wage differences: The importance of compensating differentials. *Industrial and Labor Relations Review, 38,* 426–437.

FILER, R. (1989). Occupational segregation, compensating differentials, and comparable worth. In R. Michael, H. Hartmann, & B. O'Farrell (Eds.), *Pay equity: Empirical inquiries* (pp. 153–170). Washington, DC: National Academy.

FISHBEIN, M., & AJZEN, I. (1975). *Belief, attitude, intention, and behavior: An introduction to theory and research.* Reading, MA: Addison-Wesley.

FISKE, A. P., HASLAM, N., & FISKE, S. T. (1991). Confusing one person with another: What errors reveal about the elementary forms of social relations. *Journal of Personality and Social Psychology, 60,* 656–674.

FISKE, S. T., BERSOFF, D. N., BORGIDA, E., DEAUX, K., & HEILMAN, M. E. (1991). Social science research on trial: Use of sex stereotyping research in *Price Waterhouse v. Hopkins. American Psychologist, 46,* 1049–1060.

FISKE, S. T., & STEVENS, L. E. (1993). What's so special about sex? Gender stereotyping and discrimination. In S. Oskamp & M. Costanzo (Eds.), *Gender issues in contemporary society* (pp. 173–196). Newbury Park, CA: Sage.

FISKE, S. T., & TAYLOR, S. E. (1984). *Social cognition.* New York: Random House.

FOLGER, R. (1987). Reformulating the preconditions of resentment. A referent congitions model. In J. C. Masters & W. P. Smith (Eds.), *Social comparison, social justice, and relative deprivation* (pp. 183–215). Hillsdale, NJ: Erlbaum.

FORSYTH, D. R. (1990). *Group dynamics* (2nd ed.). Monterey, CA: Brooks-Cole.

FOWLKES, M. R. (1987). Role combinations and role conflict: Introductory perspective. In F. J. Crosby (Ed.), *Spouse, parent, worker: On gender and multiple social roles* (pp. 3–10). New Haven, CT: Yale University Press.

FRABLE, D.E.S. (1989). Sex typing and gender ideology: Two facets of the individual's gender psychology that go together. *Journal of Personality and Social Psychology, 56,* 95–108.

FRABLE, D.E.S., & BEM, S. L. (1985). If you are gender schematic, all members of the opposite sex look alike. *Journal of Personality and Social Psychology, 49,* 459–468.

FRANK, E. (1988). Business students' perceptions of women in management. *Sex Roles, 19,* 107–118.

FRANKE, R., & LEARY, M. R. (1991). Disclosure of sexual orientation by lesbians and gay men: A comparison of private and public processes. *Journal of Social and Clinical Psychology, 10,* 262–269.

FREEDMAN, S. M., & PHILLIPS, J. S. (1988). The changing nature of research on women at work. *Journal of Management, 14,* 231–251.

FRENCH, M. (1992). *The war against women.* New York: Summit Books.

FRIEDAN, B. (1963). *The feminine mystique.* New York: Norton.

FRIEDMAN, L. (1989). Mathematics and the gender gap: A meta-analysis of recent studies on sex differences in mathematical tasks. *Review of Educational Research, 59,* 185–213.

FURNHAM, A., & SINGH, A. (1986). Memory for information about sex differences. *Sex Roles, 15,* 479–486.

FURSTENBERG, F. F., Jr. (1988). Child care after divorce and remarriage. In E. M. Hetherington & J. D. Arasteh (Eds.), *Impact of divorce, singleparenting, and stepparenting on children* (pp. 245–261). Hillsdale, NJ: Erlbaum.

GALLUP REPORT. (1987, December). *U.S. women endorse jobs, marriage, and children.* (Rep. No. 267, pp. 24–25).

GARLEN, H. (1982). Attributions for the success and failure of female managers: A replication and extension. *Psychology of Women Quarterly, 7,* 155–162.

GASTIL, J. (1990). Generic pronouns and sexist language: The oxymoronic character of masculine generics. *Sex Roles, 23,* 629–643.

GEARY, D. C. (1989). A model for representing gender differences in the pattern of cognitive abilities. *American Psychologist, 102,* 1155–1157.

GEIS, F. L. (1993). Self-fulfilling prophecies: A social psychological view of gender. In A. E. Beall & R. J. Sternberg (Eds.), *The psychology of gender* (pp. 9–54). New York: Guilford Press.

GEIS, F. L., BROWN, V., JENNINGS, J., & PORTER, N. (1984). TV commercials as achievement scripts for women. *Sex Roles, 10,* 513–525.

GENTILE, D. A. (1993). Just what are sex and gender, anyway? A call for a new terminological standard. *Psychological Science, 4,* 120–122.

GERBNER, G., & GROSS, L. (1976). Living with television: The violence profile. *Journal of Communication, 26,* 173–199.

GERHART, B., & RYNES, S. (1991). Determinants and consequences of salary negotiations by male and female MBA graduates. *Journal of Applied Psychology, 76,* 256–262.

GIBBONS, J. L., STILES, D. A., & SHKODRIANI, G. M. (1991). Adolescents' attitudes toward family and gender roles: An international comparison. *Sex Roles, 25,* 625–643.

GILLIGAN, C. (1982). *In a different voice: Psychological theory and women's development.* Cambridge, MA: Harvard University Press.

GLASS, G. V., McGAW, B., & SMITH, M. L. (1981). *Meta-analysis in social research.* Newbury Park, CA: Sage.

GLASS, J., & CAMARIGG, V. (1992). Gender, parenthood, and job-family compatibility. *American Journal of Sociology, 98,* 131–151.

GLICK, P. (1991). Trait-based and sex-based discrimination in occupational prestige, occupational salary, and hiring. *Sex Roles, 25,* 351–378.

GLICK, P., ZION, C., & NELSON, C. (1988). What mediates sex discrimination in hiring decisions? *Journal of Personality and Social Psychology, 55,* 178–186.

GOFFMAN, I. (1977). The arrangement between the sexes. *Theory and Society, 4,* 301–332.

GOLDBERG, C. (1974). Sex roles, task competence, and conformity. *Journal of Psychology, 86,* 157–164.

GOLDBERG, C. (1975). Conformity to majority types as a function of task and acceptance of sex-related stereotypes. *Journal of Psychology, 89,* 25–37.

GOLUB, S. (1976). The effect of premenstrual anxiety and depression on cognitive function. *Journal of Personality and Social Psychology, 34,* 99–104.

GONDOLF, E. W. (1988). Who are those guys? Toward a behavioral typology of batterers. *Violence and Victims, 3,* 187–203.

GOOD, G. E, & MINTZ, L. M. (1990). Gender role conflict and depression in college men: Evidence for compounded risk. *Journal of Counseling and Development, 69*, 17–21.

GOOD, G. F., GILBERT, L. A., & SCHER, M. (1990). Gender aware therapy: A synthesis of feminist therapy and knowledge about gender. *Journal of Counseling Psychology, 68*, 376–380.

GORE, S., & MANGIONE, T. W. (1983). Social roles, sex roles and psychological distress: Additive and interactive models of sex differences. *Journal of Health and Social Behavior, 24*, 300–312.

GOTTLIEB, B. H., & WAGNER, F. (1991). Stress and support processes in close relationships. In J. Eckenrode (Ed.), *The social context of coping* (pp. 165–188). New York: Plenum Press.

GOVE, W. (1972). The relationship between sex roles, marital status, and mental illness. *Social Forces, 51*, 34–44.

GOVE, W., & TUDOR, J. (1973). Adult sex roles and mental illness. In J. Huber (Ed.), *Changing women in a changing society.* Chicago: University of Chicago Press.

GRADY, K. (1979). Androgyny reconsidered. In J. H. Williams (Ed.), *Psychology of women: Selected Readings* (pp. 172–177). New York: Norton.

GREENHAUS, J. H., & PARASURAMAN, S. (1993). Job performance attributions and career advancement prospects: An examination of gender and race effects. *Organizational Behavior and Human Decision Processes, 55*, 273-297.

GUNTER, N. C., & GUNTER, B. G. (1990). Domestic division of labor among working couples: Does androgyny make a difference? *Psychology of Women Quarterly, 14*, 355–370.

GUTEK, B. A., & COHEN, A. G. (1987). Sex ratios, sex role spillover, and sex at work: A comparison of men's and women's experience. *Human Relations, 40*, 97–115.

GUTEK, B. A., & MORASCH, B. (1982). Sex-ratios, sex-role spillover, and sexual harassment of women at work. *Journal of Social Issues, 38*, 55–74.

HABERFELD, Y. (1992). Employment discrimination: An organizational model. *Academy of Management Journal, 35*, 161–180.

HACKER, H. M. (1981). Blabbermouths and clams: Sex differences in self-disclosure in same-sex and cross-sex friendship dyads. *Psychology of Women Quarterly, 5*, 385–401.

HALL, D. T. (1990, Winter). Promoting the work/family balance: An organizational change approach: *Organizational Dynamics*, pp. 5–18.

HALL, J. A. (1978). Gender effects in decoding nonverbal cues. *Psychological Bulletin, 85*, 845–875.

HALL, J. A. (1984). *Nonverbal sex differences: Communication accuracy and expressive style.* Baltimore: Johns Hopkins University Press.

HALPERN, D. F. (1992). *Sex differences in cognitive abilities* (2nd ed.). Hillsdale, NJ: Erlbaum.

HAMILTON, D. L. (1981). Illusory correlation as a basis for stereotyping. In D. L. Hamilton (Ed.), *Cognitive processes in stereotyping and intergroup behavior.* Hillsdale, NJ: Erlbaum.

HAMILTON, D. L., & GIFFORD, R. (1976). Illusory correlation in interpersonal perception: A cognitive basis of stereotypic judgments. *Journal of Experimental Social Psychology, 12*, 392–407.

HAMILTON, D. L., & ROSE, T. (1980). Illusory correlation and the maintenance of stereotypic beliefs. *Journal of Personality and Social Psychology, 39*, 832–845.

HAMPSON, E., & KIMURA, D. (1988). Reciprocal effects of hormonal fluctuations on human motor and perceptual-spatial skills. *Behavioral Neuroscience, 102,* 456–495.

HARDESTY, C., BOKEMEIER, J. (1989). Finding time and making do: Distribution of household labor in nonmetropolitan marriages. *Journal of Marriage and the Family, 51,* 253–267.

HARDING, S. (1986). *The science question in feminism.* Ithaca, NY: Cornell University Press.

HARGREAVES, D. (1987). *The psychology of sex roles.* New York: Cambridge University Press..

HASTIE, R. (1981). Schematic principles in human memory. In E. T. Higgins, C. P. Herman, & M. P. Zanna (Eds.), *Social cognition: The Ontario Symposium* (Vol. 1, pp. 39–70). Hillsdale, NJ: Erlbaum.

HAWKINS, A. J., & ROBERTS, T. A. (1992). Designing a primary intervention to help dual-earner couples share housework and childcare. *Family Relations, 41,* 169–177.

HAYS, R. B. (1988). Friendship. In S. Duck (Ed.), *Handbook of personal relationships: Theory, research, and interventions* (pp. 391–408). New York: Wiley.

HEILMAN, M. E. (1983). Sex bias in work settings: The lack of fit model. In L. L. Cummings & B. M. Staw (Eds.), *Research in organizational behavior* (Vol. 5, pp. 269–298). Greenwich, CT: JAI Press.

HEILMAN, M. E. (1994). Affirmative action: Some unintended consequences for working women. *Research in Organizational Behavior, 16,* 125–169.

HEILMAN, M. E., BLOCK, C. J., & LUCAS, J. A. (1992). Presumed incompetent? Stigmatization and affirmative action efforts. *Journal of Applied Psychology, 77,* 536–544.

HEILMAN, M. E., BLOCK, C. J., MARTELL, R. F., & SIMON, M. C. (1989). Has anything changed? Current conceptions of men, women, and managers. *Journal of Applied Psychology, 74,* 935–942.

HEILMAN, M. E., LUCAS, J., & KAPLOW, S. (1990). Self-derogating consequences of sex-based preferential selection: The moderating role of initial self-confidence. *Organizational Behavior and Human Decision Processes, 46,* 202–216.

HEILMAN, M. E., & MARTELL, R. F. (1986). Exposure to successful women: Antidote to sex discrimination in applicant screening decisions? *Organizational Behavior and Human Decision Processes, 37,* 376–390.

HEILMAN, M. E., RIVERO, J. C., & BRETT, J. F. (1991). Skirting the competence issue: Effects of sex-based preferential selection on task choices of women and men. *Journal of Applied Psychology, 76,* 99–105.

HEILMAN, M. E., SIMON, M. C., & REPPER, D. P. (1987). Intentionally favored, unintentionally harmed? Impact of sex-based preferential selection on self-perceptions and self-evaluations. *Journal of Applied Psychology, 72,* 62–68.

HEISTER, G., LANDIS, T., REGARD, M., & SCHROEDER-HEISTER, P. (1989). Shift of functional cerebral asymmetry during the menstrual cycle. *Neuropsychologia, 27,* 871–880.

HELGESON, V. S. (1990). The role of masculinity in a prognostic predictor of heart attack severity. *Sex Roles, 22,* 755–774.

HELLWEGE, D. R., PERRY, K., & DOBSON, J. (1988). Perceptual differences in gender ideas among heterosexual and homosexual males and females. *Sex Roles, 19,* 735–746.

HENLEY, N. M. (1989). Molehill or mountain? What we know and don't know about sex bias in language. In M. Crawford & M. Gentry (Eds.), *Gender and thought: Psychological perspectives* (pp. 59–78). New York: Springer-Verlag.

HEPBURN, C. (1985). Memory for the frequency of sex-typed versus neutral behaviors: Implications for the maintenance of sex stereotypes. *Sex Roles, 12,* 771–776.

HEREK, G. M. (1984). Beyond 'homophobia': A social psychological perspective on attitudes toward lesbians and gay men. *Journal of Homosexuality, 10,* 1–21.

HEWLETT, B. S. (1992). Husband-wife reciprocity and the father-infant relationship among Aka pygmies. In B. S. Hewlett (Ed.), *Father-child relations: Cultural and biosocial contexts* (pp. 153–176). New York: Aldine de Gruyter.

HEWSTONE, M. (1990). The 'ultimate attribution error?' A review of the literature on intergroup causal attribution. *European Journal of Social Psychology, 20,* 311–335.

HIGGINS, C. A., & DUXBURY, L. E. (1992). Work-family conflict: A comparison of dual-career and traditional-career men. *Journal of Organizational Behavior, 13,* 389–411.

HILLER, D. V., & DYEHOUSE, J. (1987). A case for banishing 'dual-career marriages' from the research literature. *Journal of Marriage and the Family, 49,* 787–795.

HILTON, J. M., & HALDEMAN, V. A. (1991). Gender differences in the performance of household tasks by adults and children in single-parent and two-parent, two-earner families. *Journal of Family Issues, 12,* 114–130.

HILTON, T. L., & BERGLUND, G. W. (1974). Sex differences in mathematics achievement—a longitudinal study. *Journal of Educational Research, 67,* 232–237.

HITT, M. A., & KEATS, B. W. (1984). Empirical identification of the criteria for effective affirmative action programs. *Journal of Applied Behavioral Science, 20,* 203–222.

HOCHSCHILD, A. (1989). *The second shift.* New York: Viking Press.

HOFFMAN, C., & HURST, N. (1990). Gender stereotypes: Perception or rationalization? *Journal of Personality and Social Psychology, 58,* 197–208.

HOFSTEDE, G. (1984). *Culture's consequences: International differences in work-related values.* Newbury Park, CA: Sage.

HOLLANDER, E. P. (1983). Women and leadership. In H. H. Blumenfield, A. P. Hare, V. Kent, & M. Davies (Eds.), *Small groups and social interaction* (Vol. 1, pp. 423–429). New York: Wiley.

HOLTZEN, D. W., & AGRESTI, A. A. (1990). Parental responses to gay and lesbian children: Differences in homophobia, self-esteem, and sex-role stereotyping. *Journal of Social and Clinical Psychology, 9,* 390–399.

HORNER, M. S. (1969, June). Fail: Bright women. *Psychology Today,* p. 36.

HORT, B. E., LEINBACH, M. D., & FAGOT, B. I. (1991). Is there coherence among the cognitive components of gender acquisition? *Sex Roles, 24,* 195–207.

HOWARD, J., & ROTHBART, M. (1980). Social categorization and memory for ingroup and outgroup behavior. *Journal of Personality and Social Psychology, 38,* 301–310.

HUBBARD, R. (1990). The political nature of 'human nature.' In D. L. Rhode (Ed.), *Theoretical perspectives on sexual difference* (pp. 63–73). New Haven, CT: Yale University Press.

HUDAK, M. A. (1993). Gender schema theory revisited: Men's stereotypes of American women. *Sex Roles, 28,* 279–293.

HUI, C. H., & TRIANDIS, H. C. (1986). Individualism-collectivism: A study of cross-cultural researchers. *Journal of Cross-Cultural Psychology, 17,* 225–248.

HUSTON, A. C. (1983). Sex-typing. In P. H. Mussen & E. M. Hetherington (Eds.), *Handbook of child psychology* (Vol. 4, pp. 387–467). New York: Wiley.

HYDE, J. S. (1984a). Children's understanding of sexist language. *Developmental Psychology, 20,* 697–706.

HYDE, J. S. (1984b). How large are gender differences in aggression: A developmental meta-analysis. *Developmental Psychology, 20,* 722–736.

HYDE, J. S. (1986). Gender differences in aggression. In J. A. Hyde & M. C. Linn (Eds.), *The psychology of gender: Advances through meta-analysis.* Baltimore: Johns Hopkins University Press.

HYDE, J. S. (1991). *Half the human experience: The psychology of women* (4th ed.). Lexington, MA: D. C. Heath and Company.

HYDE, J. S. (1992). Gender and sex: So what has meta-analysis done for me? *The Psychology Teacher Network Newsletter, 2,* 2–6.

HYDE, J. S., FENNEMA, E., & LAMON, S. J. (1990a). Gender differences in mathematics performance: A meta-analysis. *Psychological Bulletin, 107,* 139–155.

HYDE, J. S., FENNEMA, E., & LAMON, S. J. (1990b). Gender comparisons of mathematics attitudes and affect: A meta-analysis. *Psychology of Women Quarterly, 14,* 299–324.

HYDE, J. S., & FROST, L. A. (1993). Meta-analysis in the psychology of women. In F. L. Denmark & M. A. Paludi (Eds.), *Psychology of women: A handbook of issues and theories* (pp. 67–104). Westport, CT: Greenwood Press.

HYDE, J. S., & LINN, M. C. (1986). *The psychology of gender: Advances through meta-analysis.* Baltimore: Johns Hopkins University Press.

HYDE, J. S., ROSENBERG, B. G., & BEHRMAN, J. (1977). Tomboyism. *Psychology of Women Quarterly, 2,* 73–75.

ICKES, W. (1993). Traditional gender roles: Do they make, and then break, our relationships? *Journal of Social Issues, 49,* 71–85.

ICKES, W., & BARNES, R. D. (1978). Boys and girls together—and alienated: On enacting stereotyped sex roles in mixed-sex dyads. *Journal of Personality and Social Psychology, 78,* 669–683.

ICKOVICS, J. R. (1989). Is any job better than no job at all? The social psychological consequences of underemployment for women. *Dissertation Abstracts International, 50,* 5926B. (University Microfilms No. 90–09, 214)

ILGEN, D. R., & YOUTZ, M. A. (1986). Factors affecting the evaluation and development of minorities in organizations. *Personnel and Human Resources Management, 4,* 307–337.

ILYAS, Q.S.M. (1990). Determinants of perceived role conflict among women in Bangladesh. *Sex Roles, 22,* 237–248.

ISHII-KUNTZ, M. (1993). Japanese fathers: Work demands and family roles. In J. C. Hood (Ed.), *Men, work, and family* (pp. 45–67). Newbury Park, CA: Sage.

JACKLIN, C. N. (1989). Female and male: Issues of gender. *American Psychologist, 44,* 127–133.

JACKSON, L. A., GARDNER, P. D., & SULLIVAN, L. A. (1992). Explaining gender differences in self-pay expectations: Social comparison standards and perceptions of fair pay. *Journal of Applied Psychology, 77,* 651–663.

JACKSON, L. A., & GRABSKI, S. V. (1988). Perceptions of fair pay and the gender wage gap. *Journal of Applied Social Psychology, 18,* 606–625.

JACOBS, J. A. (1992). Women's entry into management: Trends in earnings, authority, and values among salaried managers. *Administrative Science Quarterly, 37*, 282–301.

JACOBS, J. A., & STEINBERG, R. (1990). Compensating differentials and the male-female wage gap: Evidence from the New York State Comparable Worth Study. *Social Forces, 69*, 439–468.

JACOBS, J. E. (1987). *Parents' gender role stereotypes and perceptions of their child's ability: Influences on the child.* Unpublished doctoral dissertation, University of Michigan, Ann Arbor.

JANKOWIAK, W. (1992). Father-child relations in urban China. In B. S. Hewlett (Ed.), *Father-child relations: Cultural and biosocial contexts* (pp. 345–363). New York: Aldine de Gruyter.

JENNINGS (WALSTEDT), J., GEIS, F. L., & BROWN, V. (1980). Influence of television commercials on women's self-confidence and independent judgment. *Journal of Personality and Social Psychology, 38*, 203–210.

JOHNSON, J., & ETTEMA, J. S. (1982). *Positive images: Breaking stereotypes with children's television.* Beverly Hills: Sage.

JOHNSON, J. T., & SHULMAN, G. A. (1988). More alike than meets the eye: Perceived gender differences in subjective experience and its display. *Sex Roles, 19*, 67–79.

JONES, B. H., & MCNAMARA, K. (1991). Attitudes toward women and their work roles: Effects of intrinsic and extrinsic religious orientations. *Sex Roles, 24*, 21–29.

JONES, D. C. (1991). Friendship satisfaction and gender: An examination of sex differences in contributors to friendship satisfaction. *Journal of Social and Personal Relationships, 8*, 167–185.

JONES, G. P., & DEMBO, M. H. (1989). Age and sex role differences in intimate friendships during childhood and adolescence. *Merrill-Palmer Quarterly, 35*, 445–462.

JUNN, E. N., BEASON, K., ENDO, L., VON ROTZ, D., & LACAYO, A. (1994, August). *Portrayals of love, marriage, and sexuality in Walt Disney's animated films.* Paper presented at the American Psychological Association meeting, Los Angeles.

KAGAN, J. (1964). Acquisition and significance of sex-typing and sex-role concepts and attitudes. In M. L. Hoffman & L. W. Hoffman (Eds.), *Review of child development research.* New York: Sage.

KAHLE, J. B., MATYAS, M. L., & CHO, H. (1985). An assessment of the impact of science experiences on the career choices of male and female biology students. *Journal of Research in Science and Teaching, 22*, 385–384.

KAHNEMAN, D., SLOVIC, P., & TVERSKY, A. (1982). *Judgment under uncertainty: Heuristics and biases.* New York: Cambridge University Press.

KALIN, R., & TILBY, R. (1978). Development and validation of a sex-role ideology scale. *Psychological Report, 42*, 731–738.

KALIN, R., HEUSSER, C., EDWARDS, J. (1982). Cross-national equivalence of a sex-role ideology scale. *Journal of Social Psychology, 116*, 141–142.

KANDEL, D. B., DAVIES, M., & RAVEIS, V. H. (1985). The stressfulness of daily social roles for women: Marital, occupational and household roles. *Journal of Health and Social Behavior, 26*, 64–78.

KANTER, R. M. (1976). The impact of hierarchical structures on the work behavior of women and men. *Social Problems, 23*, 415–430.

KANTER, R. M. (1977). *Men and women of the corporation.* New York: Basic Books.

KAPLAN, A., BROOKS, B., McCOMB, A. L., SHAPIRO, E. R., & SODANO, A. (1983). Women and anger in psychotherapy. *Women and Therapy, 2,* 29–40.

KATZENSTEIN, M. F. (1989). Organizing against violence: Strategies of the Indian women's movement. *Pacific Affairs, 62,* 53–71.

KENRICK, D. T. (1987). Gender, genes, and the social environment: A biosocial interactionist perspective. In P. Shaver & C. Hendrick (Eds.), *Sex and gender: Review of personality and social psychology* (Vol. 7, pp. 14–43). Beverly Hills, Sage.

KENRICK, D. T. (1988). Biology: Si! Hard-wired ability: Maybe no. *Behavioral and Brain Sciences, 11,* 199–200.

KENRICK, D. T., SADALLA, E. K., GROTH, G., & TROST, M. R. (1990). Evolution, traits, and the stages of human courtship: Qualifying the parental investment model. *Journal of Personality, 58,* 97–116.

KERIG, P. K., ALYOSHINA, Y. Y., & VOLOVICH, A. S. (1993). Gender-role socialization in contemporary Russia. *Psychology of Women Quarterly, 17,* 389–408.

KIBRIA, N., BARNETT, R. C., BARUCH, G. K., & MARSHALL, N. L. (1990). Homemaking-role quality and the psychological well-being and distress of employed women. *Sex Roles, 22,* 327–347.

KILMARTIN, C. T. (1994). *The masculine self.* New York: Macmillan.

KIMBALL, M. M. (1986). Television and sex-role attitudes. In T. Williams (Ed.), *The impact of television: A natural experiment in three communities.* Orlando, FL: Academic Press.

KIMBALL, M. M. (1989). A new perspective on women's math achievement. *Psychological Bulletin, 105,* 198–214.

KIMMEL, M. S. (1987). The contemporary 'crisis' of masculinity in historical perspective. In H. Brod (Ed.), *The making of masculinities* (pp. 121–154). Boston, MA: Allen & Unwin.

KIMMEL, M. S. (1992). Issues for men in the 1990's. *University of Miami Law Review, 46,* 671–683.

KIMMEL, M. S. (1994). Masculinity as homophobia: Fear, shame, and silence in the construction of gender identity. In H. Brod and M. Kaufman (Eds.), *Theorizing masculinities* (pp. 119–141). Thousand Oaks, CA: Sage.

KIMMEL, M. S., & KAUFMAN, M. (1994). Weekend warriors: The new men's movement. In H. Brod and M. Kaufman (Eds.), *Theorizing masculinities* (pp. 274–288). Thousand Oaks, CA: Sage.

KING, W. C., JR., MILES, E. W., & KNISKA, J. (1991). Boys will be boys (and girls will be girls): The attribution of gender role stereotypes in a gaming situation. *Sex Roles, 25,* 607–623.

KITE, M. E., & DEAUX, K. (1987). Gender belief systems: Homosexuality and the implicit inversion theory. *Psychology of Women Quarterly, 11,* 83–96.

KLEIN, H. M., & WILLERMAN, L. (1979). Psychological masculinity and femininity and typical and maximal dominance expression in women. *Journal of Personality and Social Psychology, 37,* 2059–2070.

KOHLBERG, L. A. (1966). A cognitive-development analysis of children's sex-role concepts and attitudes. In E. E. Maccoby (Ed.), *The development of sex differences* (pp. 82–172). Stanford, CA: Stanford University Press.

KONRAD, A. M. (1988). *Explaining the male-female earnings differential.* Unpublished manuscript, Department of Human Resource Administration, School of Business and Management, Temple University, Philadelphia.

204 REFERENCES

KONRAD, A. M., & CANNINGS, K. (1993, May). *Climbing the management hierarchy: Does family really have more impact on women?* Paper presented at the annual meeting of the Eastern Academy of Management, Providence, RI.

KONRAD, A. M., & CANNINGS, K. (1994). Of mommy tracks and glass ceilings: A case study of men's and women's careers in management. *Relations Industrielles, 49,* 303–334.

KONRAD, A. M., & LINNEHAN, F. (1993). *The implementation and effectiveness of equal opportunity employment.* Unpublished manuscript. Department of Human Resource Administration, School of Business and Management, Temple University, Philadelphia.

KONRAD, A. M., & PFEFFER, J. (1991). Understanding the hiring of women and minorities in educational institutions. *Sociology of Education, 64,* 141–157.

KOPPER, B. A., & EPPERSON, D. L. (1991). Women and anger: Sex and sex-role comparisons in the expression of anger. *Psychology of Women Quarterly, 15,* 7–14.

KOTTKE, J. L. (1988). Can androgyny be assessed with a single scale? *Psychological Reports, 63,* 987–991.

KRANAU, E. J., GREEN, V., & VALENCIA-WEBER, G. (1982). Acculturation and the Hispanic woman: Attitudes, sex-role behavior, and demographics. *Hispanic Journal of Behavioral Sciences, 4,* 21–40.

KRAUSE, N. (1983). Conflicting sex-role expectations, housework dissatisfaction, and depressive symptoms among full-time housewives. *Sex-Roles, 9,* 1115–1125.

KRAVITZ, D. A., & PLATANIA, J. (1993). Attitudes and beliefs about affirmative action: Effects of target and of respondent sex and ethnicity. *Journal of Applied Psychology, 78,* 928–938.

KREMER, J., & CURRY, C. (1987). Attitudes toward women in Northern Ireland. *Journal of Social Psychology, 127,* 531–533.

KRULEWITZ, J. E., & NASH, J. E. (1980). Effects of sex role attitudes and similarity on men's rejection of male homosexuals. *Journal of Personality and Social Psychology, 38,* 67–74.

KUHN, D., NASH, S., & BRUCKEN, L. (1978). Sex role concepts of two- and three-year-olds. *Child Development, 49,* 445–451.

KUPERS, T. A. (1993). *Revisioning men's lives: Gender, intimacy, and power.* New York: Guilford Press.

KURDEK, L. A. (1993). The allocation of household labor in gay, lesbian, and heterosexual married couples. *Journal of Social Issues, 49,* 127–139.

KUSHELL, E., & NEWTON, R. (1986). Gender, leadership style, and subordinate satisfaction: An experiment. *Sex Roles, 14,* 203–209.

LACROIX, A. Z., & HAYNES, S. G. (1987). Gender differences in the health effects of workplace roles. In R. C. Barnett, L. Biener, & G. K. Baruch (Eds.), *Gender and stress* (pp. 96–121).

LAFRANCE, M., & CARMEN, B. (1980). The nonverbal display of psychological androgyny. *Journal of Personality and Social Psychology, 38,* 36–49.

LAFROMBOISE, T. D., Heyle, A. M., & Ozer, E. J. (1990). Changing and diverse roles of women in American Indian cultures. *Sex Roles, 22,* 455–486.

LAGERSPETZ, K.M.J., BJORKQVIST, K., & PELTONEN, T. (1988). Is indirect aggression typical of females? Gender differences in aggressiveness in 11- to 12-year-old children. *Aggressive Behavior, 14,* 403–414.

LAMB, M. E. (1981). Father and child development: An integrative overview. In

M. E. Lamb (Ed.), *The role of the father in child development* (pp. 1–70). New York: Wiley.

LAMB, M. E., FRODI, A. M., HWANG, C. P., FRODI, M., & STEINBERG, J. (1982). Mother- and father-infant interaction involving play and holding in traditional and nontraditional Swedish families. *Developmental Psychology, 18,* 215–221.

LANGLOIS, J. H., & DOWNS, A. C. (1980). Mothers, fathers, and peers and socialization agents of sex-typed play behaviors in young children. *Child Development, 51,* 1237–1247.

LAPIERE, R. T. (1934). Attitudes vs. action. *Social Forces, 13,* 230–237.

LARWOOD, L., SZWAJKOWSKI, E., & ROSE, S. (1988). Sex and race discrimination resulting from manager-client relationships: Applying the rational bias theory of managerial discrimination. *Sex Roles, 18,* 9–29.

LATANÉ, B. (1981). The psychology of social impact. *American Psychologist, 36,* 343–356.

LAVINE, L. O., & LOMBARDO, J. P. (1984). Self-disclosure: Intimate and nonintimate disclosures to parents and best friends as a function of Bem sex-role category. *Sex Roles, 11,* 760–768.

LAWRENCE, F., DRAUGHN, P., TASKER, G., & WOZNIAK, P. (1987). Sex differences in household labor time: A comparison of rural and urban couples. *Sex Roles, 17,* 489–501.

LEBRA, T. S. (1984). *Japanese women: Constraint and fulfillment.* Honolulu: University of Hawaii.

LEINBACH, M. D., & FAGOT, B. I. (1986). Acquisition of gender labels: A test for toddlers. *Sex Roles, 15,* 655–666.

LEMKAU, J. P., & LANDAU, C. (1986). The 'selfless syndrome': Assessment and treatment considerations. *Psychotherapy, 23,* 227–233.

LEONARD, A. S. (1991). Homophobia, heterosexism, and judicial decision-making. *Journal of Gay and Lesbian Psychotherapy, 1,* 65–91.

LERNER, M. J. (1980). *The belief in a just world: A fundamental delusion.* New York: Plenum Press.

LEWIS, R. A. (1978). Emotional intimacy among men. *Journal of Social Issues, 34,* 108–121.

LEVANT, R. F. (1992). Toward the reconstruction of masculinity. *Journal of Family Psychology, 5,* 379–402.

LIBEN, L. S., & SIGNORELLA, M. L. (1980). Gender-related schemata and constructive memory in children. *Child Development, 51,* 563–574.

LINN, M. C. (1985). Gender equity in computer learning environments. *Computers and the Social Sciences, 1,* 19–27.

LINN, M. C. (1986). Meta-analysis of studies of gender differences: Implications and future directions. In J. S. Hyde & M. C. Linn (Eds.), *The psychology of gender: Advances through meta-analysis* (pp. 210–232). Baltimore: Johns Hopkins University Press.

LINN, M. C., & PETERSON, A. C. (1986). A meta-analysis of gender differences in spatial ability: Implications for math and science achievement. In J. S. Hyde & M. C. Linn (Eds.), *The psychology of gender: Advances through meta-analysis* (pp. 67–101). Baltimore: Johns Hopkins University Press.

LIPS, H. M. (1991). *Women, men, and power.* Mountain View, CA: Mayfield.

LIPSEY, M. W., & WILSON, D. B. (1993). The efficacy of psychological, educational, and behavioral treatment. *American Psychologist, 48,* 1181–1209.

LOCKSLEY, A., & COLTEN, M. E. (1979). Psychological androgyny: A case of mistaken identity? *Journal of Personality and Social Psychology, 37,* 1017–1031.

LOTT, B. (1991). Social psychology: Humanist roots and feminist future. *Psychology of Women Quarterly, 15,* 505–519.

LOTT, B., & MALUSO, D. (1993). The social learning of gender. In A. E. Beall & R. J. Sternberg (Eds.), *The psychology of gender* (pp. 99–126). New York: Guilford Press.

LOVDAL, L. T. (1989). Sex role messages in television commercials: An update. *Sex Roles, 21,* 715–724.

LOW, B. S. (1989). Cross-cultural patterns in the training of children: An evolutionary perspective. *Journal of Comparative Psychology, 103,* 311–319.

LUBINSKI, D., TELLEGEN, A., & BUTCHER, J. N. (1981). The relationship between androgyny and subjective indicators of emotional well-being. *Journal of Personality and Social Psychology, 40,* 722–730.

LYTTON, H., & ROMNEY, D. M. (1991). Parents' differential socialization of boys and girls: A meta-analysis. *Psychological Bulletin, 109,* 267–296.

MACCOBY, E. E. (1990). Gender and relationships: A developmental account. *American Psychologist, 45,* 513–520.

MACCOBY, E. E., & JACKLIN, C. N. (1974). *The psychology of sex differences.* Stanford, CA: Stanford University Press.

MACCOBY, E. E., & JACKLIN, C. N. (1987). Gender segregation in childhood. *Advances in Child Development and Behavior, 20,* 239–287.

MACKAY, D. (1980). Prescriptive grammar and the pronoun problem. *American Psychologist, 35,* 444–449.

MACKIE, D. M., ALLISON, S. T., WORTH, L. T., & ASUNCION, A. G. (1992a). The generalization of outcome-biased counter-stereotypic inferences. *Journal of Experimental Social Psychology, 28,* 43–64.

MACKIE, D. M., ALLISON, S. T., WORTH, L. T., & ASUNCION, A. G. (1992b). The impact of outcome biases on counterstereotypic inferences about groups. *Personality and Social Psychology Bulletin, 18,* 44–51.

MAJOR, B., FEINSTEIN, J., & CROCKER, J. (1994). Attributional ambiguity of affirmative action. *Basic and Applied Social Psychology, 15,* 113–142.

MAJOR, B., & FORCEY, B. (1985). Social comparisons and pay evaluations: Preferences for same-sex and same-job wage comparisons. *Journal of Experimental Social Psychology, 21,* 393–405.

MAJOR, B., & KONAR, E. (1984). An investigation of sex differences in pay expectations and their possible causes. *Academy of Management Journal, 27,* 777–791.

MAJOR, B., McFARLIN, D. B., & GAGNON, D. (1984a). Overworked and underpaid: On the nature of gender differences in personal entitlement. *Journal of Personality and Social Psychology, 47,* 1399–1412.

MAJOR, B., VANDERSLICE, V., & McFARLIN, D. B. (1984b). Effects of pay expected on pay received: The confirmatory nature of expectations. *Journal of Applied Social Psychology, 14,* 399–412.

MAJORS, R. (1990). Cool pose: Black masculinity and sports. In M. A. Messner & D. F. Sabo (Eds.), *Sport, men, and the gender order: Critical feminist perspective* (p. 109–113). Champaign, IL: Human Kinetics Books.

MAJORS, R., & BILLSON, J. M. (1992). *Cool pose.* New York: Lexington.

MANSFIELD, P. K., KOCH, P. B., HENDERSON, J., VICARY, J. R., COHN, M., & YOUNG, E. W. (1991). The job climate for women in traditionally male blue-collar occupations. *Sex Roles, 25,* 63–79.

MARGOLIS, D. R. (1993). Women's movements around the world: Cross-cultural comparisons. *Gender and Society, 7,* 379–399.

MARKUS, H., & ZAJONC, R. B. (1985). The cognitive perspective in social psychology. In G. Lindzey & E. Aronson (Eds.), *Handbook of social psychology* (3rd ed., Vol. I). New York: Random House.

MARSH, H. W., & BYRNE, B. M. (1991). Differentiated additive androgyny model: Relations between masculinity, femininity, and multiple dimensions of self-concept. *Journal of Personality and Social Psychology, 61,* 811–828.

MARTIN, B. A. (1989). Gender differences in salary expectations when current salary information is provided. *Psychology of Women Quarterly, 13,* 87–96.

MARTIN, C. L. (1987). A ratio measure of sex stereotyping. *Journal of Personality and Social Psychology, 52,* 489–499.

MARTIN, C. L. (1989). Children's use of gender-related information in making social judgments. *Developmental Psychology, 35,* 80–88.

MARTIN, C. L. (1990). Attitudes and expectations about children with nontraditional and traditional gender roles. *Sex Roles, 22,* 151–165.

MARTIN, C. L. (1993). Theories of sex typing: Moving toward multiple perspectives. *Monographs of the Society for Research in Child Development, 58,* 75–85.

MARTIN, C. L., & HALVERSON, C. F., Jr. (1981). A schematic processing model of sex typing and stereotyping in children. *Child Development, 52,* 1119–1134.

MARTIN, C. L., & HALVERSON, C. F., Jr. (1983a). The effects of sex-typing schemas on young children's memory. *Child Development, 54,* 563–574.

MARTIN, C. L., & HALVERSON, C. F., Jr. (1983b). Gender constancy: A methodological and theoretical analysis. *Sex Roles, 9,* 775–790.

MARTINKO, M. J., & GARDNER, J. (1983). A methodological review of sex-related access discrimination problems. *Sex Roles, 9,* 825–839.

MASON, K. O., & BUMPASS, L. L. (1975). Women's sex role ideology. *American Journal of Sociology, 80,* 1212–1219.

MASSENGILL, D., & DiMARCO, N. (1979). Sex-role stereotypes and requisite management characteristics: A current replication. *Sex Roles, 5,* 561–569.

MATSUMOTO, D. (1994). People: Psychology from a cross-cultural perspective. Belmont, CA: Brooks-Cole.

MATYAS, M. L. (1987). Keeping undergraduate women in science and engineering: Contributing factors and recommendations for action. In J. Z. Daniels & J. B. Kahle (Eds.), *Contributions to the fourth GASAT conference* (Vol. 3, pp. 112–122). Washington, DC: National Science Foundation.

MAUPIN, H. E., & FISHER, R. J. (1989). The effects of superior female performance and sex-role orientation on gender conformity. *Canadian Journal of Behavioural Science, 21,* 55–69.

MAUPIN, R. J. (1993). How can women's lack of upward mobility in accounting firms be explained? *Group and Organization Management, 18,* 132–152.

McADOO, H. P. (1983). Societal stress: The black family. In H. C. McCubbin & C. R. Figley (Eds.), *Stress and the family* (pp. 178–187). New York: Brunner/Mazel.

McANINCH, C. B., MANOLIS, M. B., MILICH, R., & HARRIS, M. J. (1993). Impression formation in children: Influence of gender and expectancy. *Child Development, 64,* 1492–1506.

McCARTY, P. (1986). Effects of feedback on self-confidence of men and women. *Academy of Management Journal, 20,* 840–846.

McDONALD, S. M. (1989). Sex bias in the representation of male and female characters in children's picture books. *Journal of Business and Psychology, 130,* 389–401.

McFarlin, D. B., Frone, M., Major, B., & Konar, E. (1989). Predicting career-entry pay expectations: The role of gender-based comparisons. *Journal of Business and Psychology, 3,* 331–340.

McGhee, P. E., & Frueh, T. (1980). Television viewing and the learning of sex role stereotypes. *Sex Roles, 6,* 179–188.

McHugh, M. C., Koeske, R. D., & Frieze, I. H. (1986). Issues to consider in conducting nonsexist psychological research: A guide for researchers. *American Psychologist, 41,* 879–890.

Meehan, A. M., & Janik, L. M. (1990). Illusory correlation and the maintenance of sex role stereotypes in children. *Sex Roles, 22,* 83–95.

Meehan, A. M., & Overton, W. F. (1986). Gender differences in expectancies for success and performance on Piagetian tasks. *Merrill-Palmer Quarterly, 32,* 427–441.

Messner, M. (1987). The meaning of success: The athletic experience and the development of male identity. In H. Brod (Ed.), *The making of masculinities: The new men's studies* (pp. 193–210). Boston: Allen & Unwin.

Miller, C. L. (1987). Qualitative differences among gender-stereotyped toys: Implications for cognitive and social development in girls and boys. *Sex Roles, 16,* 473–487.

Miller, D. T., Taylor, B., & Buck, M. L. (1991). Gender gaps: Who needs to be explained? *Journal of Personality and Social Psychology, 61,* 5–12.

Mischel, W. (1970). Sex typing and socialization. In P. H. Mussen (Ed.), *Carmichael's manual of child psychology* (Vol. 2). New York: Wiley.

Model, S. (1982). Housework by husbands: Determinants and implications. In J. Aldous (Ed.), *Two paychecks: Life in dual-earning families* (pp. 193–206). Beverly Hills: Sage.

Moghaddam, F. M., Taylor, D. M., & Wright, S. C. (1993). *Social psychology in cross-cultural perspective.* New York: Freeman.

Moore, M. L. (1992). The family as portrayed on prime-time television, 1947–1990: Structure and characteristics. *Sex Roles, 26,* 41–61.

Morin, S. F., & Garfinkle, E. M. (1978). Male homophobia. *Journal of Social Issues, 34,* 29–47.

Morrison, A. M., & Von Glinow, M. A. (1990). Women and minorities in management. *American Psychologist, 45,* 200–208.

Morrison, A. M., White, R. P., & Van Velsor, E. (1987). *Breaking the glass ceiling: Can women reach the top of America's largest corporations?* New York: Addison-Wesley.

Moscovici, S. (1985). Social influence and conformity. In G. Lindgey & E. Aronson (Eds.), *The handbook of social psychology* (3rd ed., Vol. 2), pp. 347–412. New York: Random House.

Moulton, J. M., Robinson, G. M., & Elias, C. (1978). Sex bias in language use: Neutral pronouns that aren't. *American Psychologist, 33,* 1032–1036.

Mullis, R. L., & McKinley, K. (1989). Gender-role orientation of adolescent females: Effects on self-esteem and locus of control. *Journal of Adolescent Research, 4,* 506–516.

Munroe, R. H., Shimmin, H. S., & Munroe, R. L. (1984). Gender understanding and sex role preference in four cultures. *Developmental Psychology, 20,* 673–682.

Munroe, R. L., & Munroe, R. H. (1975). *Cross-cultural human development.* Monterey, CA: Brooks/Cole.

MUNROE, R. L., & MUNROE, R. H. (1992). Fathers in children's environments: A four culture study. In B. S. Hewlett (Ed.), *Father-child relations: Cultural and biosocial contexts* (pp. 213–230). New York: Aldine de Gruyter.

MURRELL, A. J., DIETZ-UHLER, B. L., & DOVIDIO, J. F. (1994). Aversive racism and resistance to affirmative action. *Basic and Applied Social Psychology, 15,* 71–86.

MURRELL, A. J., FRIEZE, I. H., & FROST, J. L. (1991). Aspiring to careers in male- and female-dominated professions. *Psychology of Women Quarterly, 15,* 103–126.

MYERS, D. G. (1990). *Social psychology* (3rd ed.). New York: McGraw-Hill.

NACOSTE, R. B. (1990). Sources of stigma: Analyzing the psychology of affirmative action. *Law and Policy, 12,* 175–195.

NATIONAL RESEARCH COUNCIL. (1990). *Who cares for America's children: Child care policy for the 1990's.* Washington, DC: National Academy Press.

NELSON, D. L., QUICK, J. C., HITT, M. A., & MOESEL, D. (1990). Politics, lack of career progress, and work/home conflict: Stress and strain for working women. *Sex Roles, 23,* 169–184.

NEWPORT, F. (1993, October). Americans now more likely to say: Women have it harder than men. *The Gallup Poll Monthly.*

NIEVA, V. G., & GUTEK, B. A. (1980). Sex effects on evaluation. *Academy of Management Review, 5,* 267–276.

NIEVA, V. G., & GUTEK, B. A. (1981). *Women and work: A psychological perspective.* New York: Praeger.

NIGRO, G. N., HILL, D. E., GELBEIN, M. E., & CLARK, C. L. (1988). Changes in the facial prominence of women and men over the last decade. *Psychology of Women Quarterly, 12,* 225–235.

NISBETT, R. E., & ROSS, L. (1980). *Human inference: Strategies and shortcomings.* Englewood Cliffs, NJ: Prentice-Hall.

NKOMO, S. M., & COX, T., JR. (1989). Gender differences in the upward mobility of black managers: Double whammy or double advantage? *Sex Roles, 21,* 825–839.

NOE, R. A. (1988). Women and mentoring: A review and research agenda. *Academy of Management Review, 13,* 65–78.

NSAMENANG, B. A. (1992). Perceptions of parenting among the Nso of Cameroon. In B. S. Hewlett (Ed.), *Father-child relations: Cultural and biosocial contexts* (pp. 321–344). New York: Aldine de Gruyter.

NUSSBAUM, M. (1992). Human functioning and social justice: In defense of Aristotelian essentialism. *Political Theory, 20,* 202–246.

O'HERON, C. A., & ORLOFSKY, J. L. (1987). Stereotypic and nonstereotypic sex role trait and behavior orientation: Implications for personal adjustment. *Journal of Personality and Social Psychology, 52,* 1034–1042.

O'HERON, C. A., & ORLOFSKY, J. L. (1990). Stereotypic and nonstereotypic sex role trait and behavior orientations, gender identity, and psychological adjustment. *Journal of Personality and Social Psychology, 58,* 134–143.

OKIN, S. M. (1989). *Justice, gender, and the family.* New York: Basic Books.

O'LEARY, V. E., & DONOGHUE, J. M. (1978). Latitudes of masculinity: Reactions to sex-role deviance in men. *Journal of Social Issues, 34,* 17–28.

O'LEARY, V. E., UNGER, R. K., & WALLSTON, B. S. (Eds.). (1985). *Women, gender and social psychology.* Hillsdale, NJ: Erlbaum.

OLSON, J. E., & FRIEZE, I. H. (1987). Income determinants for women in business. In A. H. Stromberg, L. Larwood, & B. A. Gutek (Eds.), *Women and work: An annual review* (Vol. 2, pp. 173–206). Newbury Park, CA: Sage.

O'NEIL, J. M. (1981). Patterns of gender role conflict and strain: Sexism and fear of femininity in men's lives. *The Personnel and Guidance Journal, 60,* 203–210.

O'NEIL, J. M. (1990). Assessing men's gender role conflict. In D. Moore & F. Leafgren (Eds.), *Problem solving strategies and interventions for men in conflict* (pp. 23–38). Alexandria, VA: American Association for Counseling and Development.

O'NEIL, J. M., & EGAN, J. (1992). Men's and women's gender role journeys: A metaphor for healing, transition, and transformation. In B. R. Wainrib (Ed.), *Gender issues across the life cycle* (pp. 107–123). New York: Springer-Verlag.

O'NEIL, J. M., GOOD, G. E., & HOLMES, S. (1995). Fifteen years of theory and research on men's gender role conflict: New paradigms for empirical research. In R. Levant and W. Pollack (Eds.), *Foundations for a new psychology of men.* New York: Basic Books.

O'NEIL, J. M., HELMS, B. J., GABLE, R. K., DAVID, L., & WRIGHTSMAN, L. S. (1986). Gender-role conflict scale: College men's fear of femininity. *Sex Roles, 14,* 335–350.

O'NEIL, J. M., & ROBERTS CARROLL, M. (1987). *A six day workshop on gender conflict and strain: Helping men and women take the gender role journey.* Storrs, CT: University of Connecticut, Department of Educational Psychology, Counseling Psychology Program. (ERIC Document Reproduction Service No. ED 275 963)

O'NEIL, J. M., & ROBERTS CARROLL, M. (1988a). *Evaluation of gender role workshop: Three years of follow up data.* Storrs, CT: University of Connecticut, Department of Educational Psychology, Counseling Psychology Program. (ERIC Document Reproduction Service No. ED 287 121)

O'NEIL, J. M., & ROBERTS CARROLL, M. (1988b). A gender role workshop focuses on sexism, gender role conflict, and the gender role journey. *Journal of Counseling and Development, 67,* 193–197.

ORLOFSKY, J. L. (1977). Sex-role orientation, identity formation, and self-esteem in college men and women. *Sex Roles, 3,* 561–575.

ORLOFSKY, J. L., RAMSDEN, M. W., & COHEN, R. S. (1982). Development of the revised Sex-Role Behavior Scale. *Journal of Personality Assessment, 46,* 632–638.

OSKAMP, S. (1991). *Attitudes and opinions.* Englewood Cliffs, NJ: Prentice-Hall.

PACHECO, A. (1981). A study of sex role attitudes, job investment, and job satisfaction of women faculty at the University of Puerto Rico, Rio Piedras (Doctoral dissertation, New York University, 1981). *Dissertation Abstracts International, 42,* 3032A.

PADAVIC, I., & RESKIN, B. F. (1990). Men's behavior and women's interest in blue-collar jobs. *Social Problems, 37,* 613–627.

PARKE, R. D., & NEVILLE, B. (1987). Teenage fatherhood. In S. L. Hofferth & C. D. Hayes (Eds.), *Risking the future: Adolescent sexuality, pregnancy, and childbearing* (pp. 145–173). Washington, DC: National Academy Press.

PARKE, R. D., & TINSLEY, B. R. (1981). The father's role in infancy: Determinants of involvement in caregiving and play. In M. E. Lamb (Ed.), *The role of the father in child development* (pp. 429–457). New York: Wiley.

PARSONS, J. E., KACZALA, C. M., & MEECE, J. L. (1982). Socialization of achievement attitudes and beliefs: Classroom influences. *Child Development, 53,* 322–339.

PEDERSEN, F. A., ANDERSEN, B. J., & CAIN, R. L. (1980). Parent-infant and husband-wife interactions observed at age 5 months. In F. A. Pedersen (Ed.), *The fa-*

ther-infant relationship: Observational studies in the family setting (pp. 71–86). New York: Praeger.

PEDHAZUR, E. J., & TETENBAUM, T. J. (1979). Bem Sex Role Inventory: A theoretical and methodological critique. *Journal of Personality and Social Psychology, 37,* 996–1016.

PENA, M. (1991). Class, gender, and machismo: The 'treacherous women' folklore of Mexican male workers. *Gender and Society, 5,* 30–46.

PEPLAU, L. A., & GORDON, S. L. (1983). The intimate relationships of lesbians and gay men. In E. R. Allgeier & N. B. McCormick (Eds.), *Changing boundaries: Gender roles and sexual behavior* (pp. 226–244). Palo Alto, CA: Mayfield.

PERETTI, P. O., & SYDNEY, T. M. (1985). Parental toy choice stereotyping and its effects on child toy preference and sex-role typing. *Social Behavior and Personality, 12,* 213–216.

PERRY, D. G., & BUSSEY, K. (1979). The social learning theory of sex differences: Imitation is alive and well. *Journal of Personality and Social Psychology, 37,* 1699–1712.

PERRY, D. G., PERRY, L. C., & WEISS, R. J. (1989). Sex differences in the consequences that children anticipate for aggression. *Developmental Psychology, 25,* 312–319.

PERRY-JENKINS, M., SEERY, B., & CROUTER, A. C. (1992). Linkages between women's provider-role attitudes, psychological well-being, and family relationships. *Psychology of Women Quarterly, 16,* 311–329.

PETERSON, B., MAJOR, B., COZZARELLI, C., & CROCKER, J. (1988, April). *The social construction of gender differences in values.* Paper presented at the annual meeting of the Eastern Psychological Association, Buffalo, NY.

PETTIGREW, T. F. (1979). The ultimate attribution error: Extending Allport's cognitive analysis of prejudice. *Personality and Social Psychology Bulletin, 5,* 461–476.

PETTIGREW, T. F., & MARTIN, J. (1987). Shaping the organizational context for black American inclusion. *Journal of Social Issues, 43,* 41–78.

PFOST, K. S., & FIORE, M. (1990). Pursuit of nontraditional occupations: Fear of success or fear of not being chosen. *Sex Roles, 23,* 15–24.

PHARES, V. (1992). Where's poppa? The relative lack of attention to the role of fathers in child and adolescent psychopathology. *American Psychologist, 47,* 656–664.

PHELAN, S. (1993). (Be) Coming out: Lesbian identity and politics. *Signs, 18,* 765–790.

PIERCY, M. (1976). *Woman on the edge of time.* New York: Fawcett Crest.

PIKE, R. (1954). *Language in relation to a united theory of human behavior.* Glendale, CA: Summer Institute of Linguistics.

PILIAVIN, J. A., DOVIDIO, J. F., GAERTNER, S. L., & CLARK, R. D., III (1981). *Emergency intervention.* New York: Academic Press.

PILIAVIN, J. A., & UNGER, R. K. (1985). The helpful but helpless female: A myth or reality? In V. E. O'Leary, R. K. Unger, & B. S. Wallston (Eds.), *Women, gender and social psychology* (pp. 149–189). Hillsdale, NJ: Erlbaum.

PITCHER, E., & SCHULTZ, L. (1983). *Boys and girls at play: The development of sex roles.* New York: Bergin & Garvey.

PLECK, J. H. (1976). The male sex role: Definitions, problems and sources of change. *Journal of Social Issues, 32,* 155–163.

PLECK, J. H. (1977). The work-family role system. *Social Problems, 24,* 417–428.

PLECK, J. H. (1978). Males' traditional attitudes toward women: Contemporary issues in research. In J. Sherman and F. Denmark (Eds.), *The psychology of women: New directions in research* (pp. 617–644). New York: Psychological Dimensions.

PLECK, J. H. (1981, September). Prisoners of manliness. *Psychology Today,* pp. 69–80.

PLECK, J. H. (1983). Husbands' paid work and family roles: Current research issues. In H. Z. Lopata & J. H. Pleck (Eds.), *Research in the interweave of social roles: Families and jobs* (Vol. 3, pp. 251–333). Greenwich, CT: JAI Press.

PLECK, J. H. (1985). *Working wives/Working husbands.* Beverly Hills: Sage.

PLECK, J. H. (1987). The theory of male sex-role identity: Its rise and fall, 1936 to the present. In H. Brod (Ed.), *The making of masculinities* (pp. 21–38). Boston: Allen & Unwin.

PLECK, J. H. (1993). Are 'family-supportive' employer policies relevant to men? In J. C. Hood (Ed.), *Men, work, and family* (pp. 217–237). Newbury Park, CA: Sage.

PLECK, J. H., SONENSTEIN, F. L., & KU, L. C. (1993a). Masculinity ideology and its correlates. In S. Oskamp & M. Costanzo (Eds.), *Gender issues in contemporary society* (pp. 85–110). Newbury Park, CA: Sage.

PLECK, J. H., SONENSTEIN, F. L., & KU, L. C. (1993b). Masculinity ideology: Its impact on adolescent males' heterosexual relationships. *Journal of Social Issues, 49,* 11–30.

PLUMB, P., & COWAN, G. (1984). A developmental study of de-stereotyping and androgynous activity preferences of tomboys, nontomboys, and males. *Sex Roles, 10,* 703–712.

PODILCHAK, W. (1990). Fatherhood today: Men's changing role in the family. *Journal of Comparative Family Studies, 21,* 125–127.

POGREBIN, L. C. (1993, November/December). The stolen spotlight syndrome: You can always count on a male 'me too.' *Ms. Magazine, 96.*

POMERLEAU, A., BOLDUC, G. M., & COSSETTE, L. (1990). Pink or blue: Environmental gender stereotypes in the first two years of life. *Sex Roles, 22,* 359–367.

POWELL, G. N. (1987). *Women and men in organizations.* Newbury Park, CA: Sage.

POWELL, G. N. (1990). One more time: Do female and male managers differ? *Academy of Management Executive, 4,* 68–75.

POWELL, G. N., & BUTTERFIELD, D. A. (1984), If 'good managers' are masculine, what are 'bad managers?' *Sex Roles, 10,* 477–484.

POWELL, G. N., & MAINIERO, L. A. (1992). Cross-currents in the river of time: Conceptualizing the complexities of women's careers. *Journal of Management, 18,* 215–237.

POWLISHTA, K. K. (1990, April). *Children's biased views of male and female traits.* Paper presented at the second annual convention of the American Psychological Society, Dallas.

PRESLAND, P., & ANTILL, J. K. (1987). Household division of labour: The impact of hours worked in paid employment. *Australian Journal of Psychology, 39,* 273–291.

PURCELL, P., & STEWART, L. (1990). Dick and Jane in 1989. *Sex Roles, 22,* 177–185.

PUTNAM, L. L., & McCALLISTER, L. (1980). Situational effects of task and gender on nonverbal display. In D. Nimno (Ed.), *Communication yearbook, 4.* New Brunswick, NJ: Transaction.

QUATTRONE, G. A. (1986). On the perception of a group's variability. In S. Worchel & W. G. Austin (Eds.), *Psychology of intergroup relations* (2nd ed., (pp. 25–48). Chicago: Nelson-Hall.

RACHELS, J. (1993). *The elements of moral philosophy* (2nd ed.). New York: McGraw-Hill.

RAGINS, B. R., & COTTON, J. L. (1993). Gender and willingness to mentor in organizations. *Journal of Management, 19,* 97–111.

RAGINS, B. R., & SUNDSTROM, E. (1989). Gender and power in organizations: A longitudinal perspective. *Psychological Bulletin, 105,* 51–88.

RAYMOND, C. L., & BENBOW, C. (1986). Gender differences in mathematics: A function of parental support and student sex typing? *Developmental Psychology, 22,* 808–819.

REID, H. M., & FINE, G. A. (1992). Self-disclosure in men's friendships: Variations associated with intimate relations. In P. M. Nardi (Ed.), *Men's friendships* (pp. 132–152). Newbury Park, CA: Sage.

REIS, H. T., SENCHAK, M., & SOLOMON, B. (1985). Sex differences in the intimacy of social interaction: Further examination of potential explanations. *Journal of Personality and Social Psychology, 48,* 1204–1217.

REPETTI, R. L., MATTHEWS, K. A., & WALDRON, I. (1989). Employment and women's health: Effects of paid employment on women's mental and physical health. *American Psychologist, 44,* 1394–1401.

RIGGIO, R. E., & ZIMMERMAN, J. (1991). Social skills and interpersonal relationships: Influences on social support seeking. In W. H. Jones & D. Perlman (Eds.), *Advances in personal relationships* (Vol. 2, pp. 133–155). London: Jessica Kingsley.

ROBBINS, T. L., & DENISI, A. S. (1993). Moderators of sex bias in the performance appraisal process: A cognitive analysis. *Journal of Management, 19,* 113–126.

ROBERTS, D., & BACHEN, C. (1981). Mass communication effects. *Annual Review of Psychology, 32,* 307–356.

RODIN, J., & ICKOVICS, J. R. (1990). Women's health: Review and research agenda as we approach the 21st century. *American Psychologist, 45,* 1018–1034.

ROGERS, S. C. (1985). Gender in Southwestern France: The myth of male dominance revisited. *Anthropology, 9,* 65–86.

ROGOFF, B. (1981). The relation of age and sex to experiences during childhood in a highland community. *Anthropology UCLA, 11,* 25–41.

ROOPNARINE, J. L., & AHMEDUZZAMAN, M. (1993). Puerto Rican fathers' involvement with their preschool-aged children. *Hispanic Journal of Behavioral Sciences, 15,* 96–107.

ROSARIO, L. (1982). The self-perception of Puerto Rican women toward their societal roles. In R. E. Zambrana (Ed.), *Work, family, and health: Latina women in transition* (pp. 95–107). New York: Hispanic Research Center.

ROSENTHAL, R. (1991). *Meta-analytic procedures for social research* (rev. ed.). Newbury Park, CA: Sage.

ROSENTHAL, R., & RUBIN, D. B. (1982). Further meta-analytic procedures for assessing cognitive gender differences. *Journal of Educational Psychology, 74,* 706–712.

ROSS, C. E., MIROWSKY, J., & ULBRICH, P. (1983). Distress and the traditional female role: A comparison of Mexicans and Anglos. *American Sociological Review, 48,* 567–578.

Ross, L. D. (1977). The intuitive psychologist and his shortcomings: Distortions in the attribution process. In L. Berkowitz (Ed.), *Advances in experimental social psychology* (Vol. 10, pp. 174–214). New York: Academic Press.

Rothbart, M., Evans, M., & Fulero, S. (1979). Recall for confirming events: Memory processes and the maintenance of social stereotypes. *Journal of Experimental Social Psychology, 15,* 343–353.

Rothbart, M., Fulero, S., Jensen, C., Howard, J., & Birrell, B. (1978). From individual to group impressions: Availability heuristics in stereotype formation. *Journal of Experimental Social Psychology, 14,* 237–255.

Rothbart, M., & Lewis, S. (1988). Inferring category attributes from exemplary attributes: Geometric shapes and social categories. *Journal of Personality and Social Psychology, 55,* 861–872.

Rubin, J. Z., Pruitt, D. G., & Kim, S. H. (1994). *Social conflict: Escalation, stalemate, and settlement* (2nd ed.). New York: McGraw-Hill.

Ruble, D. N., Balaban, T., & Cooper, J. (1981). Gender constancy and the effects of sex-typed televised toy commercials. *Child Development, 52,* 667–673.

Ruble, D. N., & Ruble, T. L. (1982). Sex stereotypes. In A. G. Miller (Ed.), *In the eye of the beholder: Contemporary issues in stereotyping* (pp. 188–252). New York: Praeger.

Ruble, D. N., & Stangor, C. (1986). Stalking the elusive schema: Insights from developmental and social-psychological analyses of gender schemas. *Social Cognition, 4,* 227–261.

Ruble, T. L., Cohen, R., & Ruble, D. N. (1984). Sex stereotypes: Occupational barriers for women. *American Behavioral Scientist, 27,* 339–356.

Russell, G. (1978). The father role and its relation to masculinity, femininity, and androgyny. *Child Development, 49,* 1174–1181.

Russell, G. (1986). Primary caretaking and role-sharing fathers. In M. E. Lamb (Ed.), *The father's role: Applied perspectives,* (pp. 29–57). New York: Wiley.

Russell, G., & Radin, N. (1983). Increased paternal participation: The father's perspective. In M. E. Lamb & A. Sagi (Eds.), *Fatherhood and family policy* (pp. 139–166). Hillsdale, NJ: Erlbaum.

Rytina, N. (1983). Tenure as a factor in the male-female earnings gap. *Monthly Labor Review, 107,* 32–34.

Sabo, D., & Jansen, S. C. (1992). Images of men in sport media: The social reproduction of gender order. In S. Craig (Ed.), *Men, masculinity, and the media* (pp. 169–186). Beverly Hills, CA: Sage.

Sadker, M., & Sadker, D. (1982). *Sex equity handbook for schools.* New York: Longman.

Sapadin, L. A. (1988). Friendship and gender: Perspectives of professional men and women. *Journal of Social and Personal Relationships, 5,* 387–403.

Sarason, B. R., Sarason, I. G., Hacker, T. A., & Basham, R. B. (1985). Concommitants of social support: Social skills, physical attractiveness, and gender. *Journal of Personality and Social Psychology, 49,* 469–480.

Saurer, M. K., & Eisler, R. M. (1990). The role of masculine gender role stress in expressivity and social support network factors. *Sex Roles, 23,* 261–271.

Scarr, S. (1984). *Mother care, other care.* New York: Basic Books.

Scarr, S., & McCartney, K. (1983). How people make their own environments: A theory of genotype-environment effects. *Child Development, 54,* 424–435.

Scarr, S., Phillips, D., & McCartney, K. (1989). Working mothers and their families. *American Psychologist, 44,* 1402-1409.

SCHEIN, V. E. (1973). The relationship between sex role stereotypes and requisite management characteristics. *Journal of Applied Psychology, 57,* 95–100.

SCHEIN, V. E. (1975).The relationship between sex role stereotypes and requisite management characteristics among female managers. *Journal of Applied Psychology, 60,* 340–344.

SCHEIN, V. E., & MUELLER, R. (1992). Sex role stereotyping and requisite management characteristics: A cross-cultural look. *Journal of Organizational Behavior, 13,* 439–447.

SCHEIN, V. E., MUELLER, R., & JACOBSON, C. (1989). The relationship between sex role stereotypes and requisite management characteristics among college students. *Sex Roles, 20,* 103–111.

SEAVEY, C., KATZ, P., & ZALK, S. (1975). Baby X: The effect of gender labels on adult responses to infants. *Sex Roles, 1,* 103–109.

SEDNEY, M. A. (1989). Conceptual and methodological sources of controversies about androgyny. In R. K. Unger (Ed.), *Social constructions of gender.* Amityville, NY: Baywood Press.

SEGINER, R., KARAYANNI, M., & MAR'I, M. (1990). Adolescents' attitudes toward women's role: A comparison between Israeli Jews and Arabs. *Psychology of Women Quarterly, 14,* 119–133.

SELKOW, P. (1985). Male-female differences in mathematical ability: A function of biological sex or perceived gender role? *Psychological Reports, 57,* 551–557.

SERBIN, L. A., POWLISHTA, K. K., & GULKO, J. (1993). The development of sex typing in middle childhood. *Monographs of the Society for Research in Child Development, 58,* 1–74.

SEYFRIED, B., & HENDRICK, C. (1973). When do opposites attract: When they are opposite in sex role attitudes. *Journal of Personality and Social Psychology, 25,* 15–20.

SHAFFER, D. R., PEGALIS, L., & CORNELL, D. P. (1991). Interactive effects of social context and sex role identity on female self-disclosure during the acquaintance process. *Sex Roles, 24,* 1–19.

SHAKIN, M., SHAKIN, D., & STERNGLANZ, S. H. (1985). Infant clothing: Sex labeling for strangers. *Sex Roles 12,* 955–964.

SHARPE, M. J., & HEPPNER, P. P. (1991). Gender role, gender-role conflict, and psychological well-being in men. *Journal of Counseling Psychology, 38,* 323–330.

SHAVER, P., & FREEDMAN, J. (1976, October). Your pursuit of happiness. *Psychology Today,* pp. 26–29, 31–32, 75.

SHEHAN, C. L. (1984). Wives' work and psychological well-being: An extension of Gove's social role theory of depression. *Sex Roles, 11,* 881–888.

SHELTON, B. A., & JOHN, D. (1993). Ethnicity, race, and difference: A comparison of white, black, and hispanic men's household labor time. In J. C. Hood (Ed.), *Men, work, and family* (pp. 131–150). Newbury Park, CA: Sage.

SHERIF, M. (1937). An experimental approach to the study of attitudes. *Sociometry, 1,* 90–98.

SHERROD, D. (1989). The influence of gender on same-sex friendships. In C. Hendrick (Ed.), *Review of personality and social psychology: Vol. 10. Close relationships* (pp. 164–186). Newbury Park, CA: Sage.

SHIRAKAWA, Y., SHIRAISHI, T., & SUKEMUNE, S. (1992). Current research on gender roles in Japan. *Psychologia, 35,* 193–200.

SHUMAKER, S. A., & HILL, D. R. (1991). Gender differences in social support and physical health. *Health Psychology, 10*, 102–111.

SIAVELIS, R. L., & LAMKE, L. K. (1992). Instrumentalness and expressiveness: Predictors of heterosexual relationship satisfaction. *Sex Roles, 26*, 149–159.

SIDOROWICZ, L. S., & LUNNEY, G. S. (1980). Baby X revisited. *Sex Roles, 6*, 67–73.

SIEGEL, L. S. (1968). The development of the ability to process information. *Journal of Experimental Child Psychology, 6*, 368–383.

SIEMIENSKA, R. (1986). Women and social movements in Poland. *Women & Politics, 6*, 5–35.

SIGNORIELLI, N. (1989). Television and conceptions about sex roles: Maintaining conventionality and the status quo. *Sex Roles, 21*, 341–360.

SILBER, L. (1990). Negotiating sexual identity: Non-lesbians in a lesbian feminist community. *Journal of Sex Research, 27*, 131–140.

SINGLETON, C. H. (1987). Biological and social explanations of sex-role stereotyping. In D. J. Hargreaves & A. M. Cooley (Eds.), *The psychology of sex roles* (pp. 3–26). New York: Harper & Row.

SISTRUNK, F., & McDAVID, J. W. (1971). Sex variable in conformity behavior. *Journal of Personality and Social Psychology, 86*, 11–22.

SKRYPNEK, B. J., & SNYDER, M. (1982). On the self-perpetuating nature of stereotypes about women and men. *Journal of Experimental Social Psychology, 18*, 277–291.

SLUSHER, M. P., & ANDERSON, C. A. (1987). When reality monitoring fails: The role of imagination in stereotype maintenance. *Journal of Personality and Social Psychology, 52*, 653–662.

SMETANA, J. G., & LETOURNEAU, K. J. (1984). Development of gender constancy and children's sex-typed free play behavior. *Developmental Psychology, 20*, 691–696.

SMITH, M. J. (1982). *Persuasion and human action.* Belmont, CA: Wadsworth.

SNELL, W. E., Jr. (1989). Development and validation of the Masculine Behavior Scale: A measure of behaviors stereotypically attributed to males vs. females. *Sex Roles, 21*, 749–767.

SNODGRASS, S. E. (1985). Women's intuition: The effect of subordinate role on interpersonal sensitivity. *Journal of Personality and Social Psychology, 49*, 146–155.

SNOW, M. E., JACKLIN, C. N., & MACCOBY, E. E. (1983). Sex-of-child differences in father-child interaction at one year of age. *Child Development, 54*, 227–232.

SNYDER, M. (1981). On the self-perpetuating nature of social stereotypes. In D. L. Hamilton (Ed.), *Cognitive processes in stereotyping and intergroup behavior.* Hillsdale, NJ: Erlbaum.

SNYDER, M., & URANOWITZ, S. W. (1978). Reconstructing the past: Some cognitive consequences of person perception. *Journal of Personality and Social Psychology, 36*, 941–950.

SNYDER, R., VERDERBER, K. S., LANGMEYER, L., & MYERS, M. (1992). A reconsideration of self and organization-referent attitudes as 'causes' of the glass ceiling effect. *Group & Organization Management, 17*, 260–278.

SOH, C. S. (1993). Sexual equality, male superiority, and Korean women in politics: Changing gender relations in a 'patriarchal democracy.' *Sex Roles, 28*, 73–90.

SORENSEN, G., & VERBRUGGE, L. M. (1987). Women, work, and health. *Annual Review of Public Health, 8*, 235–251.

SOTO, E., & SHAVER, P. (1982). Sex-role traditionalism, assertiveness, and symptoms of Puerto Rican women living in the United States. *Hispanic Journal of Behavioral Sciences, 4,* 1–19.

SPENCE, J., & HELMRICH, R. (1981). Androgyny vs. gender schema: A comment on Bem's gender schema theory. *Psychological Review, 88,* 365–368.

SPENCE, J., HELMRICH, R., & STAPP, J. (1974). The personal attributes questionnaire: A measure of sex role stereotypes and masculinity-femininity. *JSAS Catalog of Selected Documents in Psychology, 4,* 43.

SPENCE, J., HELMRICH, R., & STAPP, J. (1975). Ratings of self and peers on sex role attributes and their relation to self-esteem and conceptions of masculinity and femininity. *Journal of Personality and Social Psychology, 32,* 29–39.

SPENCE, J. T., & HELMRICH, R. (1978). *Masculinity and femininity: Their psychological dimensions, correlates, and antecedents.* Austin: University of Texas Press.

SPRAFKIN, C., SERBIN, L. A., DENIER, C., & CONNOR, J. M. (1983). Sex-differentiated play: Cognitive consequences and early interventions. In M. B. Liss (Ed.), *Social and cognitive skills: Sex roles and children's play.* New York: Academic Press.

STANGOR, C., LYNCH, L., DUAN, C., & GLASS, B. (1992). Categorization of individuals on the basis of multiple social features. *Journal of Personality and Social Psychology, 62,* 207–218.

STANGOR, C., & RUBLE, D. N. (1987). Development of gender role knowledge and gender constancy. In L. Liben & M. Signorella (Eds.), *Children's gender schemata* (pp. 5–22). San Francisco: Jossey-Bass.

STANGOR, C., & RUBLE, D. N. (1989). Differential influences of gender schemata and gender constancy on children's information processing and behavior. *Social Cognition, 7,* 353–372.

STAPLEY, J. C., & HAVILAND, J. M. (1989). Beyond depression: Gender differences in normal adolescents' emotional experiences. *Sex Roles, 20,* 295–308.

STEEVES, H. L. (1987). Feminist theories and media studies. *Critical studies in mass Communication, 4,* 95–135.

STEIL, J. M., & TURETSKY, B. A. (1987). Marital influence levels and symptomatology among wives. In F. J. Crosby (Ed.), *Spouse, parent, worker: On gender and multiple roles* (pp. 74–90). New Haven, CT: Yale University Press.

STERIKER, A. B., & KURDEK, L. A. (1982). Dimensions and correlates of third through eighth graders' sex-role self-concepts. *Sex Roles, 8,* 915–929.

STEVENS, G. E. (1984). Women in business: The view of future male and female managers. *Journal of Business Education, 59,* 314–317.

STOCKARD, J., & WOOD, W. (1984). The myth of female underachievement: A reexamination of sex differences in academic achievement. *American Education Research Journal, 21,* 825–838.

STORMS, M. D., STIVERS, M. L., LAMBERS, S. M., & HILL, C. A. (1981). Sexual scripts for women. *Sex Roles, 7,* 699–707.

STRATE, L. (1992). Beer commercials: A manual on masculinity. In S. Craig (Ed.), *Men, masculinity, and the media* (pp. 78–92). Beverly Hills: Sage.

STROH, L. K., BRETT, J. M., & REILLY, A. (1992). All the right stuff: A comparison of female and male managers' career progression. *Journal of Applied Psychology, 77,* 251–260.

SUGISAKI, K. (1986). From the moon to the sun: Women's liberation in Japan. In L. B. Iglitzin & R. Ross (Eds.), *Women in the world: 1975–1985, the women's decade.* Santa Barbara, CA: ABC-Clio.

SWIM, J., BORGIDA, E., MARUYAMA, G., & MYERS, D. G. (1989). Joan McKay vs. John

McKay: Do gender stereotypes bias evaluations? *Psychological Bulletin, 105,* 409–429.

SWITZER, J. Y. (1990). The impact of generic word choices: An empirical investigation of age-and-sex-related differences. *Sex Roles, 22,* 69–82.

SYMONS, D. (1985). Darwinism and contemporary marriage. In K. Davis (Ed.), *Contemporary marriage: Comparative perspectives on a changing institution.* New York: Russell Sage.

TAJFEL, H. (1981). *Human groups and social categories: Studies in social psychology.* Cambridge, England: Cambridge University Press.

TAJFEL, H. (1982). Social psychology of intergroup relations. *Annual Review of Psychology, 33,* 1–39.

TAJFEL, H., & TURNER, J. C. (1979). An integrative theory of social conflict. In W. Austin & S. Worschel (Eds.), *The social psychology of intergroup relations* (pp. 33–47). Monterey, CA: Brooks-Cole.

TAVRIS, C. (1992). *The mismeasure of woman.* New York: Simon & Schuster.

TAVRIS, C., & OFFIR, C. (1977). *The longest war: Sex differences in perspective.* New York: Harcourt Brace Jovanovich.

TAVRIS, C., & WADE, C. (1984). *The longest war: Sex differences in perspective.* New York: Harcourt Brace Jovanovich.

TAYLOR, A. (1983). Conceptions of masculinity and femininity as a basis for stereotypes of male and female homosexuals. *Journal of Homosexuality, 9,* 37–53.

TAYLOR, M. C., & HALL, J. A. (1982). Psychological androgyny: Theories, methods, and conclusions. *Psychological Bulletin, 92,* 347–366.

TAYLOR, S. E. (1981). A categorization approach to stereotyping. In D. L. Hamilton (Ed.), *Cognitive processes in stereotyping and intergroup behavior.* Hillsdale, NJ: Erlbaum.

TAYLOR, S. E., & FALCONE, H. T. (1982). Cognitive bases of stereotyping: The relationship between categorization and prejudice. *Personality and Social Psychology Bulletin, 8,* 426–432.

TAYLOR, S. E., FISKE, S. T., ETOCOFF, N. L., & RUDERMAN, A. J. (1978). Categorical and contextual bases of person memory and stereotyping. *Journal of Personality and Social Psychology, 36,* 778–793.

THOITS, P. A. (1987). Negotiating roles. In F. J. Crosby (Ed.), *Spouse, parent, worker: On gender and multiple roles* (pp. 11–22). New Haven, CT: Yale University Press.

THOMPSON, C. A. (1992). Lesbian grief and loss issues in the coming out process. *Women and Therapy, 12,* 175–185.

THOMPSON, D. F., MOLISON, L., & ELLIOT, M. (1988). *Adult selection of children's toys.* Paper presented at the annual meeting of the Eastern Psychology Association, Buffalo, NY.

THOMPSON, E. H., JR., & PLECK, J. H. (1986). The structure of male role norms. *American Behavioral Scientist, 29,* 531–543.

THORNE, B., & LURIA, Z. (1986). Sexuality and gender in children's daily worlds. *Social Problems, 33,* 176–190.

TIGER, L., & SHEPHER, J. (1975). *Women in the kibbutz.* New York: Harcourt Brace.

TILBY, P. J., & KALIN, R. (1980). Effects of sex-role deviant lifestyles in otherwise normal persons on the perception of maladjustment. *Sex Roles, 6,* 581–592.

TOCH, H. (1992). *Violent men: An inquiry into the psychology of violence.* Washington, DC: American Psychological Association.

TODD-MANCILLAS, W. R. (1981). Masculine generics = sexist language. *Communication Quarterly, 29,* 107–115.

TORRES-MATRULLO, C. (1980). Acculturation, sex-role values and mental health among mainland Puerto Ricans. In A. M. Padilla (Ed.), *Acculturation theory, modes and some new findings* (pp. 111–137). Boulder, CO: Westview Press.

TRIANDIS, H. C. (1994). *Culture and social behavior.* New York: McGraw-Hill.

TSAI, S. L., & WAHLBERG, H. J. (1979). Mathematics achievement and attitude productivity in junior high school. *Journal of Educational Research, 76,* 267–272.

TULANANDA, O., YOUNG, D. M., & ROOPNARINE, J. L. (1994). Thai and American fathers' involvement with preschool-aged children. *Early Child Development and Care, 97,* 123–133.

TURNER, J. C. (1987). *Rediscovering the social group: A self-categorization theory.* Oxford, England: Basil Blackwell.

TURNER, J. C., & BROWN, R. (1978). *Rediscovering the social group: A self-categorization theory.* Oxford, England: Basil Blackwell.

TURNER, M. E., & PRATKANIS, A. R. (1994). Affirmative action as help: A review of recipient reactions to preferential selection and affirmative action. *Basic and Applied Social Psychology, 15,* 43–70.

TURNER, M. E., PRATKANIS, A. R., & HARDAWAY, T. (1991). Sex differences in reactions to preferential selection: Towards a model of preferential selection as help. *Journal of Social Behavior and Personality, 6,* 797–814.

TVERSKY, A., & KAHNEMAN, D. (1974). Judgment under uncertainty. *Science, 185,* 1124–1131.

UNGER, R. K. (1988). Imperfect reflections of reality: Psychology constructs gender. In R. T. Hare-Mustin & J. Maracek (Eds.), *Making a difference: Psychology and the construction of gender* (pp. 102–149). New Haven, CT: Yale University Press.

UNGER, R. K., & CRAWFORD, M. (1992). *Women & Gender: A feminist psychology.* New York: McGraw-Hill.

UNGER, R. K., & CRAWFORD, M. (1993). Sex and gender. The troubled relationship between sex and gender. *Psychological Science, 4,* 122–124.

UNITED NATIONS. (1985). *The state of the world's women.* Oxford, England: New Internationalist Publications.

UNITED NATIONS. (1991). *The world's women: Trends and statistics, 1970–1990.* New York: United Nations.

U.S. DEPARTMENT OF COMMERCE. (1991). *Statistical abstracts of the United States.* Washington, DC: U.S. Department of Commerce.

U.S. DEPARTMENT OF COMMERCE. (1993). *Statistical abstracts of the United States.* Washington, DC: U.S. Department of Commerce.

U.S. DEPARTMENT OF LABOR. (1990, October). *Facts on working women: Earnings differences between men and women.* Washington, DC: U.S. Department of Labor.

U.S. DEPARTMENT OF LABOR. (1991a, January). *Facts on working women: Women in skilled trades and in other manual labor occupations.* Washington, DC: U.S. Department of Labor.

U.S. DEPARTMENT OF LABOR. (1991b). *A report on the Glass Ceiling Initiative.* Washington, DC: U.S. Department of Labor.

U.S. DEPARTMENT OF LABOR. (1993). *Facts on working women: 20 facts on women workers.* Washington, DC: U.S. Department of Labor.

VALDEZ, R. L., & GUTEK, B. A. (1987). Family roles: A help or hindrance for working women? In B. A. Gutek and L. Larwood (Eds.), *Women's career development* (pp. 157–169). Beverly Hills: Sage.

VANDEBERG, L. R., & STRECKFUSS, D. (1992). Prime-time television's portrayal of women and the world of work: A demographic profile. *Journal of Broadcasting & Electronic Media, 36,* 195–208.

VASQUEZ-NUTTALL, E., ROMERO-GARCIA, I., & DeLEON, B. (1987). Sex roles and perceptions of femininity and masculinity of Hispanic women: A review of the literature. *Psychology of Women Quarterly, 11,* 409–425.

VISS, D. C., & BURN, S. M. (1992). Divergent perceptions of lesbians: A comparison of lesbian self-perceptions and heterosexual perceptions. *The Journal of Social Psychology, 132,* 169–178.

VONK, R., & ASHMORE, R. D. (1992). The multifaceted self: Androgyny reassessed by open-ended self-descriptions. *Social Psychology Quarterly, 56,* 278–287.

VREDENBURG, K., KRAMES, L., & FLETT, G. L. (1986). Sex differences in the clinical expression of depression. *Sex Roles, 14,* 37–49.

WAINRIB, B. R. (1992). Successful women and househusbands: The old messages die hard. *Psychotherapy in Private Practice, 11,* 11–19.

WALKER, I., & MANN, L. (1987). Unemployment, relative deprivation, and social protest. *Personality and Social Psychology Bulletin, 13,* 275–283.

WEBER, R., & CROCKER, J. (1983). Cognitive processes in the revision of stereotypic beliefs. *Journal of Personality and Social Psychology, 45,* 961–967.

WEISNER, T. S., & WILSON-MITCHELL, J. E. (1990). Non-conventional family lifestyles and sex typing in sex-year-olds. *Child Development, 61,* 1915–1933.

WELCH, M. R., & PAGE, B. M. (1981). Sex differences in childhood socialization patterns in African societies. *Sex Roles, 7,* 1163–1173.

WELLER, R. H. (1968). The employment of wives, dominance and fertility. *Journal of Marriage and the Family, 30,* 437–442.

WENTZEL, K. R. (1988). Gender differences in math and english achievement: A longitudinal study. *Sex Roles, 18,* 691–699.

WHITELY, B. E. (1990). The relationship of heterosexuals' attributions for the causes of homosexuality to attitudes toward lesbians and gay men. *Personality and Social Psychology Bulletin, 16,* 369–377.

WHITING, B. B., & EDWARDS, C. P. (1988). *Children of different worlds: The formation of social behavior.* Cambridge, MA: Harvard University Press.

WICKER, A. W. (1969). Attitudes versus actions: The relationship of verbal and overt behavioral responses to attitude objects. *Journal of Social Issues, 25,* 41–78.

WILDER, D. A. (1981). Perceiving persons as a group: Categorization and intergroup relations. In D. L. Hamilton (Ed.), *Cognitive processes in stereotyping and intergroup behavior.* Hillsdale, NJ: Erlbaum.

WILEY, M. G., & ESKILSON, A. (1983). Scaling the corporate ladder: Sex differences in expectations for performance, power and mobility. *Social Psychology Quarterly, 46,* 351–359.

WILEY, M. G., & ESKILSON, A. (1988). Gender and family/career conflict: Reactions of bosses. *Sex Roles, 19,* 445–465.

WILLIAMS, E., RADIN, N., & ALLEGRO, T. (1992). Sex role attitudes of adolescents reared primarily by their fathers: An 11-year follow-up. *Merrill-Palmer Quarterly, 38,* 457–476.

WILLIAMS, J. E., & BEST, D. L. (1986). Sex stereotypes and intergroup relations. In S. Worshel & W. G. Austin (Eds.), *Psychology of intergroup relations* (pp. 244–259). Chicago: Nelson-Hall.

WILLIAMS, J. E., & BEST, D. L. (1990a). *Measuring sex stereotypes: A thirty-nation study* (rev. ed.). Beverly Hills: Sage.

WILLIAMS, J. E., & Best, D. L. (1990b). *Sex and psyche: Gender and self viewed cross-culturally.* Beverly Hills: Sage.

WILSON, E. O. (1978). *On human nature.* Cambridge, MA: Harvard University Press.

WINSTEAD, B. A., DERLEGA, V. J., & WONG, P.T.P. (1984). Effects of sex-role orientation on behavioral self-disclosure. *Journal of Research in Personality, 38,* 541–553.

WISE, E., & RAFFERTY, J. (1982). Sex bias and language. *Sex Roles, 8,* 1189–1196.

WRIGHT, P. H. (1982). Men's friendships, women's friendships and the alleged inferiority of the latter. *Sex Roles, 8,* 1–20.

YEE D., & ECCLES, J. S. (1988). Parent perceptions and attributions for children's math achievement. *Sex Roles, 19,* 317–333.

YODER, J., & ANIAKUDO, P. (1994, August). *African-American women firefighters in triple jeopardy.* Paper presented at the 102nd Annual Convention of the American Psychological Association, Los Angeles.

YOGEV, S. (1981). Do professional women have egalitarian marital relationships? *Journal of Marriage and Family, 43,* 865–871.

ZAMMICHIELI, M. E., GILROY, F. D., SHERMAN, M. F. (1988). Relation between sex-role orientation and marital satisfaction. *Personality and Social Psychology Bulletin, 14,* 747–754.

ZANNA, M., CROSBY, F., & LOEWENSTEIN, G. (1987). Male reference groups and discontent among female professionals. In B. A. Gutek and L. Larwood (Eds.), *Woman's career development* (pp. 28–41). Beverly Hills: Sage.

ZICK, C. D., & MCCULLOUGH, J. L. (1991). Trends in married couples' time use: Evidence from 1977–78 and 1987–88. *Sex Roles, 24,* 459–487.

ZIGLER, E. F., & LANG, M. E. (1990). *Child care choices: Balancing the needs of children, families, and society.* New York: Free Press.

Author Index

Subject Index